THE TOWN THAT WAS MURDERED

Ellen Wilkinson reading in her Bloomsbury flat
during the summer of 1940.
*Courtesy of South Shields Museum & Art Gallery,
Tyne & Wear Archives & Museums*

THE TOWN THAT WAS MURDERED

The Life Story of Jarrow

Ellen Wilkinson

with an Introduction by Matt Perry

MERLIN PRESS

First published in 1939 by Victor Gollancz Ltd
This edition, with a new introduction, published 2019 by
Merlin Press Ltd
Central Books Building
Freshwater Road
Dagenham
RM8 1RX

Introduction © Matt Perry, 2019

ISBN 978-0-85036-749-2

A CIP record of this book is available from the British Library

Printed in the UK by Imprint Digital, Exeter

Contents

Introduction to this edition by Matt Perry		vii
Introduction to the first edition		1
1.	Earliest Jarrow	5
2.	Capitalism Starts Operations	10
3.	Jarrow Colliery and Its Martyrs	17
4.	Pit Life Ends in Jarrow	30
5.	The Rise of Palmer's Shipyard	43
6.	'Making' Jarrow	53
7.	Labour Fights Palmer	62
8.	Fifty Years of Palmerstown	78
9.	Palmer's After the War	92
10.	N.S.S. Cuts Jarrow's Lifeline	109
11.	The Fight for the Steelworks	132
12.	Jarrow Marches	147
13.	The Town of Initials	164
14.	How Charity Helps	174
15.	Housing and Health	181
16.	The Rates and the Child	192
17.	Unemployment in Jarrow Now	199
18.	Conclusions	210

Introduction to New Edition

Matt Perry

In October 1936, two hundred jobless men marched from their shipyard town on Tyneside to London, vainly hoping that public sympathy would make the government do something to alleviate their plight. The Jarrow Crusade, as the march organisers called it, continues to capture the public imagination: Three examples suffice. Eighty years after the event, music journalist and broadcaster Stuart Maconie followed the Crusaders' footsteps in order to write what became a bestselling reflection on the state of British society.[1] In Jarrow itself, in July 2018, the Mayor of South Tyneside unveiled a blue plaque at its old council building to Joe Symonds, one of the march organisers and later MP for Whitehaven. In the BBC documentary *Before Grenfell*, a local resident's testimony that her grandfather had been a 'Jarrow walker' encapsulated the background to the Grenfell Tower disaster, in which 71 council tenants lost their lives. For the film-makers, the connection to the Crusade perfectly framed the long-standing neglect of working-class residents in London's wealthiest borough. This is because Jarrow resonates with other places – such as Grenfell or Orgreave or Hillsborough – that reveal the class character of British society, being sites of palpable injustice where the differentials of power and wealth manifest themselves in open and shocking ways.

How the Jarrow Crusade came to acquire this status is answered in Ellen Wilkinson's *The Town That Was Murdered*. This socialist classic is the story of the Crusade, the history of the town and a portrayal of its social conditions during the depression of the 1930s. In a way, like her second novel, *The Town That Was Murdered* is also a whodunit, with Ellen Wilkinson as the detective, piecing together the crime and discovering the culprits. Well before the concept of moral hazard, the decisions that transformed Jarrow into a derelict ruin was, for her, criminal, resulting in a heavy toll of suffering and death. As such, this book can reach out to three generations' experiences of unemployment, economic crisis and austerity: the Crusade generation of the 1930s, the Thatcher generation of the 1980s and the present generation, many of them Jeremy Corbyn-supporting millenials. This book can speak to these three apparently distinct constituencies and find a receptive audience because of the uncomfortable truths and concerted injustices it exposes.

Despite this, *The Town That Was Murdered* has fallen out of print and its place in the literature of the 1930s is uncertain. The obvious comparison is another Left Book Club volume: George Orwell's *Road to Wigan Pier* (1937). His standing as one of the twentieth century's greatest novelists has ensured that *The Road to Wigan Pier* would remain continuously in print, thereby allowing it to occupy the territory of 1930s social comment. This is not to say that this is undeserved. Orwell writes in a breezy, seemingly effortless, prose. Yet this alone does not explain *The Town That Was Murdered's* neglect. Wilkinson deploys a clear punchy style that is rich in metaphor, blending seasoned journalism and the cadences and vividness of her public meeting rhetoric. A more likely explanation for the greater success of *The Road to Wigan Pier* is paradoxically Orwell's class position. This allows him to connect with his reader more intimately than with his subjects in distressed Lancashire. The result is a more observational and conversational voice sharing surprises and ironies with other outsiders in his encounters with the northern working class. Ellen Wilkinson's voice is that of the insider, knowing Jarrow or Lancashire not on the basis of a literary assignment but from birth. Given this immersive quality, she is able to access Jarrow and the Durham coalfield's political culture, folklore and collective tradition in a way that a baffled Orwell simply cannot. Moreover, as a public school educated intellectual who fought in Spain, Orwell also conforms to a romantic masculine ideal that is of its time and can be safely consigned to the 1930s. Ellen Wilkinson defies such categorisation and awkwardly asserts the continuities of class struggles and capitalism's destructive powers in a manner that is uncomfortable for a liberal middle-class audience.

The book's title is a story in itself. It can be traced back to 1922 and Ellen Wilkinson's efforts to understand the 'hunger and misery behind lace curtains and aspidistra plants' of the crisis in her native Lancashire's cotton industry.[2] Urging workers to fight the employers' plans, she explained the chaos in the cotton industry as an interaction of big finance, industrial reorganisation, global competition, the political influence of cotton barons, and the conservative mentality of the unions, whose members had bought shares in the industry to secure their futures. She made the impassioned observation that the people were suffering unnecessarily from the supposedly objective functioning of the economy. Her developing analysis of industrial crisis crossed the Pennines to Middlesbrough and its steel industry when she became one of the town's Members of Parliament. She highlighted the everyday human consequences of the crisis, asking why children were dying due to malnutrition and why mothers were unprotected in national health insurance when their occupation was more dangerous than working in a factory. After 1932, when she became Jarrow's prospective parliamentary candidate, her approach found a new home and a yet more dramatic language. Here emerged the rhetoric of a town that was murdered in the Crusade's public meetings on the way to London, and famously at its Hyde Park demonstration on 1 November 1936.[3]

The Town That Was Murdered was Ellen Wilkinson's last book, written, as she put it, in a successful race to finish before Hitler launched war.[4] While more famous for her participation in the Jarrow Crusade and her term as Minister of Education (1945-47), her neglected political thought and journalistic career deserve a place in the history of British socialism. She wrote two novels, major political analyses of war and fascism as well as developing a distinctive journalistic style, contributing to over a dozen periodicals in a political spectrum from the *Daily Mail* to *All Out* (the newspaper of the Red International of Labour Unions). She covered such diverse issues as Hitler's militarisation of the Rhineland and the impact of domestic electrical appliances upon women's lives. Her political itinerary is equally remarkable. Her first political employment was for the suffrage movement just before the Great War. The shopworkers' union – the Amalgamated Union of Cooperative Employees – recruited her as a national organiser in 1915, for whom she led a series of wartime equal pay strikes.[5] With peace, she remained a union official, which provided her route into the Commons in 1924, representing Middlesbrough East until 1931 and then Jarrow, from 1935 until her death.

However, the idea that her legacy is mainly as a 'trailblazer for women in parliament' as Rachel Reeves, Leeds West Labour MP, described it, sells (the 4 foot 10) Ellen Wilkinson short.[6]

Her reputation and popularity rested upon her combative and campaigning approach to politics outside as much as inside parliament, earning her the nickname 'Red Ellen'. The diminutive Mancunian was involved in great trade union struggles, the women's movement, the protests against unemployment as well as international solidarity with anti-fascists (especially from Germany and Spain) and anti-imperialists (notably in Ireland, India and China). There was much more to Ellen Wilkinson than meets the eye. She travelled the globe supporting campaigns against injustice. She had met Lenin and Trotsky, visited Gandhi in jail, defied the Nazi authorities to warn that the German army was to march into the Rhineland, spoke to the strikers occupying US car plants and French department stores for union recognition and decent pay. She joined the Churchill-Attlee coalition government during the Second World War with responsibility for air raid shelters and was Minister of Education in the Labour Government of 1945. At the Ministry, she raised the school leaving age to 16 and introduced free school milk.

Sadly, much of her activity is forgotten, her achievements eroded or overturned. Thus, free school milk ended when Margaret Thatcher got Ellen Wilkinson's old cabinet job and playgrounds chanted 'Thatcher, Thatcher, milk snatcher' up and down the country. You might say 'what Ellen Wilkinson giveth, Margaret Thatcher taketh away'. We are left with the flashbulb moment of the Jarrow Crusade illuminating Ellen Wilkinson, the rest of her life is left in darkness. Reading *The Town That Was Murdered* reveals that, while occasionally distinctly anachronistic, Ellen Wilkinson's thought remains uncannily prescient and timely.

The Town That Was Murdered might be understood to have four parts. The first looks at Jarrow's early history (synonymous with the Venerable Bede, England's first historian (673-735), and the monastic settlement he established there) and the industrial revolution. Regarding the latter, *The Town That Was Murdered* examined Jarrow's early nineteenth-century reincarnation as a pit village. She charted the lack of regulation, poor drainage and rough deal that miners received, with low wages, fines and the servile status of the annual bond. She reconstructed the 1831, 1832 and 1844 strikes in the Durham coalfield, through her motif of the anonymous heroes of which movements are made. She paid tribute in turn to Thomas Hepburn for establishing the Northern Union of Pitmen, a milestone in mining trade unionism, to William Jobling, unjustly and barbarically executed on the gibbet during the 1832 strike, to the 'seven lads of Jarrow' sentenced, like the celebrated 'Tolpuddle martyrs', to transportation to the penal colony of Australia for trade union activity. She stressed that solidarity and class struggle came from practical necessity rather than theory: 'The courage that was born of facing death daily in the slaughter-pits of this period was needed by the leaders, who were grown in the ranks of the miners.'[7] They faced victimisation, persecution and historical oblivion. Even today, the local labour movement has sought to maintain this tradition. The Durham Miners' Association continues to conduct an annual ceremony at St Mary's Church cemetery, Heworth, at Hepburn's grave and in July 2018 there was a commemoration in honour of the Jarrow transportees.[8]

With their focus upon coal, these chapters hint at Wilkinson's work during the General Strike of 1926 and her relationship with the Durham Miners' Association, who first invited her to speak at their annual Gala the following year. She regularly attended the event as a County Durham MP. The Durham Miners' Gala continues to the present and Ellen Wilkinson's face features on the remade Follonsby Miners' Lodge banner, a former pit in her Jarrow constituency.[9] She described the event as a 'baptism in trade union solidarity' for the young people in the coalfield.[10] The Gala – which remains the largest regular event on the labour movement calendar in the UK – in recent years has swelled with the enthusiasm for Jeremy Corbyn's leadership of the Labour Party. In 2016, during Owen Smith's leadership challenge, the DMA assembled those MPs who had rallied to the beleaguered Corbyn.[11] The Labour leader addressed the issues facing the movement after the Brexit vote, putting an internationalist case in a region that voted heavily for Brexit and not dismissing working-class Brexit supporters as a homogeneous racist block. The following year occurred in the exuberant aftermath of the 2017 election result, in which everyone expected Corbyn's humiliation but Theresa May lost her overall majority. The crowd chanted 'Oh, Jeremy Corbyn' and the greatest cheer went up when he declared New Labour to be dead. Demonstrating the resilience of class politics, over 100,000 continue to attend the 'Big Meeting' that first took place in 1871. The continued vitality of the Gala is symptomatic of the spent fortunes of New Labour and the advocates of the service model of trade unionism, in which cheap credit cards attract new individual members rather than an approach focused upon collective workplace organisation. In discussing Jarrow's mining past, Ellen Wilkinson sought to distil the lessons of working-class history for her contemporary audience. The Gala plays a similar function today. Sometimes wrongly perceived as nostalgic, the Gala has become a model of how to retain a mass platform for the renewal of socialist politics, working-class identity and trade unionism.

The second part of the book examines Jarrow's transformation into a shipbuilding and company town under the dominion of Sir Charles Mark Palmer. After the closure of Jarrow's colliery, the rise of Palmer's shipyard signalled Jarrow's great capitalist revival. Palmer was initially a colliery manager for John Bowes, the illegitimate son of the Earl of Strathmore, one of the great land and mine owners of the Durham coalfield. His family seats, Gibside and the Bowes Museum, are today popular North East of England visitor attractions. Through developing the steam-powered iron ship to reduce transport costs and overcome sail's dependence upon the weather, Palmer saved the London market for the northeast coalfield and laid the basis for iron shipbuilding on the Tyne. Palmer also helped to pioneer naval armour-plating with his 'iron clad' ships. Palmer epitomised the kind of Victorian entrepreneur that George Osborne believed ought to be celebrated when the then Conservative Chancellor of the Exchequer announced his plan for a Great Exhibition of the North.

As Ellen Wilkinson observed, the heroic ideal of the industrialist barely matched the realities. With expansion, the nature of the business underwent a transformation facilitated by changes in company law and limited liability; from being a personally owned business, it became a joint stock company possessed by wealthy shareholders outside Jarrow. During Jarrow's new phase of industrial capitalism based on shipbuilding, its population leapt from 3,500 in 1851 to 33,000 in 1891, becoming a migrant town with large contingents of Scots and Irish. Challenging the image of Palmer cultivated over the decades as a great benefactor, Wilkinson observed that he saw no obligation to provide his company town with decent housing or social amenities. There was no water supply until 1864. This was the 'pirate period of nineteenth century capitalism' with squalor, epidemics and slums.

Palmer's entered the First World War with debts and having skipped dividend payments. Wilkinson concluded the 'fifty years of Palmerstown' with war's end. She evoked the town's optimism that accompanied peace and victory. The knowing contrast and the devastating emotional reversal to come when its shipyard closed cleverly framed the reader's sense of injustice at Jarrow's demise. The story of Palmer's after the war provided a telling indictment of the capitalist system. Wilkinson dramatised the hubris of the modern industrial colossus. During the boom, the company rewarded shareholders with bonus dividends, encouraging new investors. Yet when the boom ended, so too did the dividends, and the small investors – including many of Palmer's workers – lost their life's savings when the clever money deserted the firm. For the workers, the acquisition of shares in Palmer's was an investment in something real, in their own town and in their futures; it was inconceivable to them that this might fail. For the rich, Wilkinson observed, the motive was simply greed. Wilkinson emphasised that Palmer's remained a sound shipbuilder with a high reputation that was able to secure its share of available work remaining the second largest shipbuilder on the Tyne, but fell due to the chaos of the markets.

The third part of the book explores the end of the shipyard and the protest march. In 1930, Sir James Lithgow persuaded fellow shipbuilding employers to establish the holding company the National Shipbuilders Security Ltd (NSS) to restore prices through cutting shipbuilding capacity. The NSS decision to close (or 'sterilise' in its neutral euphemism) Palmer's included a 40-year moratorium on shipbuilding at the yard. Wilkinson observed: 'And so, in a dull court-room in London on the last day of June 1933, the fate of Jarrow was decided. [...] An unknown company, its real backers hidden, cut Jarrow's lifeline.'[12] Wilkinson then recounted the cruel drama of the denial of a modern steelworks for Jarrow, blocked as it was by the steel industry and the banks. In a case that she rehearsed in public meetings the length of the Jarrow Crusade, big business in the shape of the organisations of steel and shipbuilding employers had conspired to 'murder' Jarrow. The town's apparent salvation '[t]he Jarrow Steelworks was dead ... strangled at birth.' The language stands out as emotive only because we are conditioned to think – then as now – that such decisions (in neoliberal rhetoric 'tough decisions' or 'hard choices'), which are always taken behind closed doors, are inevitable, necessary, even courageous, and blind to their human consequences. As today, euphemism soothes the harsh realities of economic crisis.

The fourth and final part of the book examined the devastating after-effects for the town. Ellen Wilkinson carefully spelled out Jarrow's social conditions: the inadequate relief, the difficulties for the council to raise money from the local rates, the exceptionally high maternal and infant mortality and the slum housing. Connecting Jarrow's story to the case for socialism, she concluded that, though profiteers might ravage a town and move on elsewhere, the workers remain amid the ruins.

Unexpected affinities with our present predicament recur throughout the book, connecting us to the narrative. Since the late 1970s, an entire field of academic scholarship has arisen to address the global phenomenon of deindustrialisation. Ellen Wilkinson's book might well be considered a founding text of this field. She forensically detailed the catastrophic loss of industry and its relation to the sense of place. The loss of industry in the 1930s or since the 1970s is so disastrous that metaphors of life and death routinely accompany deindustrialisation from the rustbelt of the US to northern France or the depressed areas of the UK. The Marxist geographer David Harvey explained that the combination of mass unemployment and deindustrialisation, with the attendant loss of skilled unionised jobs, has 're-empowered capital' at the expense of labour globally.[13] Moreover, many commentators have pointed to deindustrialisation to explain the unexpected turns of events that have caught them off guard, be that the rise of the neo-fascism across Europe (including the British far right of the British National Party, English Defence League and their successors), the 'Brexit' referendum result, or the election of Donald Trump.[14] Ellen Wilkinson was well aware of the reactionary turn in politics that mass unemployment and workplace closure could bring, having visited Germany during the July 1932 breakthrough election for the Nazis, when unemployment stood at 8 million. From that point, she took the threat of fascism in Britain seriously, as she did the looming menace of world war when British Foreign Secretaries complacently appeased Hitler and Mussolini. That Oswald Mosley's British Union of Fascists were blaming Jewish people for unemployment or overcrowding and offering false solutions to the crisis rendered, for her, the efforts to identify the actual decision-makers who sealed Jarrow's fate all the more important.

That is why Ellen Wilkinson devoted five pages to the closed mentality and elite connections of Sir James Lithgow who set up the NSS. He sought to block nationalisation, deregulate industry and undermine the unions. She tried to convince us of the psychology of the industrialist and structural forces that he personified: 'Lithgow stands for capitalism, and the maintenance of private profit-making, with no apology for the results. To him the man who can make a profit is the only factor really worth considering in national life.'[15]

All this has an uncanny familiarity to later generations who have faced workplace closure. Lithgow was to the 1930s what Sir Ian MacGregor was to the 1980s, the latter doing for steel and coal what Lithgow had done in shipbuilding. Both developed similar notoriety in trade union quarters. It is ironic, then, that their paths had crossed. As he revealed in his memoirs, MacGregor learned how to manage from Lithgow. MacGregor was taken on at the age of 23 at Lithgow's firm in the very year of the Jarrow Crusade. The head of the National Coal Board reminisced fondly: 'he was the one – my first great mentor.'[16]

The Town That Was Murdered is also a plea against British society's inequalities and injustices. After a decade of austerity and three decades of neo-liberalism, the geographical, material and health inequalities today parallel those articulated in *The Town That Was Murdered*. In her chapter 'Rates and the Child', Ellen Wilkinson highlighted how local government finances made austerity worst in the areas of greatest need as a consequence of the inadequate revenue that could be raised there. In line with 'ratepayer' opinion, the Baldwin government had introduced the De-Rating Act of 1929 that had undermined the finances of local government and resulted in dramatic discrepancies between the ability to raise money in wealthy and depressed areas. Ellen Wilkinson had warned in 1929 that the full 'terrible' effects would only be felt for the 'coalfields and Northern industrial towns' in five to seven years' time.[17] In Jarrow, an additional penny would net as little as £350, whereas in Westminster, it would increase the borough's revenue by £42,000.[18] Today, the mechanism is different. Since the 1980s, cuts in central government grants to local authorities have decimated the capacities of local democracy, denying the possibility of compensating for these loses at the municipal level through 'rate-capping' and then the Council Tax (via the debacle of the Community Charge or Poll Tax). Caught between mandatory responsibilities and reduced budgets, councils have eaten into their reserves and have long been incapable of responding to the housing crisis. At least in the 1930s, the Labour councils could build council houses.

As with the Household Means Test and the Genuinely Seeking Work Clause during the interwar era, the unemployed have been a major target of the austerity drive since the global crash of 2008.[19] Ellen Wilkinson described the scrutiny of women who were entitled to unemployment insurance to be 'something like an inquisition' and the Genuinely Seeking Work Clause as an 'insult to our people'.[20] In the folklore of the Crusade is a joke that debunks the perennial search for the 'scrounger'. After their day's exertions, sometimes the marchers would be given a small amount of spending money from the kitty to relax in a public house. On one such occasion, the landlord opined that people from Jarrow would not accept a job if it was offered to them. A marcher replied: 'Well, it just goes to show you don't want to believe everything you hear. We were told that you watered the beer but we don't believe a word of it.' Since the 2008 crash, the expectations for work search have become increasingly stringent, with the requirement to prove 35 hours a week of active job search. The benefits system has become more punitive with the sanctions increasing in October 2012 from one to four weeks for missing a job centre appointment. Between 2010 and 2015, the National Audit Office revealed that a quarter of Job Seekers' Allowance (JSA) claimants received such suspensions of benefit. Ironically, given that Ken Loach's film *I, Daniel Blake* was set in Newcastle, the exercise of this punitive stance operated according to a postcode lottery with sanctions being ten times higher in the North East of England, than the South East.[21] Whilst all this is going on, governments have responded to criticism with neoliberal soundbites of 'incentivising work' (that is what wages do) or 'restoring fairness' or quoting decontextualised figures of overall (usually 'record') spending.[22] At the same time, fly-on-the-wall documentaries, conservative election slogans and newspaper headlines caricature or denounce the 'shirkers' and 'scroungers' on benefits. All of this would be sadly familiar to Ellen Wilkinson who railed against the humbug of the press and government, the injustices and inequalities of policy and the counter-productive quality of budget cuts.

The introduction of Universal Credit from 2013 – replacing Job Seekers'

Allowance and incorporating work-related benefit – was part of a wider raft of reforms to cut income to the poorest. This deliberate attempt to make the poor pay for the crisis found cover under the rhetoric of 'poverty plus a pound', a mendacious notion that providing additional income to the poor would do nothing to arrest poverty.[23] A family benefits cap (introduced in 2012 and lowered in 2016), a benefits freeze (of four years from April 2016, constituting a real terms cut) together with benefit cuts and reassessments for the disabled (through the Employment Support Allowance and the Work Capacity Assessments) have all reduced the income of the unemployed, low-income families and the disabled. In June 2017, the High Court heard a case that four single mothers brought on the grounds that they were forced to choose between buying food and paying rent. The Court condemned the benefit cap for causing 'real misery' for their children.[24] As with the Means Test investigators of the 1930s, austerity intrudes into the homes of the poor. The Social Fund that provided loans and grants for big ticket items like boilers or fridges was closed and the responsibility shunted onto local councils alongside cuts in the proportion to be paid for such household expenditures. Relief for Council Tax underwent similar devolution to council administration and cuts in funding. The 'spare room subsidy' – or bedroom tax – penalised those on benefit according to their domestic living arrangements.[25] Unsurprisingly, this package of cuts has coincided with a surge in mental illness amongst the unemployed. In March 2017, an NHS survey of GPs revealed that 15.2% of the unemployed suffered from severe or extreme anxiety or depression, roughly growing by half in a four-year period.

While Ellen Wilkinson focused upon a single town, she was aware that austerity was a national and global phenomenon, having criticised the way in which economic orthodoxy and international finance capital had forced Ramsay MacDonald, the Labour Prime Minister, in the late summer of 1931 to surrender and impose cuts on the unemployed. That debacle led to the Second Labour government's collapse. At the Palace's request, MacDonald formed the cross-party National government, splitting the Parliamentary Labour Party in so doing. She dealt with 'that dreadful betrayal' in *The Town That Was Murdered* through the protest march from Jarrow to Seaham in January 1934, to lobby the Prime Minister in his constituency. For her, it was tragic that he 'knew the real cause of the evils of which we told him … but had run away at the moment of trial that he had himself forecast so accurately years before.'[26]

After the Second World War, when Keynesianism was in the ascendant, the great powers established institutions (the World Bank, International

Monetary Fund and General Agreement on Trade and Tariffs) intended to prevent a crisis on the scale of the 1930s, but these bodies have with the passage of time perversely morphed into the conduits of neoliberal dogma and austerity. Since 1979, one country after another has fallen victim to 'structural adjustment' demanded by those institutions. The most spectacular recent case – the third bailout of the Greek economy of 2015 – provided an insider's account of the negotiations with the 'troika' (the International Monetary Fund, the European Commission and the European Central Bank). Yanis Varoufakis, the Greek Finance Minister, described how the troika ignored democratic mandates and prioritised the security of German, French, Dutch and British banks over the well-being of the Greek people. The latter have suffered in ways comparable to the suffering to the effects of the depression of the 1930s: GDP fell by 28%, unemployment rose to 27%, pensions cut by 20% to 60%. Varoufakis pointedly observed that 'Austerity is a morality play pressed into service of legitimising cynical wealth transfers from the have-nots to the haves during times of crisis.'[27] Like Varoufakis, Ellen Wilkinson traced both the complicity of individuals and their concealment behind an array of initials, acronyms and cant. More so than Varoufakis, she outlined the structural forces of global capitalism at work that sealed Jarrow's fate in an accessible way to a popular audience. The world economy's institutional architecture poses a direct challenge to opponents of neoliberalism seeking political office – such as Jeremy Corbyn or Bernie Saunders in the US – namely, that they are not bent to its will and that they do not follow similar paths to those taken by the second Labour or the Syriza governments.

At an ideological level, austerity's victims have to deal with the claim, then as now, that 'there is', as Margaret Thatcher asserted, 'no alternative'. Though millennials might puzzle about all the fuss regarding her, Thatcher's legacy is very real within the Conservative Party and beyond. Indeed, she connects three eras of austerity. Thatcher herself lived through the 1930s; but in a place very different from Jarrow. Grantham was a wealthy market town in Lincolnshire. In her memoirs, she nostalgically evoked the town's social harmony: thrifty people reaping the rewards of hard work, bound together through support for the Empire and the monarchy. These pages suggest that her 1930s childhood were a formative moment, shaping her personal morality and political outlook. Even the unemployed were 'respectable' and – though none numbered amongst her friends – their children were 'neatly turned out', because of their parents' 'spirit of self-reliance and independence'.[28] Of course, her memoirs set up this sentimental ideal of a deserving, loyal and godly poor who knew their place as a knowing comparison. This is how working-class people should behave, unlike the unruly trade unionists she was determined to crush in later life or those who allegedly preferred to sit on the dole than, as her Employment Secretary put it, get on their bike and find work.

As with Ellen Wilkinson, Thatcher's father was a Methodist lay preacher. Unlike Richard Wilkinson, Alfred Roberts was also a 'ratepayers" (i.e. Conservative) councillor, then chairman of the Finance Committee and eventually Mayor in 1945-6. He was active in the Rotary Club and local charity. Ellen Wilkinson criticised the function of charity – read David Cameron's 'big society' – in relation to unemployment in the 1930s. For all its good intention, its source was a belated attack of middle-class conscience, often clumsily patronising the poor. In her experience, unemployed workers did not want charity, they wanted work. The Jarrow Crusade did not pass through Grantham but, if it had, Ellen Wilkinson would have spoken at the public meeting. She would have compared Grantham's infant mortality, which stood at 24 per 1,000 with Jarrow's at 104 per 1,000.[29] Red Ellen would not have blushed while pointing out to a Grantham audience that a child born in the Lincolnshire town was four times more likely to survive to its first year than an infant born to the fathers amongst the Jarrow marchers present in the meeting hall.

So, cossetted in a childhood fantasy of what the 1930s were like, and consequently immune to the sufferings of those deemed to be responsible for their own fate, Margaret Thatcher sought to roll back the welfare state. Other Conservative cabinet members, Rhodes Boyson and Norman Tebbitt, articulated their own versions of this myth of the 1930s.[30] Indeed, the elections of Margaret Thatcher and Ronald Reagan in the US signalled a turning point in relation to the principal themes of *The Town That Was Murdered* and the post-war consensus in favour of a welfare state, to which it in no small way contributed. The welfare state made Britain a more equal society. In 1937, the top half a per cent of the UK population accounted for 9% of the after-tax income. The Beveridge plan for social services launched during the Second World War prompted four decades of declining inequality, so that by 1978 that same top half a per cent drew only 2.4% of after-tax income. Two decades later, that figure had leapt to 7.2%.[31] A final connection between Ellen Wilkinson and Margaret Thatcher is that while the latter's father was notorious for molesting female shop assistants, it was Ellen Wilkinson's job to persuade women shopworkers to join a union and she pressed for her union to address the 'male manager problem', as she euphemistically called what is now known as sexual harassment in the workplace.[32]

Surveying the current state of the world, the claim that there is no alternative to neoliberalism imposes a responsibility upon the historian. Not much is really new about neoliberalism. The Treasury orthodoxy of the 1930s resembled neoliberalism, somewhat repackaged intellectually. Indeed, neoliberalism as an ideology is conventionally traced back to von Hayek's *Road to Serfdom* (1944). This warned of the totalitarianism of the welfare state and mixed economy or 'collectivism' that would cause a new age of servitude and economic degeneration. Hayek's intervention was a reaction to the consensus shifting away from classical economics. *The Road to Serfdom* was perhaps the most spectacular piece of flawed economic and political forecasting, given that the 'new serfdom' of welfare capitalism and Keynesian regulation stabilised democracy in the West and ushered in historically unparalleled economic growth for three decades until the twin recessions of the 1970s hit. During the long boom, the liberal or social democratic critics of unregulated markets such as Karl Polanyi, John Maynard Keynes, William Beveridge and T.H. Marshall were in the intellectual ascendant. It was only during the 1970s that neoliberalism gained hold inside the British Conservative Party and the American Republicans and from there, it has spread to the world. That said, the anti-welfarist aspect of the neoliberal agenda is older still than Hayek.

Taking the longer view, *The Town That Was Murdered* connects across the decades with the recurrent 'condition of England' question and the great debate launched about the reform of the Poor Law at the time of the French Revolution. The book makes the case for equality and welfare just as Thomas Paine, William Godwin and Condorcet had in the 1790s. These debates run into the present, with the neo-liberal hegemony being constructed on the arguments of Thomas Malthus, Edmund Burke and Alexis de Tocqueville. Malthus argued for the outright abolition of the poor laws altogether, to allow the 'killing frost' of winter to keep the population in check. Anticipating the turn from welfare to charity in the three periods of austerity, Alexis de Tocqueville proposed philanthropy in the place of welfare entitlement.[33] After Grey's Liberal administration introduced the Poor Law Amendment Act of 1834, such beliefs condemned the poor domestically to the degradation of the workhouse and in the Empire consigned colonial subjects to famine.[34]

Ellen Wilkinson was certainly familiar with this debate – not least Fredrick Engels's *Condition of the Working-Classes in England* based on the situation in her place of birth, Manchester – but preferred to communicate to her political audience in terms of working-class experience. For instance, in a radio broadcast shortly after becoming Minister of Education, she noted the persistent residue in Lancashire working-class families – like her own – of the hardships associated with the cotton famine of the 1860s.[35] These nineteenth-century arguments have mutated into the debate about neoliberalism and austerity today with many of the original positions being easily detectable.

Today in Britain, there has been a decade of austerity. *The Town That Was Murdered* surveys the effects of industrial closure and a decade of austerity upon a single community. History does not simply repeated itself like a genetic clone. Human engineering produced Dolly the Sheep, just as human hands constructed neoliberal capitalism, deregulation and the crash of 2008. The architects of the welfare state would be horrified to see the return of the soup kitchen, which the foodbank is in modified form, upon which today 1.3 million people rely.[36] Church Action on Poverty dramatised the situation with a campaign adapting the famous 1979 Conservative Party election poster replacing the words 'Britain isn't working' with 'Britain isn't eating'; it depicted a queue of people now at a food bank rather than a labour exchange.[37] At the same time, we should not allow the distorting lens of the past to ignore that Jarrow's poverty lay amid the affluence for some of the late 1930s. For every Jarrow, there is a Grantham; for every Richmond, a Tower Hamlets. Indeed, today the North East of England is not one big derelict shipyard. A couple of miles down the road from Jarrow is the Nissan plant at Sunderland. The North East has witnessed a culture-led regeneration strategy with the construction of such landmarks as the Angel of the North, the Sage Gateshead and the Baltic Centre for Contemporary Art.[38] Yet these sites of investment should not mask how such regeneration often relies upon gentrification, marketing new commodified lifestyles, the 'rebranding' of place identity, geographically uneven economic benefits and exclusion of industrial work and displacement of long-standing residents.[39]

For a place like Jarrow, on the periphery of these monumental Newcastle-Gateshead projects, the economic uplift is less apparent. According to Public Health England, South Tyneside (the local authority within which Jarrow sits) has health 'significantly worse that the England average' in the following categories: children in low income families, long-term unemployment, diabetes, hip fractures in people aged 65 or over, life expectancy, mortality under the age of 75 for cardiovascular illness or cancer.[40] South Tyneside is among the 20% most deprived areas of England. The effects on public health are not restricted to a small number of particularly deprived localities. Sir Michael Marmot, Director of the Institute of Health Equity, has reported that the improvements in life expectancy in the UK that have been rising since 1850 ground to a halt in 2010.[41] Office of National Statistics projections from 2018 now anticipate a decline in life expectancy.[42] Kate Pickett of York University also highlighted the relationship between austerity, stress levels and worsening health. Again with health, coalition and Conservative governments indulge in the rhetoric of investment of 'record' sums of money, while health inequalities widen. Equally, as with the 1930s and the discourse of mothers 'wrong-feeding' their children to sidestep child malnutrition, the government is keen to emphasise the self-inflicted nature of the poor health of those on low incomes through high-profile campaigns about smoking, obesity and alcohol.

The Town That Was Murdered documents the effects of mass unemployment upon health, prior to the establishment of the National Health Service. It does so in a way that humanises the consequences of the austerity, drawing the human implications of the pages of statistics that Registrars-General and Medical Officers of Health produced. *The Town That Was Murdered* ought also to be seen as part of a wider campaign over public health during the 1930s that stretched from the protests of the unemployed to a minority of the medical profession that challenged the complacency and conservatism of their colleagues.

For Ellen Wilkinson, socialism meant equality, saying those socialists who refused to admit this were snobs or fools: 'A snob, if you cannot bear to think of a world where there isn't someone for you to cringe to, and with less money whom you can patronise; or a fool if you haven't grasped that the first essential of the gospel you are supposed to be preaching.'[43] Despite government neglect of inequality, academics have challenged spiralling social, economic and health inequalities. Danny Dorling explains the persistence of social inequality as a consequence of elitism, prejudice and exclusion rather than natural talents or economic rationality.[44] He shows that a North-South Divide in wealth, health and educational attainment cuts urban Britain in two. The line runs between the Humber and the Severn. Coming from a medical science background and using statistical comparison, Richard Wilkinson and Kate Pickett outlined how more equal societies performed much better in terms of physical and mental health, educational attainment, social mobility and crime, concluding that greater equality is better for everyone. Economists such as Joseph Stiglitz and Thomas Piketty have indicated the adverse consequences of inequality upon growth, consumption, the environment and the stability of the world economy. Piketty observed that, with the exception of the dislocation that two world wars caused, capitalism naturally tended towards widening inequalities and diminishing growth. Inequality, at its present exorbitant levels, thus explains the morbid growth rates and seriously destabilised the global economy. He also identifies the political consequences of this skewed wealth distribution. As the wealthy enrich themselves, their political influence increases, creating a vicious circle of low top tax rates and low growth. Furthermore, inequity increasingly undermines the most basic social justice necessary for democracy to function.

Inequality has become a global problem. In 2018, we learned from Oxfam that 42 individuals have the same wealth as half the world's population. In the same year, the first *World Inequality Report* underlined the growing scale of between-country (though India and China have closed the gap in national income with the most advanced) and within-country inequality since 1980.[45] In her day, Ellen Wilkinson was demanding that something be done about it.

Conclusion

Ellen Wilkinson had an exceptional talent for humanising the consequences of capitalism. Be they Basque children fleeing the fascist bombing during the Spanish Civil War, or her malnourished constituents on the Means Test, or victims of Nazi repression, Wilkinson treated those suffering the injustices of the 1930s as human beings and persuaded others to do likewise. She went further arguing that all these victims could resist injustice just as the Jarrow marchers did. It is a radical thing to do. Connecting Jarrow's story to the case for socialism, she concluded that, though profiteers might ravage a town and move on elsewhere, the workers have a stronger attachment to place:

> They were crowded into hovels, their children starved and died, and on their sacrifice great capital has been accumulated. It is now time that the workers took control of this country of ours. It is time that they planned it, organised it and developed it so that all might enjoy the wealth.

Some might say that all this is no longer relevant today, that those who look to an industrial past are indulging in nostalgia. In 2018, that 780,000 work on a zero hour contract seems like a novelty. Yet the 'gig economy' operated at the morning hiring at shipyards and the docks in the 1930s. The decline in trade union membership from 13.2 million in 1979 to 5.6 million in 2018 seems unprecedented. Yet we forget the collapse in trade unionism after the highpoint of 1919 and the anti-union legislation that following the general strike of 1926.

So perhaps Ellen Wilkinson's message of socialism, the rights of the most vulnerable, her commitment to women's liberation, her robust anti-fascism, her opposition to war, her trade unionism and her attitude to protest return us to a past rich in parallels to our present.

NOTES

1. Stuart Maconie, *Long Road from Jarrow: A Journey Through Britain Then and Now*, Ebury, London, 2016. It became The Sunday Times Bestseller.
2. *All Out*, 8 September 1923.
3. Matt Perry, 'The Town that Was Murdered: Martyrs, Heroes and the Urbicide of Jarrow' in Keith Laybourn and Quentin Outram (eds), *Secular Martyrdom in Britain and Ireland*, Palgrave Macmillan, Cham, 2018. 203-225.
4. She had some assistance from George Bishop (who was working with her on Spanish work) regarding the chapters on shipping and iron and steel. Seeley G. Mudd Manuscript Library Princeton University (SGMML) Louis Fischer Papers (LF) 13 16 Wilkinson to Louis Fischer, 14 January 1939.
5. Matt Perry, '"Industrial unionism for women": Ellen Wilkinson and the unionisation of shop workers, 1915–18' in Lucy Bland and Richard Carr (eds.), *Labour, British radicalism and the First World War*, Oxford University Press, Oxford, 2018, pp. 126-44.
6. Ellen Wilkinson, *Division Bell Mystery*, British Library Publishing, London, 2018, p. 11.
7. Ellen Wilkinson, *The Town That Was Murdered*, Gollancz, London, 1939, p. 28.
8. The transportation was commemorated on 28 July 2018: http://ucunorthern.org.uk/event/seven-men-of-jarrow/
9. *The Journal*, 14 July 2012. http://www.thejournal.co.uk/news/north-east-news/tony-benn-keeps-durham-miners-4406634 [last accessed 21 August 2018].
10. *ribune*, 16 July 1937.
11. *The Chronicle*, 12 June 2017 https://www.chroniclelive.co.uk/news/north-east-news/jeremy-corbyn-speak-durham-miners-13173073 [last accessed 23 August 2018].
12. Wilkinson, *The Town*, p. 158.
13. David Harvey, *The Enigma of Capital and the Crises of Capitalism*, Profile, London, 2010, p. 131.
14. Explaining these phenomena as the political aftershocks of deindustrialisation, Steven High, Lachlan MacKinnon and Andrew Perchard (eds), *The Deindustrialized World: Confronting Ruination in Postindustrial Places*, UBC Press, Vancouver, 2017, p. 20.
15. Wilkinson, *The Town*, p. 146.
16. Ian McGregor, *The Enemies Within: the Story of the Miners' Strike 1984-5*, Fontana Collins, London, 1987, p. 29.
17. Ellen Wilkinson, '1924-1929 five years of class war', *The Plebs*, May 1929, pp. 99-101.
18. Wilkinson, *The Town*, p. 250.
19. Stewart Lansley and Joanna Mack, *Breadline Britain: The Rise of Mass Poverty*, Oneworld Publications, 2015, pp.121-34.
20. *All Power*, May 1922. On the GSWC, *New Leader*, 26 July 1929.
21. D. Webster, Evidence to the Work and Pension Committee: the Role of the Jobcentre Plus in the Reformed Welfare, 2014, quoted in Stewart Lansley, Joanna Mack, *Breadline Britain: the Rise of Mass Poverty*, Oneworld Publications, London, 2015, p. 128.
22. *The Independent*, 16 July 2017.
23. Lansley, Mack, *Breadline Britain*, p. 6.
24. Patrick Butler, 'Benefit cap on lone parents of under-twos is unlawful, court rules', *The Guardian*, 22 June 2017 at https://www.theguardian.com/society/2017/jun/22/benefit-cap-lone-parents-under-twos-unlawful-court

25 S. Moffatt, S. Lawson, R. Patterson, E. Holding, A. Dennison, S. Sowden, J. Brown, 'A qualitative study of the impact of the UK 'bedroom tax'', *Journal of Public Health*, Volume 38, Issue 2, 1 June 2016, pp. 197–205.
26 Wilkinson, *The Town*, p. 196.
27 Yannis Varoufakis, *Adults in the Room: My Battle with Europe's Deep Establishment*, Bodley Head, London 2017.
28 Thatcher, Margaret. *The Path to Power*, HarperCollins Publishers, 1995, pp. 19-24.
29 *Registrar-General's Statistical Review of England and Wales for the Year 1936*, New Annual Series, no. 16, HMSO: London, 1937, pp.80 & 90.
30 Rhodes Boyson, 'The shadow of failure behind Labour's Jarrow nostalgia', *Daily Telegraph*, 3 June 1981.
31 A.B. Atkinson and W. Salverda, 'Top incomes in the Netherlands and the UK over the Twentieth Century', *Journal of European Economic Association*, 3, 4, 2005, pp. 883-913.
32 Keith Nuthall, 'Thatcher's dad: mayor, preacher, groper', *The Independent*, 22 June 1997 https://www.independent.co.uk/news/thatchers-dad-mayor-preacher-groper-1257249.html [last accessed 22 August 2018]. *Co-operative Employé*, October 1915. AUCE Special circular from Wilkinson, 14 January 1918.
33 Alexis de Tocqueville, *Memoir on Pauperism*, IEA, London, 1997.
34 Mike Davis, *Late Victorian Holocausts: El Niño Famines and the Making of the Third World*, Verso, London, 2001.
35 *The Listener*, 29 November 1945.
36 May Bulman, Food bank use in UK reaches highest rate on record as benefits fail to cover basic costs', The Independent, 24 April 2018. https://www.independent.co.uk/news/uk/home-news/food-bank-uk-benefits-trussell-trust-cost-of-living-highest-rate-a8317001.html [last accessed, 22 August 2018].
37 Church Action on Poverty, Britain Isn't Eating - the message will hit the road, http://www.church-poverty.org.uk/news/britainisnteating [last accessed, 1 September 2018].
38 Natasha Vall, *Cultural Region: North East England, 1945–2000*, Manchester University Press, Manchester, 2011.
39 Harvey, *Enigma*, p. 131. Tracy Neumann, 'Goodbye, Steeltown', in Steven High, Lachlan MacKinnon and Andrew Perchard (eds), *The Deindustrialized World: Confronting Ruination in Postindustrial Places*, UBC Press, Vancouver, 2017, p. 203.
40 Health Summary for South Tyneside, 4 July 2017 at www.healthprofiles.info [last accessed, 1 September 2018].
41 Michael Marmot, Peter Goldblatt, Jessica Allen , et al. *Fair Society Healthy Lives (The Marmot Review)*, 2010 http://www.instituteofhealthequity.org/resources-reports/fair-society-healthy-lives-the-marmot-review [last accessed 22 August 2018].
42 Danny Dorling and Stuart Gietel-Basten, 'A century of improving life expectancies in the UK is now officially over', I News, 5 December 2017 at https://inews.co.uk/opinion/century-improving-life-expectancies-uk-now-officially/ [last accessed, 28 August 2018].
43 Ellen Wilkinson, 'The magnificent obvious: Shaw's tourist guide to capitalism', *Plebs*, 1928, p. 126.
44 Daniel Dorling, *Injustice: Why Social Inequality Still Exists*, Policy, Bristol, 2011.
45 Facundo Alvaredo, L. Chancel, T. Piketty, E. Saez, and G. Zucman, eds., *World Inequality Report 2018*, Belknap Press of Harvard University Press, Cambridge, Mass., 2018.

Introduction

THE POVERTY of the poor is not an accident, a temporary difficulty, a personal fault. It is the permanent state in which the vast majority of the citizens of any capitalist country have to live. That is the basic fact of the class struggle, which not all the well-meant efforts of Personal Service Leagues and Social Service Councils can gloss over. Class antagonism cuts as deeply to the roots of capitalist society as ever it did. Men are regarded as mere instruments of production, their labour a commodity to be bought and sold. In capitalist society vast changes can be made which sweep away the livelihood of a whole town overnight, in the interest of some powerful group, who need take no account of the social consequences of their decisions. These are the facts at the base of the modern labour movement.

Generalizations are not proof. The idea of this book is to take one town, which has been through the whole process – the rise of capitalist industry, its heyday, and the rationalization period after the first world war – and to give a picture of capitalism at work. For this purpose the ancient town of Jarrow serves as a curiously complete example.

Its history dates from the days when Agricola built a fort there to protect his ships anchored in the mouth of its River Don. In the days of Bede it was a centre of European learning. Jarrow has seen the rise and fall of a great coal industry, the growth of one of the great shipyards of Europe … and its extinction. For in its heyday Palmer's Shipyard at Jarrow led the way in shipbuilding technique. At the end of the war it had a payroll of ten thousand men. Twenty years later, a blue official paper, addressed "Palmer's Shipyard, Ellison Street, Jarrow", was returned, with the postman's pencilled scrawl, "Not known. Gone away!" – the last letter of the Palmer file at Somerset House.

The bitterness of the passing of this great enterprise is that its fall was due to no national emergency, but to serve the immediate interest of a certain group. The story of what that group did to one of the national assets of this country forms part of the story of Jarrow. For this town is an illustrated footnote to British working-class history. Every stage of the class struggle in Britain has been fought out there in turn. It has had its martyrs, from Will

Jobling hanged on the gibbet at Jarrow Slake, the young miners deported in the 1831 strike, Andrew Gourlay, hero of the Nine Hours' Movement in the shipyards, and then when everything had gone, the march of the forgotten men to London.

One thing is constant through the whole story of Jarrow – through boom and slump, through so-called prosperity and the consequent distress – and that is the poverty of the working people of Jarrow. They built vast fortunes for others. They remained at subsistence level ... and many are now below even that. Any one of a dozen towns could tell something of the story, but just because Jarrow has gone through the whole process, it serves as well as any to show how, in practice, the class struggle is waged.

A personal note must be added. Work on this book was started in the Summer Parliamentary recess last year. Crisis followed crisis, calling M.P.s to the House of Commons and to work on the platform. By May 1939, when the last chapters were being written, things seem to develop into a race between Hitler and me – whether he would get his war before I finished my book. That race I won.

To friends on Tyneside, and my constituents: may I apologetically remind them that this is not a guide-book to Jarrow or a complete history of the town. It is a biography with a thesis. Much interesting detail has had to be left out, including such important movements as the Co-operative Society in Jarrow and the work of the Friendly Societies. One lady allowed me to borrow some useful papers, on condition that I told how good her grandfather had been to the strikers in 1870. Alas, that and similar promises could not be fulfilled. For the research on which the shipping and iron and steel chapters are based I am indebted to George S. Bishop, a brilliant student of the London School of Economics who has, since taking his degree, been working on a study of conditions in the distressed areas. Without his sound research, and his help even after the crisis had claimed him for heavy organizing and press work, this book could not have been written in the time available. He is not of course to be saddled with any responsibility for the opinions expressed in the book. The staff of the Jarrow Town Hall have been very helpful. The Town Clerk and the Medical Officer of Health granted the loan of reports which, particularly for the early days, give information otherwise unobtainable. Special thanks are due to the Chief Librarian at Wigan Public Library for the loan of documents about the 1844 strike in Durham. I hand on the fact of the existence of this unique collection to anyone working on early mining conditions. The Librarian of the House of Commons Library helped me to secure pamphlets about the struggles of the 1870s. For all that is known of the earliest history of Jarrow in

Roman and medieval times I have to thank Mr. J. D. Rose, whose collection of documents is unique, and whose deep knowledge of the subject makes me regret that I have had to treat this part of the story so sketchily. Mr. Peter Fanning of Newcastle lent me an interesting collection of pre-war press cuttings about Jarrow. The older town councillors, particularly Alderman J. W. Gordon, dived into their memories and their boxes for information of the pre-war period. Unemployed men have sat round the fire of their club and talked to me about their struggles of the present day. This study is necessarily incomplete. As I realized when half way through the work, such a task really needs a whole group of people working on different aspects of the problem. But perhaps this attempt may encourage some Left Book Club groups to start on a study of their own town. Much precious working-class history is waiting to be studied. Documents are available now that may easily be thrown away because their value is not realized. No working class has a richer history than the British workers, or offers a more fascinating field for research.

CHAPTER ONE

Earliest Jarrow

JARROW'S FIRST export was not battleships but Christianity. Germany was first converted to the faith by missionaries educated in the monastery of St. Paul which was founded in Jarrow in A.D. 681. Three years later, in the year of its dedication, a boy of seven years, called Bede, was placed in the care of its Abbot. This boy, who lived all his long life there till he died in 735, made Jarrow a centre of learning known throughout Europe. "First among English scholars, first among English theologians, first among English historians, it is in the monk of Jarrow that English literature strikes its roots. In the six hundred scholars who gathered round him for instruction, he is the father of our national education," is J. R. Green's description of Bede. As well as being a scholar, "the glory of the Saxon Church" Bede was a statesman, with a wide influence over the North. A letter of his, written in the last year of his life, shows him vigorously organizing from Jarrow, " to stem the growing anarchy in Northumbria ". To Bede, and the high prestige of the Jarrow school of learning, we owe the introduction into England of the Gregorian Calendar, with the B.C. and A.D. reckoning, to take the place of the old A.U.C. – " from the founding of the city of Rome".

A little way out of the present town of Jarrow, on a square of land by the River Don and Jarrow Slake, overlooking the Tyne, there stands a squat little church with a curious square tower. It is grimy with industrial soot. The churchyard, though carefully tended now, is grimy, too. But if you stand by the Saxon doorway, your feet will be on land that for 1225 years has been continuously the site of Christian service.

Jarrow from the first had unusually direct contact with Rome. The Romanesque plan of the foundations, and the little Romanesque windows in the chancel date to Benedict Biscop, the founder of the Cell of Jarrow. He travelled frequently to Rome and brought back from one of his journeys, the glazed windows for Jarrow Church … the first of their kind in Britain. Bede was very impressed by them, and tells us of their beauty and how glazing was an unknown art then in Britain. The glass has gone, but the window holes remain. The church, alas, was "restored" in the 18th century, but the original dedicatory stone of A.D. 684 is fixed in the west wall.

Built on the banks of the Tyne, the ease of communication which this gave with the continent had helped to bring the scholars in Bede's time. Next it brought the pirates. In 794 the monastery was plundered. Three years later it was burned. Each time the monks came back when the pirates went, and made it habitable again. In 870 it was again plundered and burned. Again the monks came back. Next came the scourge by Christians. When William the Conqueror laid the north country waste in 1069-70, it is recorded, "The monastery at Jarrow had been fired, and the treasures which in the precipitancy of flight were left at Durham had been plundered and profaned." But again the monks came back. The Black Death ravaged the little village that through all misfortune huddled round the monastery walls. Still services were carried on. The persistence of these humble monks of Jarrow, their determination to keep the memory of Bede a living tradition, sometimes against the frowns of the wealthy and influential monastery at Durham, gives a human link to the scattered notes of calamities through seven centuries. This story ends in 1540, when the monastery at Jarrow, listed as being worth £40 7s. 6d. (about equal to £800 of our money), was dissolved. Henry VIII gave the manor of Jarrow to a Lord Eure.

Lord Northbourne, one of the present ground landlords of Jarrow, remarked that "Jarrow has no history except that associated with Bede and Palmer". These are big names ... but the history of a town is not that of its famous men only, but the story of the tenacity of its unknown fighters in the struggle for existence. Jarrow, and the little string of towns along the Tyne, started to grow from the stagnation of the centuries with the first beginnings of capitalism in England. In the accounts at Durham Cathedral, there is a note of a coal-mine in Jarrow producing coal in 1618.

The first industries at Jarrow, and on Tyneside therefore, were small enterprises arising from the fact of easily worked coal being found so near the sea. There was a considerable salt-producing industry in the seventeenth and eighteenth centuries. At first with primitive hand-pumps, then, after 1720, when an agency for them was established at nearby Chester-le-Street, with the new steam pumps, sea water was pumped at high tide into tanks on the river banks at Jarrow. It was then evaporated by coal fires lighted underneath the tanks.

But development of the little towns like Jarrow and Shields was not easy in these early days. Newcastle, with its "charters" and "liberties", was the jealous big city watching any developments along the river very suspiciously. For that matter the fight, in 1939, is still going on. Traditional quarrels linger. This bitterness, dating from the seventeenth century, and with a good bit of fuel added to the flames since, made it impossible to have South Shields included in the scheme for the Unification of Tyneside put forward by the Royal Commission of 1937.

Newcastle had become the centre of a considerable export trade of salt and coal to London. Roads were bad: railways as yet non-existent. Sea was the only transport. With great difficulty, Benjamin Ellison, a Jarrow merchant, managed to get a licence from Newcastle Corporation about 1750 to "build a Quay from Jarrow Pans, westward to Black Point". When this was built, salt could be exported direct from Jarrow, and coal too. So the riverside village began to build wooden ships ... an industry that developed so quickly that in a few years the Jarrow Yard was building ships for the wooden Navy. A repairing yard was started next to the building yard. Sails and ropes were needed. ... There are records of a colony of 40 sail-cloth weavers, independent and tough, near the river. Unfortunately nothing survives from which it is possible to build a picture of their standard of living. The ropes for the rigging and the hundred different needs of a sailing-ship were also at first made by small independent craftsmen and their families. Then a rope-works was started. No actual wage-figures are extant, but in the town the memory of the badly-paid rope-makers contrasts with references to the relative prosperity of the independent sail-cloth weavers.

Coal-mining started seriously in Jarrow with the beginning of the nineteenth century. Demands for shipments of coke increased from the iron-smelters of the South. Middlesbrough, with its great iron industry, was as yet a tiny village clustered round the Church of St. Hilda. Coke-making developed in Jarrow because it was seen that the waste heat from the ovens could be used to heat the salt-pans. The coke ovens spread for more than a mile along the river bank, until there were more ovens than salt-pans.

Salt is a raw material for the chemical industry. In the days of bad transport, industry followed the raw material. Between 1820 and 1840, three chemical firms were established in Jarrow. A paper mill was built in 1840 on the river bank, which used the esparto grass brought in by sea, with the local salt, chemicals, and coal. In this small but growing town, as in many similar places in the England of the early part of the century, there was a balance of trades, before the great heavy industries began to grow like beans talks, making a whole town dependent on one works. An industry, like the local pottery industry at Jarrow, could flourish for a time, then die, its labour being easily absorbed, without the utter tragedy that falls on a one-industry town when that industry goes.

Labour was first drawn into Jarrow from the immediate countryside, for any industrial wages were better than what the farmers paid. Later, the coal lords sent their agents as far as Suffolk and South Wales to recruit men. The census shows that the population of Jarrow doubled from 1801 to 1811. The further increase to 3350 by 1821 was due to the demand of the mines. It remained round about this figure, until the rapid growth of Palmer's Shipyard from 1851 onwards.

While there is no record of the wages paid to the saltworkers, the records of agricultural wages provide some guide as to what would be needed to tempt the agricultural labourer into Jarrow. In 1785 the yearly rate for a male farm labourer in Durham was £10, for a woman worker £4. By 1805, owing to the demands of the mines and the new industries, these rates had risen to £21 for a man, and £9 for a woman. In 1830 the figures show a further advance. The landworker's wage, like the miner's, included a cottage, which other workers had to pay for directly as rent. How much these wages bought we will discuss later in connection with the coal strikes in Jarrow.

No stories have come down to us of any definite labour disputes in this little town before mining started on a big scale. Unrest there must have been in plenty, for with the rise in prices which followed the Napoleonic wars, food was terribly dear. But it was not until men began to be employed together in considerable numbers that trade-unionism could take root. From an old diary it is possible to piece together a picture of social conditions in Jarrow in the early years of the nineteenth century.

> "The little gardens were well looked after, but there were no other amenities for the workmen. Apart from fighting, the only recreations were quoits and bowls, both carried on in conjunction with the public houses."

The water supply was drawn from only two sources. One was from the well in the High Street which was connected to a flour mill belonging to one of the four shopkeepers in the place. If he had not enough orders to keep his mill going, no water could be obtained. Then the only hope was the Clegg Well which was too far away for the women to go to fetch water. So the owner of the well brought it round in a water cart, at a charge of one penny per skiel (two gallons).

Drains were non-existent. Glancing through a file of the *Newcastle Courant* it is possible to trace a cholera epidemic as it swept through Europe. There is a small reference in three lines to the cholera in Europe in the summer of 1831; quite a paragraph when it reached London; half a column as it comes up through Lincoln. Then panic denials of the existence of the plague, till

210 deaths in three weeks at the end of the year in Newcastle itself cannot be ignored. A couple of columns, equal to a banner-spread in a modern paper, tells of its sweep through the Tyneside villages. Prayers against the cholera were being said in every church. By the third week in January 1832, the plague is on the wane. The *Newcastle Courant* writes complacently:

> "*One* of the most remarkable features it still exhibits. The narrow and dirty lanes in the lower parts of the town, and the confined and ill-ventilated passages which are numerous in the upper, and in which the dwellings of the poor and wretched are situated, have been, with few exceptions, the only places to which the disease has penetrated, and in which it has revelled with all its fatality ... *it might almost be inferred that it is a malady as far as regards predisposition PECULIAR to the poorer portion of the population.*"

Even the cholera was somehow the fault of the poor. It was peculiar to the people who lived in the noisome hovels. The well-to-do could take heart by the comforting thought that they had not to live in such places. A good many years were to elapse before a medical officer in Jarrow was to be practically driven out of his job for daring to suggest that foul and overcrowded conditions could actually cause the spread of zymotic disease.

CHAPTER TWO
Capitalism Starts Operations

JARROW'S FIRST capitalist promoter, Simon Temple, is still a legendary figure in the town. He had interests in all its industries – salt-pans, shipping, chemicals, glassworks. He opened the Alfred Pit in 1803, which really started the deep-seam mining on a big scale. It was he who built the first wooden frigates, the best things of their kind at that date. But the contract was a disastrous one, and started his ruin, as a battleship contract was to start his great successor on the downgrade eighty-eight years later. He bought Jarrow Slake, a natural harbour on the Tyne with great possibilities which have never to this day been properly utilized. Temple saw the advantages of the Slake. He proposed to build a great naval arsenal there at his own risk, to be financed by a tonnage tax on Tyne shipping. Newcastle and the Tyne shippers stopped that enterprise. The white-walled cottages he built for his workmen, some of which, till the clearance scheme last year, were still occupied, were a considerable improvement at that time on the wretched hovels usually provided for miners. Temple bought a nearby castle, gave a reputed Vandyk to Bede's old church, started a badly needed fever hospital, and crashed to obscurity and poverty, all in about fourteen years.

The dazzling entrepreneur, the local man who had just had a glimpse of the possibilities of the new capitalism, but had enough local feeling to want to cut a dash in his own place, vanished. The solid men, with London money and no local associations, took over. They had no time for such expensive hobbies as Vandyks to churches, model cottage and fever hospitals. Quick money was their only concern … and the tale of their work is grim.

The nature of the industry makes coal-mining the classic battle-ground of the class struggle in any country. In Britain it was the first industry to employ large numbers of men together. The cost of labour, however low the wage per man, is the highest item in the cost of production. The coal is there, underground. It must be got to the surface. The earlier and more primitive the mine, the higher the wage cost relative to all other expenses. Hence the constant pressure of the owners to drive down wages. Despite this, it was not till after a century of coal-mining that any considerable progress was made in labour-saving devices. The individual labour unit was cheap. There was always the hope of getting it still cheaper. Until electricity and compressed air came into commercial use there was no source of power underground for actual coal-getting except human muscle.

Coal from the first was a fiercely competitive industry. Even for their own most immediate interest ... to save the coal ... the owners refused to co-operate. In some 140 years of coal-getting, they have been the most short-sighted of all employers of labour. Some of the collieries in North Durham tunnelled beneath the Tyne River. In 1838, the owners of one of these, the Percy Main, though they were warned by experienced men, insisted in order to get a little quick extra profit, that the pillars of coal which had been left by the miners to support the roof of the High Main seam beneath the Tyne should be dug out.

What the men, as well as the technicians, had predicted, happened. The water came in at a rate with which the pumps could not deal. The" viewer" (manager) at Percy Main, Mr. John Buddle, the chief colliery consultant of his time, warned the neighbouring collieries of the danger. He tried to get the owners to agree to some kind of co-operative action against the water. They would not even come, or send representatives, to look at the dams he was building, and the other measures he was taking to keep down the water.

In the North Durham of 1838, as in the South Durham of 1938, the coalowners would not act together to save the priceless national asset in their hands. The significant difference is that in the early nineteenth century, the owner fought for his own hand, and frankly said that he did not see why he should pay to save his neighbour's coal, even though his own colliery was thereby endangered. A century later the owners in South Durham admitted the need for some joint action against the water, but expected the Government to pay for it.

The results of the bad tradition thus established in the earliest days of Durham mining persist to this day. Whole villages are derelict in the county, the men permanently unemployed, because the pits are flooded. Wallsend, which in the 1820s produced the finest steam coal in England, had to close down because of the flood water from Percy Main. Thirteen million tons of workable coal in the Bishop Auckland district have been lost through neglected water. If from the early days some tradition of responsibility had been established, if owners could have been made liable to keep down the water in the pits they owned when they decided to abandon them ... even if this had had to be financed by some common fund, Durham would be in a far different position to-day. But when the coal traditions were being made, the coal barons were undisputed masters, owners of life and land. No set of employers has such a record of success at keeping "interfering legislation" down to a minimum. To-day we are trying to deal with the results of their criminal folly. When a Labour Government comes to expropriate the coalowners, the amount of workable coal that has been thus destroyed, deliberately or through negligence, should be put into the debit account when compensation is being estimated. There would not be much of a balance to hand over in some areas of Durham County.

The owners who would not unite to save the coal soon learned to combine against the men. In the early days the problem was to get enough men, and then to keep them, under the conditions then existing. It was not of course imagined that the cheapest way of keeping them might, in the long run, be to treat them decently. In Durham, in the first half of the century, the coalowners, the high dignitaries of the Church of England, and the magistrates acted like men in a continual state of panic, surrounded by hordes of savages.

Between 1825 and 1850 mining was being established as a large-scale industry in Durham. As yet the men had no effective organization. The story of their treatment at this period is, therefore, a very instructive chapter in labour history. In these days of fascism, when the workers' unions have been smashed, and all effective means of protest and redress removed, the story of these earlier struggles cannot be dismissed as "All so long ago. Things are better now." Wherever workers are denied their own bulwarks against tyranny, the same kind of oppression recurs; the same kind of accusation are levied by employers against the leadership created from the ranks. The magistrates' comments on the men who led the Durham strikes of 1832 and 1844 were repeated in very much the same phrases by the Colonial Secretary, regarding Uriah Butler, the leader of the oil strikers in Trinidad in 1938. The Marquis of Londonderry of the eighteen-thirties used every device to beat starving strikers, even to preventing them getting credit in the local shops. The Marquis of to-day was for a long time one of the most consistent admirers of Herr Hitler.

As men began to be employed on a larger scale, the idea behind the employers' methods was to put them in a position where it was difficult or in fact almost impossible for them to claim even their rights under the Common Law of England. Hence the importance attached by the owners to the Yearly Bond, which was subject of dispute as early as 1765 and was not finally got rid of until 1872.

The miners engaged in Binding Day signed a bond to work for the owners of the colliery for a year. When possible, it was arranged in the bond to be just so many days short as would prevent the miner establishing residential qualifications in the parish and so entitle him to relief if he were destitute. No point was missed. The men agreed, under penalty, to work for that colliery for every working day in this period. In return they got a cottage and work in that colliery. But the right to that cottage or that work could not be enforced. If a foreman wanted to get rid of a man, there was nothing so easy as to prove that the bond had been infringed. Eviction followed dismissal that same day.

The owners agreed to find the men such work as would allow them to earn a certain minimum per fortnight, and a clause to this effect was put in the bond. Twenty-eight shillings was a usual figure in Durham at this time, but in Jarrow the men were paid 2s. less. Although the owners spoke during any dispute as though this was a guaranteed rate, it was never enforceable. The men were continually denied enforceability of the bond by the courts. Though the men were not allowed during their bond to work elsewhere when the pit was idle, there was no compulsion on the owners to pay the miner for any working day on which he was not allowed to work.

A letter sent to the *Miners' Journal* on behalf of the men of Jarrow Colliery says:

> The men of Jarrow Colliery are bound to £1 6s. 0d. per man on an average for four successive fortnights, for which they have been generally a great way short I assure you. They have been before the magistrates three different times about it, and the only proof they had against the master's bills was their pay note, that IS a small piece of paper with an account of the money that is paid to each man; but I think they are now trying their last shift which is to pay them without any notes at all. So it appears to me that they are determined to beat them next time, but I hope the magistrates will give them a hearing when they go again, when they state the truth and nothing but the truth, but it has not always been the case with them.
> Signed "ALPHA."

It was not so much this rate of wage about which the men were Concerned. However vague they were about what else was in their bond, they were clear as to that promised amount. Low as it was, it was considerably higher than they could get at any other work in the district. But throughout this period, and in fact for long after, until the system of men's checkweighers was introduced in 1861, their difficulty was to get paid the money they had actually earned. Once the employers, by alluring promises of high wages, had collected men from as far distant as Devon or Norfolk, and had induced them to sign the bond, they resented having to pay men for this terribly dangerous work any more money than by old and bad custom they paid their farm labourers. Ingenious schemes amounting to actual swindling were devised to get back as much as possible from each man's pay bill.

The standard measure for the coal the hewer sent to bank was called a corve (usually 7½ cwts.), from the basket which he filled. The colliers worked in very bad light. Until the Davy Lamp was invented and first used at Hebburn, the sister town to Jarrow, they had only the light of a single candle. If the coal in the basket was even a quart (i.e., about 2 lbs. out of 7½ cwts.) under measure, the coal in that basket was forfeited to the owner, and sometimes the man had to pay a fine as well. If a small quantity of stone or "black brass", indistinguishable from coal in such a light, was included in the corve, then also it was forfeited. The records of the time are filled with the bitter complaints of men who after working desperately hard all day to fill as many as eight baskets would find that seven of *them* were forfeit to the Owner. The fines for "bad work" would then come to more than he was paid for the correct one.

The miners tell their own story in a *Memo. of Grievances* from the Durham of 1825.

"In working the large coal we have the small coals to throw back, they are denominated by us ' dead small'; for this we get nothing though we have them to work. But this does not end the history of dead small, they are wanted for engine fires or the workmen's houses and then we have to fill them *up for nothing,* and if there should happen to be among this dead small a few stones we are fined one shilling."

The memo. goes on to complain of the "insolent and contemptuous manner in which we are generally treated by the agents and men in office". This was always a sore point among the Jarrow men.

If the miners thought they were being cheated by a fraudulent corve measure, they had to give three days' notice before the measure could be checked ... just to let the "keeker" have time to get a correct one along. What the men thought about the "keeker," the man who was paid by commission on the number of corves he found faulty, is best told by the men in a pamphlet, *A Voice from the Coalmines,* published in 1825 by the short-lived Association of the Miners of Northumberland and Durham.

"Our bond is too rigorous and contains conditions which it is impossible for us to comply with. The bond makes it imperative for us to send to bank, round or large coal at 4s. 8d. per score, an small at 2s. per score, but if the round coal should be mixed with the small coal then the poor unfortunate workman is fined 1s. or rather if the coal should be deemed so mixed by the keker whose mere assertion is quite sufficient for the purpose. Now this fine is both absurd and oppressive for no line of distinction is drawn between round and small; what the workman may deem a good corf, the keker's caprice may made a bad one.

"There is also a strong bias towards self interest in this petty spy. If he does not fine the men and show some work for his wages he must walk about his business. He knows that his masters will not pay him his wages for nothing. Therefore he

labours dilligently in his disgraceful calling to the great oppression of his fellow-men. Besides he may have a private pique at some men and by fining them he kills two birds with one stone, or in other words pleases his masters and gratifies his own bad passions.

"We can number of these officious understrappers, no less a number than eleven upon our colliery. But our fine system does not end here. If two quarts of splints or stones are found in a corf *we* are fined six pence, and if more than that quantity is found we are mercifully fined the trifling and very moderate sum of five shillings!!!

"AND SHOULD a corf want one quart of measure, that corf is forfeited to the owner. We certainly (if we had anything like fairplay) ought when a corf is short of measure to have pay for what is really produced by our labour, and when stones are accidentally found in a corf (for no man will put them in on purpose) the workman ought to have the privilege of picking them out, and at anyrate not be fined until he refuses to do so, which no man would when his own interest was so intimately concerned."

Most miners at this time could neither read nor write, yet the pamphlets and broadsheets of the period pulsate with the spirit of mining life. The men gathered in groups to hear them read. Mostly they were written by local preachers, Wesleyans and Primitive Methodists who were taught their letters at the Sunday School. Because these men were still working at the coal-face, they were able to put the miner's real views on paper as no official or lawyer could do. These local leaders were sober and moderate men. What they wrote was a careful understatement. They would have deemed any exaggeration a serious moral fault. From their writings one can feel the strength of the petty tyrants set over them. At one colliery a drunken keeker was "down on the methodies because they are sober men". His word was sufficient to deprive a man of payment for a hard day's work, simply by declaring his corves to be short measure. The worker had no appeal.

The law was mobilized on the side of the owners ...and therefore of the keeker. In addition to fines for bad work there were a list of fines which the owner, more often the "viewer" or manager, drew up himself. He acted as his own judge and the fines went into his pocket. Some were fines for offences that had no connection with the colliery at all. Fines for keeping pigs, for trespassing or stealing, and even for not doing "a fair day's work" ... a frequent cause of fine. The men bitterly complained that no standard of what was a fair day's work was laid down.

The bond could be enforced in the courts by the employers, because it was a legal document on which the men had made their mark, or signed if they could write their names. In these courts the owners and their viewers sat as magistrates and tried cases of their own men without question. Being absent from work was an offence under the bond; the penalty: three months in the House of Correction, or a fine. This clause could be and was used with deadly effect to prevent union organization spreading from pit to pit. A miner who had been elected as delegate, and who took a day off to attend a miners' meeting, even though he gave notice beforehand, not only lost his wages. He rendered himself liable for three months on the treadmill!

Behind all the struggles on individual grievances was the instinctive fight for human rights ... to be regarded as men, not mere serfs. The miners felt that they were being done down every way; that the manager who got them to sign the bond administered it as magistrate and could send them to prison for "crimes" that he himself had listed and which applied to no other men; that if they struck against the most obvious swindling, such as the fraudulent declaration of short-weight, the police, the military, the dreaded cavalry even, would be called out to whip them back to work ... with the blessing of the Lord Bishop of Durham and every well-to-do man in the county.

CHAPTER THREE
Jarrow Colliery and its Martyrs

"You SIGNED the bond. You knew what you were signing. Why do you come here and complain now?" The magistrates were fond of this sort of speech to miners who found themselves trapped by their bond. Binding Day was the miner's one day of apparent freedom ... and the last thing the colliery-owner wanted him to know was what was in his bond. If miners were in demand, beer flowed freely. The viewer would get up on a barrel or a low wall, and with hundreds of men gathered round him would hastily read out the bond. Only those men nearest to him could even hear his words. No questions could be asked while he was reading. If an intelligent miner recognized some clause as a new "try-on", he had to wait until the viewer had read the whole bond. Even then any question could be drowned by the viewer calling out, "A pound for the first man to sign, ten shillings for the second, then two and sixpence a head." In the rush to get the pound, the questioner would have no chance of anything but being marked out by the viewer as a man likely to be dangerous, who must not be allowed to sign at all.

With the keeker ready to penalize a man suspected of union tendencies, by declaring an intolerable number of his corves short, any chance of getting the men to stand together for Binding Time seemed small. Only after the men had signed did spontaneous strikes occur. When they found that some new oppressive clause had been put in without their knowing the whole pit would stop like one man. The Binding Strike of 1810, the biggest of the early strikes, occurred when the men discovered that the time conditions of the bond had been altered. This was the occasion when so many miners were arrested that the Lord Bishop of Durham obligingly lent his episcopal stables to the authorities as a concentration camp. The miners were manacled to the mangers. The leaders were ill-treated. So many men were crowded in small spaces that fever broke out. Even under these conditions they managed to resist the blandishments of the Rev. Nesfield, who was sent to recall them to a sense of their duty to God and their masters. This padre, to do him justice, worked hard later to get the worst scandals of fining put right.

It was always hunger that drove the men back. They had no resources, no permanent organization. Their only weapon was violence, on which, of course, the employers could play to get more soldiers and prove how right they were to keep such dangerous creatures in their places.

By 1825 the Association of the Colliers of Northumberland and Durham had been formed, and, despite the tyranny, the organization did spread from pit to pit. Violence may be a bad way of getting public sympathy, but the knowledge that he might be found behind a hedge with his head split open kept many a keeker within some tolerable bounds. Jarrow and Hebburn colliers had a reputation in the coal-field for having effective private methods of settling keekers, while at the neighbouring colliery of Felling the men were known as being most law-abiding ... a distinction between Jarrow and Felling that oddly enough continues to this day.

The Jarrow men were more concerned about safety than about any other conditions ... and they had need to be. Small explosions had always been common in the Jarrow pits, with a small but steady loss of life. When only two or three men lost their lives or were badly burned, it was, as Fyne points out in his *History of the Miners,* only rarely reported, except in the neighbourhood. But the tradition that Jarrow was a "slaughter pit" lingers still in the town. There were such big explosions at Jarrow, however, that they could not be kept out of the news. On January 17, 1826, thirty-four men and boys out of the forty-nine in the pit at the time lost their lives. In August 1830 a great explosion occurred that killed forty-two men and injured over a hundred. The Jarrow men complained that lives were being lost unnecessarily to save money. The owners would not go to the expense of digging an extra shaft for ventilation.

The sense of solidarity in the class struggle grows not as a matter of theory, but of practical necessity, when men are employed in great numbers under hard conditions. Leaders of courage and decision in these struggles are not the product of soft places. The courage that was born of facing death daily in the slaughter-pits of this period was needed by the leaders, who were grown in the ranks of the miners. Few names have come down to us from the earlier days. The men who led the early strikes were victimized when the men returned to work. Hunted from place to place, they either starved to death, or later, if lucky, got away to America.

Tommy Hepburn of Hetton, who lived and worked most of his life in the Jarrow-Felling area, is one of the first names to stand out among the anonymous working-class heroes of these early days. H was born in the same village as Macintosh, who had tried to get a co-operative store as an alternative to the scandalous Tommy Shop. But the owners were not having that lucrative business taken from them, and soon hounded him out of the country. Hepburn, who was a local preacher of the Primitive Methodists, was a man of rare intelligence and shrewdness of judgement. He saw that stand-up fights between owners and pitmen were leading nowhere. With the whole legal apparatus on the side of the masters, the men could not win alone. He aimed at breaking down the isolation of the men in the colliery villages. There was a fair amount of sympathetic middle-class support to be got at this time, as a result of the work of the Chartists in Newcastle and the struggle for the Reform Bill. Hepburn made a shrewd appeal to the pockets of the shop-keeping class by pointing out that the Tommy-Shop system prevented more than the merest trickle of the miners' wages coming to them. Newcastle, more then than now, was one of the leading centres of progressive politics. Hepburn spoke at some of these general political meetings, exciting sympathy by his description of the long hours and terrible conditions of the young boys in the pits.

The association of the two counties was revived in 1830 and to this day is known as Hepburn's Union among the old pitmen. It was decided to make a stand for Binding Day, April 1831. Great meetings were held, culminating in a vast demonstration of 20,000 men on Newcastle Moor. The miners walked in from Jarrow, South Shields, and from twenty miles around.

Hepburn's work was shown in the ,more sympathetic attitude of the newspapers, which, entirely dependent on middle-class support, had always denounced the men without troubling about their grievances.

The *Newcastle Courant* wrote, in a report of the meeting, which had actually been attended by the Mayor of Newcastle, who had addressed a few sympathetic words to the men and advised them to keep the peace,

> "Several persons addressed the meeting and detailed in homely but energetic language the grievances ... These did not appear to be so much connected with the prices of work as with some objectionable parts of the bond of service, the chief of which were, the power of the owners to lay the men idle on the occurrence of the most trifling accidents to pits, engines or even rail roads, after which their wages are discontinued for three days, their subjection to the caprice of the viewers and agents not only for a continuance of work, but even for the shelter of their wives and families, as they are liable to be turned out of their houses either on the completion of their bond, or on the non-fulfilment of the articles of the bond arising from mutual disagreement; the obligation they are under to remain idle for three weeks at Xmas time without any wages, and the

length of time boys are immured in the collieries to the destruction of health, and of almost every chance of education or moral welfare."

Tommy Hepburn, feeling that he had got the tide of public opinion with the men for the first time, held meetings all along the Tyne Valley appealing for a solid stand and no violence. He desperately wanted to give the public an object lesson in the quiet reasonableness of his trade-union members, as compared with the unreasonable demands of the owners. At a great meeting at Jarrow on April 22nd, to which men came in procession from Hebburn, Felling and South Shields, Hepburn impressed this on the men.

A peaceful strike did not suit the owners. Special constables were sworn in, and an excess number of yeomanry were drafted into the area. The word went out that "incidents" were inevitable ... which meant that blacklegs would be imported ... and trouble would ensue. The scab labour was imported first into Hebburn. The Jarrow men came along to lend a hand in dealing with this little problem. Corves, rolleys, loose material, anything they could lay their hands on, were flung down the shaft, "to the great terror of the men below" as a local reporter wrote at the time.

A local magistrate, Mr. Fairless, took a big part in fighting the men. He stayed with the viewer "to be on hand conveniently to read the Riot Act". Through his efforts extra soldiers were sent into the Jarrow-Hebburn area. He himself went with them to the pit-heads. His efforts were to have a tragic sequel for himself and for others in the following year.

The case of the Seven Lads of Jarrow deserves to rank with the martyrs of Tolpuddle, their contemporaries. These seven young pitmen were arrested during the strike. Five of the seven were ardent Primitive Methodists who met regularly in their "society class". The authorities tried to make a case out against them of "feloniously demanding money and meat from one Thomas Hedworth, assaulting him, and trying to steal two guns". The young men admitted that they had begged for food because they were starving, but strenuously denied the other charges, which the police made no attempt to prove. But evidence was given that the seven had been seen at strike meetings. This they admitted and declared that they were members of the Union. They were all sentenced to death, on a charge of "conspiracy". This was commuted to transportation for seven years because of their good character ... and presumably the fact that nothing but asking for food, and being members of the Union could be proved against them. They went to Botany Bay in the convict ship and never returned to England.

Twenty years later a member of the Legislative assembly of Victoria, interested as being a Primitive Methodist with relatives in Jarrow and

Hebburn, tried to find out what had become of them. They had been liberated at the end of their seven terrible years of penal servitude which they had fully served. Five of them survived, all of whom became respected members of their communities ... one of them reaching local fame as a preacher. This was the type of working-class youth the coalowners were hunting down like animals with their cavalry and police.

The case of the Seven Lads of Jarrow roused great indignation in the area. Steady and unexpected support came from the biggest Newcastle paper, influenced by certain of the business men who felt that the coal barons were going really too far, and damaging local trade. One of them politely wrote to the *Newcastle Courant*, "The station of the coalowners may have placed them too much above their dependents to perceive the abuse of power in those who hold an intermediate post, while others who have become proprietors in shares of collieries feel little interest but in the profits."

The owners were taken by surprise ... both by the strength of the resistance under Hepburn's careful leadership, and by the attitude of a middle-class public which had been attracted by the huge Chartist meetings. It was a new situation to feel themselves on the defensive against Hepburn's exposures of conditions in the pit. Lord Londonderry was heard advocating "that the fines should be left to his honour and that of his agents". Funny how through the years this family goes on saying silly things. The owners began to give way. By June work was generally resumed throughout the area, though the Jarrow Pit had a private row of its own about victimization.

There was, of course, no signed agreement. That would have implied recognition of the Union. But the main victory of the strike was the general establishment of a working day of twelve hours for boys instead of one without limit. For a time this was fairly well kept, but when the Union was weakened, the old bad habits returned. In 1842 the child-labour Commission reported on boys in the area, all from eight to twelve years old, who had at times stayed the whole twenty-four hours down the pit. No concession was given as regards fines. At Jarrow, and some other collieries, the owners offered to pay wages in money instead of tommy checks ... a promise that in J arrow was soon broken. To us, used to signed agreements, all this seems vague enough ... but the general impression of victory is best expressed by a local preacher at J arrow who included in a prayer, " And we thank thee, oh Lord, that through the strike thou hast tamed the arrogance of our keekers."

Anyway, the men felt they had won, and there was a grand victory meeting at Boldon Fell, which had, tactfully, to be described as a meeting to "thank His Majesty for his beneficent attentions to the wants of his people".

The meeting listened to speeches urging solidarity with the Union. It agreed to appoint Hepburn to be travelling organizer, and to give special attention to the educational needs of the pitboys. The miners received all the resolutions with cheers, and the demonstration was just ending when someone remembered that they were supposed to thank His Majesty for something. However, they thanked the public for their support and called it a day.

In the long rows of white miners' cottages that stretched from Jarrow Pit, and the cluster of similar ones nearby at Hebburn and Felling, hope ran high during the remaining months of 1831. True, it was terrible trying to make up the debts that had had to be contracted during the strike. It was difficult to get back into the cottages from which some had been evicted and blacklegs put in their places. There were fights in plenty about that. There was a great deal of victimization ... particularly at Jarrow. Those who had taken a prominent part in the dispute had to leave the little town, for they could get no work there. But there was a feeling of victory. "Even the hard masters of Jarrow", as a contemporary article calls them, "had to give way." There was even interest in this odd idea of Tommy Hepburn's that miners should learn to read and write. After some ten hours' gruelling hard work underground, the big fists of miners curled round lead pencils, or tired minds tried to learn the alphabet. Tommy even started a circulating library of books and pamphlets for the miners' lodges. Those who could read would spell out the page for the others. There was a feeling in Jarrow that things would be better.

The owners were considering the situation, too. They had been caught unawares, by the solidarity of the men, by an extent of organization which they had not suspected, and by the astonishing amount of public sympathy which had backed the men. They began to prepare for Binding Day, 1832. The Union must be broken. As for public opinion ... that public should learn what sort of men they had been supporting the previous year. Plenty of violence from the very beginning, whatever that scoundrel Hepburn advised. The keekers could see to that. The magistrates' courts would do their duty and make examples before the district. The legal decisions during the strike of 1832 are important in working-class history, as we shall see.

Hepburn realized that the Union would have to fight for its very existence, and he decided to fight on that ground rather than complicate the issue by demands for higher wages ... much as such demands would have been justified. At the meeting at Bolden Fell, to which the Jarrow men send a large and militant contingent, the three following resolutions were passed which are important in view of what happened.

1. "That we are authorized by the laws of our country to meet on such occasions and support each other.
2. "That as intimidation and coercion are repugnant to all sacred and civil law all our undertakings be done peaceably and orderly.
3. "That as the establishment of our system (Le., Union) hath been of great benefit to ourselves and our families, we be grateful to those who have supported us, and that we henceforward persevere in *the* ways of truth and reason."

The *Newcastle Courant,* in commenting on the orderliness of the meeting, said "there was not one word uttered tending to show a disposition to procure augmented wages, or in any way to seek advantages beyond those already obtained."

Hepburn and his colleagues were trying to help their men to struggle out of the degradation to which the hard conditions of life and work, and the appalling poverty, had forced them. The Union was the life line that pulled them up, made decent citizens of these brave men. Yet, for the sake of a little extra profit, the local landowners and the moneyed men from London who owned Jarrow Pit were preparing to use all the forces of the law, the army, the police, and the magistrates to thrust the men back into the abyss of hopelessness and poverty.

An "Open Letter" to the coalowners from a worker, most probably from one of Hepburn's immediate helpers, written just before the strike details the grievances of the men, and complains about the incorrect information about hours and wages given out by the coalowners to the public. Defending the Union from the owners' charge of being a "secret conspiracy" and a "general confederacy", whereas it was quite open, held open meetings, and the rules of the Union were widely printed, the letter goes on to say bitterly,

"The Union has done good work in supporting the widows and orphans of those whose lives have been sacrificed in the service of men who, while they rail at slavery and shudder at the use of the whip, expose their fellow creatures to extreme labour in a pestilential atmosphere, where their lives are in continual Jeopardy, and where hundreds of them perish. Yet they begrudge them their scanty pittance, and either by themselves or by their agents devise every means to plunder and oppress them."

It was a deserved sneer at some of the proprietors of the period who were shedding crocodile tears about slavery in America, while oblivious to, or even defending, the industrial atrocities in their own country ... a habit the

English still maintain to the annoyance of other nations.

The coalowners were not able to keep a completely united front. The smaller owners, who were willing to work on the 1831 basis, came to terms with their men to carry on as before. The bigger owners, and with these Jarrow owners were firmly ranged, were ready for a fight. Hepburn realized the difficulty of split forces, but met it by urging the men at work to contribute to the support of those who would have to fight.

The owners struck quickly. Detachments of troops were sent to the North-east from London. During the week of May 5th, police troops and magistrates concentrated on Jarrow. Those long white rows of miners' cottages built by Simon Temple were emptied of strikers and their families. They had no place to go. No neighbour dare take them in, even if there had been room. With great pluck they went on to the common and erected shacks out of their own furniture, with sacks and bedclothes for tent covers. Lead miners from Alston were brought in and given the cottages. Miners were brought in from South Wales on the story that the cholera epidemic had caused a shortage and that wages were high. Though far from their homes, the South Wales men refused to blackleg. They joined the strike, and spoke at the meetings. This heartened the Durham men enormously. Even to-day, there is a feeling of solidarity between Durham and South Wales at Trades Union and other Congresses which is closer than that shown by other coal-fields. A great tradition lives on.

Nicholas Fairless, that hard and elderly magistrate, was as active in this strike as in previous troubles. He was hated for various harsh judgements. The severe sentences he inflicted on the sailors on strike in South Shields as far back as 1818 were remembered.

In April 1832 he had sentenced a boy apprentice to three months' imprisonment simply for disobeying some order of his master. He had got himself hated in Hebburn during the strike of the previous year. This time, he was staying as guest with Mr. Foster, the viewer of Jarrow Colliery, so as to be on hand to read the Riot Act when required, and cover the operations of the soldiery.

William Jobling was one of the miners on strike at Jarrow. He had two children. His wife was expecting a third. He was known as a good union man, strongly on the side of Hepburn's law-abiding policy. He had an unblemished personal character. Jobling, with a friend, Ralph Armstrong, also a union man, went for a long walk to fill in one of the hot June days of the strike, and stopped at an inn on the South Shields' road for a drink. As they went out, Mr. Fairless came riding by on his pony. An argument ensued between the men, during the course of which Jobling was asked his name, and gave it. Jobling was also seen to shake hands with the magistrate. Beyond that, the evidence is completely conflicting. Mr. Fairless was later found with a wound on his head. Jobling was arrested that same evening on the sands at South Shields.

Mr. Fairless told his doctor that Jobling did not hit him, but did not prevent the other man from doing so. It seems evident that the older man, Armstrong, lost his temper and struck Mr. Fairless the blow from which he died. But the authorities had got Jobling, while Armstrong had disappeared. They were determined on an example. In the deposition put in after Mr. Fairless had died, the dead magistrate was said to have declared that Jobling held him while the other man hit him, an account which did not tally with Mr. Fairless's personal statement to his doctor.

Jobling pleaded not guilty, at his trial at Durham Assizes on August 1st. Any lawyer could have made hay of the flimsy evidence brought against him, but how could a miner on strike get a lawyer! The jury, with a coalowner as foreman, took just fifteen minutes to find him guilty. The remarks with which Mr. Justice Parkes sentenced him to death should be noted.

"To the death of that gentleman, your country is about to add the death of yourself; and it will afford another melancholy proof of the baneful effects of these combinations amongst the workmen against their employers which have prevailed for so many months in this country which have been so deeply injurious both to the public interest and the interest of those concerned."

The judge also ordered that the body should be gibbetted near the scene of the crime in accordance with an act that had only been in operation a week. Jobling's body was the first to be subjected to this revived medieval horror.

Jobling, whose manner at the trial had been impressive in its simple dignity, was hung at noon on August 3rd. He maintained his innocence and went calmly to his death. It was, of course, a public execution. Just before he was hung, a voice from the crowd called out "Farewell, Jobling". Jobling turned his head to that friendly voice, and in so doing displaced the rope ... which meant a prolonged and horrible death. His body was then covered with pitch and gibbetted at Jarrow Slake. A large military escort took the humble striker to his final humiliation. The miners swore that the body of their comrade should not hang there, so a military guard was kept by the Jarrow gibbet night and day. Leaflets were distributed in Jarrow warning the people that the punishment for removing the body would be seven years' transportation. There were protests in the Newcastle papers. The *Newcastle Courant* urged the removal of "so disgusting an exhibition", but the authorities were determined on that "example". When the soldiers could not stand the smell from the decaying body, they were removed, it being thought that no one would now go near it. But on the night of September 1st, both body and gibbet vanished ... no one ever knew how, except those whose courage in facing infection to honour their comrade's body is a reproach to the disgusting ideas of the legal authorities of the day. Most probably the body was rowed out to sea.

Jobling was regarded as a martyr by the miners who knew him, and the memory of this revenge-execution still lingers in Jarrow. A *Brief History of Jarrow* says of him : "No could have looked more unlike the typical murderer: high broad forehead, nose shapely and well-defined, full expressive lips, a clear and thoughtful eye, and of more than ordinary intelligence and respectability ... large numbers continue to believe that Jobling was unjustly accused."

Rewards of £100 and £300 were offered for the information and arrest of Ralph Armstrong. He is believed to have fled overseas. There is a local legend that he visited Jarrow as an old man thirty years later. It was believed at the time that the voice that called "Farewell, Jobling" was Ralph Armstrong's ... though that would have been foolhardy to the extreme. Had Armstrong given himself up, it would not have saved Jobling. The magistrates were out for blood, and any excuse for making examples was sufficient.

The type of justice the men were getting at Durham Assizes during this strike is worth putting on record. Just before Mr. Justice Parkes dealt with William Jobling he tried seventeen prisoners for offences arising out of the strike. Two men and one woman were sentenced to death for assaulting a blackleg. A man was given twelve months for trying to persuade a fellow-pitman not to work. Five men were given one year each for picketing South Shields Colliery. Eight men were sentenced to periods ranging from nine to twenty-one months for trying to resist ejectment during the Friar's Goose evictions, which followed the evictions at Jarrow. The records at Durham state:

"The learned judge addressed himself to the prisoners and pointed out the consequences attending the illegal combinations which existed in this county, which he said had the inevitable tendency to induce men *of otherwise irreproachable character* to break the law in a most atrocious manner. He trusted that the parties chiefly concerned in keeping up such illegal societies would speedily be brought to the punishment they deserved; and further that the severe sentences he intended to pass upon the prisoners at the bar would be a warning to them and an example to others."

After that outburst, he sentenced the seventeen before him, and proceeded with Jobling's case.

The horrible punishment of Jobling was so dramatic coupled with his known good character it led to considerable criticism in the area. A few days later, at Newcastle, Mr. Justice Parkes further delivered himself of his theory of justice. He admitted the sentences were severe, but claimed they were necessary as a deterrent.

"It matters not in what manner the Union and the combinations were got up, or in what manner they are conducted. The law will be found sufficient to put them down."

It is interesting to contrast with this severity, sentences passed on those who erred on what might be called the "right" side of the law. While trying to settle some trouble between strikers and special constables near North Shields, a miner, Cuthbert Skipsey, a respected man of great influence with the miners ... was shot dead by a constable named Weddle. At the inquest, which returned a verdict of manslaughter, the coroner refused even to allow the Press to take notes of the evidence. Weddle was tried on the same day that Jobling was hanged and sentenced to six months' imprisonment.

There is no doubt these sentences had their effect on the strikers ... especially as they were coupled with merciless hounding of strikers' leaders over the moors, which made it impossible to hold a meeting in the later days of the strike. Blacklegs were brought up from the South in large numbers. The coalowners' agents were sending up any sort of men, to break the spirit of the strikers. They evidently went to extremes, as a letter exists from a viewer to one of these agents, asking him not to send "old and obviously decrepit men". Even to resist deliberately provocative evictions, such as those at Jarrow and Friar's Goose, where sick women and newly born babies were turned out on to the road, meant facing savage sentences like those inflicted by Justice Parkes. To fight four and a half months, without a roof over the head of one's family, with practically no resources except collections from workers themselves desperately poor, is the sort of achievement which would thrill the hearts of British working-class children to-day, if they were allowed to learn their own history instead of only that of their masters. Some men were still holding out in August ... and their example was such that the owners actually proposed to set up their own friendly societies for the benefit of the miners, and to subscribe to the funds themselves ... a left-handed compliment to the work the Unions had done.

With sickness sweeping through the temporary homes, women starving and children dying from exposure and want, the men could hold out no longer. In the middle of August such men as were not marked for victimization, returned to work, having, according to a contemporary announcement in the newspapers, "abandoned all the rules of their Society or Union which interferes with the performance of their duty to their employers, retaining only such rules and regulations as belong to a benefit society, which by Act of Parliament they are authorized to establish." So they were not quite down and out. The skeleton of the Union was still there.

There was no restraint of the keekers, by the fear of the Lord or anything else this time. Jarrow Pit suffered a further wave of victimization, a further clean-out of the best union men. Some of them went to America. Those who remained to work had to lie low. During the strike Hepburn had behaved like a hero. It was due to his influence that the desperate men had not flung themselves to certain death against the soldiery. For him there was no mercy. The Union could no longer pay him the tiny wage that had been voted in suchjoy at the 1831 victory meeting. For him there was no work anywhere in the district. Starved and shabby, he tried to earn a little by selling packets of tea. The viewers and keekers were on to this at once. Any wife 'en trading with Hepburn, her man would lose his job at colliery ... which meant eviction from the home that day. Some of the men who had worked with him did starve to death. Hepburn, out of his own , poverty, had tried to plead for them ... but in vain. One would have thought that some of those middle-class sympathizers of the 1831 strike would have helped ... but there is no sympathy for the unsuccessful. The well-to-do middle class generally only likes to be in on successful labour movements. If there were individual exceptions to this attitude in 1832 as there are to-day, Hepburn did not seem able to find them. Nor did the Churches trouble themselves with the heroic fighter who was being crucified among them. Finally, Hepburn went to a viewer at the Felling Colliery with whom he had had some negotiations at the height of the men's power. That viewer knew the character of the man he had to deal with ... and showed himself as a man of some courage. "I can only give you work if you will promise to have nothing more to do with unions." Starving as he was, Hepburn hesitated. He looked away from the viewer, his heart rent with the decision he knew was inevitable. He agreed, and kept his word. He lived and worked in Felling till 1873. His tomb in Heworth churchyard is kept in good order by the miners to this day.

That old grave-yard, which has the memorial to the disaster in 1810, a witness in stone to the deaths of boys of eight and nine years in the mine, is the only place near, where the old men can sit under a tree in the sun on summer afternoons. "He was a good man, hinney ", said the men sitting there when I went to view the grave this year. "Not many like him and Jobling these times." "You forget the lad Jobling who was killed in the International Brigade, fighting the same battle in Spain", I said. The old men agreed that perhaps there were working-class heroes to-day, too.

CHAPTER FOUR

Pit Life Ends in Jarrow

THE YEARS that followed the defeat of the 1832 strike were terrible years for J arrow. However badly the miners were paid, the mere fact that they had this union sense, that beyond a point they could not be driven down without hitting back, kept their wages higher than any others in the town. But after so big a defeat, when for the time they were helpless, their misery reacted on the other workers in the area. In the Jarrow Bonds for the ten years that followed the strike, the figure of the wages that the men were supposed to be allowed to earn was still 26s. a fortnight.. But few men actually took home this amount. Deductions, fines, confiscation of carves for short weight, all brought the actual wages below the 13s. a week. Yet all the records of the time speak of the miners as being the best paid men in Jarrow, which gives some indication of the other wages of the period. A very highly skilled hewer, supposing that he had managed to avoid any fine for a quart of stone in his carve, or a pint of coal underweight, might take home 30s. for a fortnight's hard work. A budget of one of these best paid men has come down to us in a pamphlet *A Voice from the Coal-mine*.

Actually spent for man, wife and three children:

	s.	d.
2½-stone of bread at 25. 6d. per stone	6	3
1 lb. butcher meat per day at 7d.	4	1
2 pecks potatoes at 1s. per peck	2	0
Oatmeal and milk for 7 breakfasts at 4½d. each	2	7½
	14	11½

This was the budget for an unusually small family and an unusually highly paid worker, doing very heavy physical work and needing meat each day. Such a worker allowed his imagination to play on what he would really like to buy and how much it would cost to add such luxuries as pepper, cheese and sugar to the diet. Here are the suggestions:

		s.	d.
2 oz. tea at 6d. per oz.		1	0
2 lb. sugar at 8d. per lb.		1	4
1 lb. salt butter at 1s. 2d. per lb.		1	2
1 lb. cheese at 9d. per lb.			9
Pepper, salt, mustard, vinegar			4
Soap, starch. blue, etc.		1	6
Tobacco: 1½ oz. packet			5¼
1 pint of ale each day		1	9
Clothing for five persons		3	0
		11	3¼
		14	11½
	£1	6	2¾

It is the usual reply to the accusation that British capitalism built its accumulation of wealth out of unbearably low wages that simply meant semi-starvation to say, "But prices were so much less. Money would buy so much more." The prices given for this pathetic little list of luxuries show the housewife of the eighteen-thirties paying three times as much for an ounce of tea, four times for a pound of sugar, more for everything except tobacco and ale, than she would pay to-day. In addition to the heavy deductions from wages due to fines and stoppages, the miners' wages were further raided by the Tommy Shop. Part of the wages was always given in the form of "tommy" tickets which could only be exchanged at the colliery shop. Apart from prices, this was a great hardship to the women, especially if their sons or lodgers were on different shifts. The Tommy Shop in these days only opened two or three hours a week. The women had to form up in queues. If there were different men working on different collieries in the home, the women had to walk long distances to get the goods. A woman whose husband worked in the Jarrow Pit, might have a son at Hebburn Pit, and another might be "on loan to Boldon" ... for it was one of the worst of the miners' grievances that having signed on for one pit, the owners claimed the right to transfer them to others often several miles from their homes.

So great was the grievance of the Tommy Shop that the complaints have preserved for us records of the prices charged which can be compared with prices advertised by the ordinary grocers of the time. Prices for the worst cuts of meat were always 2d. and 3d. per lb. higher than were paid in Newcastle for the best cuts. Marshall, the big family grocer of Newcastle at this time, advertised his cheapest tea at 3s. per lb., Rich Pekoe at 5s. per lb.

According to the budget just given the miner's wife would pay at the rate of 8s. for the cheapest tea at the Tommy Shop.

Very coarse sugar was being sold at the Tommy Shop for 3d. and 8½d. at the time when the ordinary grocer was advertising "good moist sugar" in the *Newcastle Courant* for 6d.

On such wages, and with these prices, the miners could not possibly be adequately fed. Yet if they were caught netting a rabbit or a hare on the landlord's estate ... as of course plenty of them did ... they were punished with all the ferocity of the game laws. The Jarrow of these ten years 1832-42 was a hungry Jarrow.

Yet in these appalling conditions of semi-starvation and bad working conditions the fibre of many of these men and their wives comes out in the records. Miners are generous men, and will give all they can to a cause they believe in. Primitive Methodism, with its simple and direct emotional appeal, was a strong force in Jarrow at this time. Yet the miners could never afford to build a place of worship. In 1837, perhaps a bit ashamed of the part they had played in getting the seven lads from their own colliery transported, perhaps conscious of the strong public reaction against them because of this, the proprietors of Jarrow Colliery let the congregation have a meeting-place. The coalowners did not build it. They merely roofed in the space between two rows of pitmen's cottages at what was known as Bede Place.

Still to the Methodists it was a home of their own, this little meeting-house which would only at best hold about forty people. To men who faced death every day, and with no other outlet for their deep longings for some life better than the hell of the pit, the little sanctuary, in *the* few years they were allowed to have it, became very dear ... a real centre of hard lives. Yet they were never able to afford any furnishing. If you needed a seat you brought some stool along with you, or the kitchen form for the family.

They were stern puritans, these early Primitives ... which added to the shock in the town when five of their sons, and sons strong in the family faith, were arrested and transported in the 1832 strike. But all the time they were the backbone of the Union organization. They faced prison for their trade union, as if need be they would have gone to the stake for their faith. Their Union Lodge meetings began with a hymn, and the appeal to be loyal to the Union was couched in very similar terms to the Sunday appeals to be faithful to God. As the resistance, a century later, to Hitler has proved, the truly religious man is a stubborn man, not easily intimidated by employer or dictator. It was with a very shrewd eye to the main chance that the rich employers of later date who built the handsome nonconformist chapels, stipulated that politics (with which they classed trade unionism) should be kept out of the chapel. The two faiths together make a tough mixture.

The Jarrow employers were not having an easy time in these years. The easy-money days, when coal lay near to the surface, near to the river and the sea, and Durham had almost a monopoly of the London market, were over. The great coal-absorbing industries of the Tees and Tyne were still fifteen to twenty years in the future. New coalfields in Yorkshire and the Midlands with their cheaper freights were becoming serious competitors. Jarrow Pit had its own troubles. The management was fighting the rising water, while having to keep up dividends to meet the demands from London. They avoided taking expensive precautions, such as sinking a new shaft for ventilation. They tried to speed up production while doing nothing for safety. It was from these years that Jarrow became known as the "slaughter pit" ... and its grim reputation for accidents still lingers in the town. The owners had the men at their mercy in the years that followed 1832, and they put on the screw.

Tyneside towns, like Jarrow, with their easy access to such great centres of political agitation as Newcastle, soon responded to the propaganda of the Chartists and the beginning of socialist agitation. This gave a stimulus to the Union again. When Durham had taken a year or two to lick its wounds, the coalowners' exactions supplied all the stimulus necessary to get the Union going again.

More miners were learning to read. The stimulus which the desire to read the Bible had first given to the Methodists, was now provided by a desire to read the speeches of the Chartists and the exciting political pamphlets which began to circulate on Tyneside. Tommy Hepburn, working grimly in Felling Colliery, was bound by his word to do nothing for the Union. But he could as a local preacher, teach the miners how to read. In a quiet way, the only way left to this great organizer of the 1831 and 1832 strikes, he laid the foundation for the reputation that Felling and Follonsby Pits have to this day of being among the most thoughtful and best-read of the Tyneside miners.

The School Boards and the Education Acts were a long way in the future, but still a beginning was made to get schools in Jarrow. There were schools both for boys and girls for those who could afford to pay fees, which was not possible out of the wages earned even by miners. A parish school at the Old Church was all that was left of the great tradition of 900 years earlier ... odd how the idea of automatic progress lingers. How much use could be made of these facilities by the boys of the mining homes can be deduced from the evidence given from the Jarrow area before the Commission on the Employment of Children, 1842.

Take the case of George Hall. He went to work as a child of eight in 1842. His skull was damaged by falling against the crane handle when he was too tired to stand up. He was off work six months. Then he returned. His leg was badly cut, then he had his thigh broken, all before he was ten. At the age of seventeen he was working as a putter, could neither read nor write and earned 10s. a week. The worst explosion in Jarrow Pit was caused by a boy of eight who left a ventilating door open. He worked twelve hours in the dark, not being allowed light.

Of a group of sixteen boys, eight went down the pit at eight years, four at nine, three at seven years. One, a lucky lad, was very exceptional. He did not go down till he was eleven. Of these, six could write their names, twelve could spell out easy words, and four went to night school. They said they were called at 4 a.m., went down to start at 5, and "were loose at 5 or 5.30." They worked overtime. One or two had stayed down all the twenty-four hours, and said they liked it for the additional money. They said, "It did not hurt their health but that they want sleep very much. Working in the broken hurts them all a little. The bad air makes their heads work while, and they feel hot." That a boy could say he "liked" working twenty-four hours occasionally because of the additional money, in the complete dark and in a primitively under-ventilated mine, gives some idea of how desperately that money was needed. Learning to read was a hard job, needing determination when hours like these were worked.

That, despite all the difficulties, the miners were learning to read, made it possible to start in Newcastle a little paper called *The Miners' Journal*. Its first number is dated October 21st, 1843. In three months it was able to appear in an enlarged form as *The Miners' Advocate*. The pitmen of those days were not mealy-mouthed. There is spirit in the prospectus and early numbers. The little octavo sheet proudly announced itself as "The Miners' Journal and Scourge of Tyrants, a means by which the black deeds of owners and viewers shall be made known to the world ... destined to tell the world that the miners are the only substantial foundation of our trade and commerce, and the corner stone of our social fabric." It robustly threatens the overmen and keekers that "if any of them show any desire at the bidding of their masters, for the purpose of getting the poor men committed to prison to gratify the fiendlike propensities of a few tyrants, swear the whole truth, more than the truth, or none of the truth, it shall be made known, together with their height, weight, colour, and residence, what situation they hold and how long they have held it ... in fact it is intended to make the paper the Despots' Plague." Sad commentary on the decay of working-class forthrightness that we now call our papers the *Tribune,* the *Herald,* the *Worker,* instead of a grand challenging title like "The Despots' Plague"!

The paper was started through the influence of W. P. Roberts ... and with him a new type of workers' leader comes into the bitter class struggle of the North. A" law fund" had been started by the Miners' Association of Great Britain under the influence of Martin Jude, a worthy successor to Tommy Hepburn. The Durham and Northumberland miners raised £500, towards which the miners of Jarrow and Hebburn contributed their quota. Martin Jude and his associates had felt that just a frontal attack in the old ways of 1832 would lead to the same result. The coalowners used the fact of the signed bond as an instrument against the men, while they continually violated its provisions themselves. So it was decided to see if the miner could not appeal to the law more successfully, packed though the courts were with his class and industrial enemies.

The individual miner had been trying to fight his employers single-handed in the courts, with all the risk of victimization and eviction. The law fund would provide him with legal help. Very shrewdly it was decided not to pay fees to local solicitors, who would be as dependent on the coalowners as were the miners themselves. Instead a man was to be retained who would give his whole time to the work, and would be completely independent of the employing interests.

Everything depended on the type of man, taken from a profession so solidly against the workers. W. P. Roberts, a forceful and somewhat unconventional solicitor who had taken a prominent part in the Chartist movement in Bristol, had attracted attention by his courage in defending Chartist prisoners. He was appointed "The Miners' Attorney General" at a retainer of £1000 a year. It shows courage and imagination for men who at best were only getting 15*s.* a week to think in terms of such an enormous sum. For this, Roberts undertook to fight all possible cases before the Justices at Quarter Sessions, the Assizes and, if necessary, in the House of Lords. The miners might so easily have got a lawyer with his eye on pleasing the employers, and being taken over by them. But Roberts earned his money and justified the miners' trust.

In the bad travelling conditions of the time, he went by mail coach up and down the country. Miners suing against illegal fines, against actions to enforce unreasonable clauses of a bond, or against the various swindling practices by which wages were withheld, had the chance now of a first-class lawyer, who thus built up a long series of precedents as well as accumulating a vast amount of experience. Viewers and agents, when they knew Roberts would be presnt, could not so easily come into the court of a man who was their personal friend, and swear whatever was necessary to send an awkward union man to prison, or to get enforced some new and unheard-of condition in the bond.

The very size of the salary paid to Roberts seems to have been good publicity. It infuriated the owners that their serfs should meet them on their own ground. Every kind of charge was levelled against Roberts' personal character. Handbills were distributed at every colliery, making charges ranging from being absent on luxury trips at the miners' expense when he should have been representing them, to drunkenness and downright swindling. Roberts steadily fought every one of these charges through at meetings of the men. His work was its best testimony, and the miners backed him solidly. He was always a popular speaker. There are records of his having visited Jarrow Colliery on several occasions, for the Jarrow men were a militant crowd, meeting a notoriously hard viewer. They wrote to Roberts' paper to say that a deputation which had waited on the viewer at Jarrow Colliery to show that the tubs were 2½ pecks more than had been paid for, were kept waiting three hours at his back door on a cold morning. His carriage then came to the front door and the men were left there, standing in the cold. "Such robbery they said and contempt from the parties who are the cause of it can surely not last long."

Conditions had got so bad that it was clear that a fight would be made round Binding Day, 1844. The heavy reductions caused by the fall of prices the previous year, the fines imposed on wages reduced to starvation point, and the accumulation of petty tyranny against every miner known to be a union man made a stand inevitable. When a man could be fined for one quart of "splint" out of six hundredweights of coal, when another had been fined 22s. for absence in a period during which he could only earn 6s., things were getting beyond endurance.

The men at the head of the Durham Miners' Union were not hotheads. They were men working at the coal face and they knew what a strike would bring ... the cavalry in the area, their best men on the run before the police, they themselves subject to every form of victimization ... and certain eviction. Men do not lightly contemplate a strike under such conditions.

There was now a national Miners' Association, which brought a new sense of solidarity into the fight ... for it had always been the imported blacklegs who had, at the last, broken every strike of the Durham men. In a very dignified letter the Miners' Association put a constructive plan before the coalowners for a uniform price for coal which should ensure a reasonable return on capital to the owner and a living wage to the collier. The letters goes on to say:

"We have had this year to submit to a very great reduction in prices, and this we opine, if you as coalowners get into the path of ruinous competition by underselling each other in the market and then endeavouring to reduce the wages to still keep a market, is a process which is alike ruinous to both parties, and which must have the tendency to keep up a contentious war of strikes and stagnation."

What the miners tried to initiate in 1844 by their "simple plan" had the same aim as the Labour Government's Coal Bill of 1930. A century of misery and loss lay between, because the coalowners treated with contempt every suggestion to put order into their chaotic industry. On this occasion, the sensible and constructive proposals of the miners were left without even the courtesy of an acknowledgement.

The Jarrow men prepared for the strike with a sense of desperation in their hearts. They knew that things were going badly with their colliery. The water, rising rapidly since John Buddle had tried to get some co-operation to fight the floods from Percy Main, had been getting out of hand. The owners, realizing that the pit might soon be overwhelmed, simply concentrated on getting out as much coal as possible as cheaply as possible. Things got so bad that in January 1844 the Jarrow men posted on the walls of the district a small poster stating their grievance.

JARROW COLLIERY
Several scandalous reports have been set abroad against the men of this colliery and we think it right that these reports should be contradicted by stating the truth of our grievances.

First then:- We have been working with the tubs near four months and we have been paid for 25 pecks in each tub; on the 21st and 22nd December we measured the tubs; the average measure was 28 *pecks, 3 quarters and* 1 *pint* in each tub; and what we ask is to be paid after this rate since we measured the tubs the 21st December last.

Secondly:- Our bond states that we are to be found work so that we can earn £1 6s. per fortnight, to be calculated by four consecutive fortnights, except in case of accident; we never are allowed to earn this sum, and on the last four consecutive fortnights we were £1 4s. 6d. short; we ought each to have received £5 4s. and we have only received £3 19s. 6d. We applied for a summons and were put off for a fortnight; now we have got one and are put off again.

We want to be paid what we have earned before we go to work again; and this is all we ask for. The masters owe us for the overplus and also the

£1 4s. 6d. each man; and we think as we have worked so hard we ought to be paid.

There are many other grievances we could speak of, but this is for the present.

Jarrow, Jan. 25th, 1844.

It would seem from this poster that Jarrow men were running a strike on their own at this time. To have had to give overmeasure per tub to the extent of three pecks, three quarters and at the same time to have only received less than 10s. per week instead of the promised 13s. and that with retail prices such as we have quoted for food, was surely sufficient cause for any strike. Trouble was still on at Jarrow Pit when the National Conference of the miners was called at Glasgow in March. Jarrow sent delegates on 432 members, a sign that Jarrow Pit was still one of the larger ones in the county.

The strike, which lasted twenty weeks, without resources, without strike pay, and, once the evictions started, without even shelter, was epic in its quality. There was far less violence on the men's side than in the strikes of the 'thirties. The pleadings of the miners' leaders had that effect. "For God's sake, men, keep the peace, or you will smash the Union" was the constant advice of W.P. Roberts in his paper and in his speeches. The evictions were carried out in a particularly brutal way in order to provoke the men into giving the excuse for reprisals.

The usual method was for one of the colliery agents, with a police officer, and a gang of hired men, to walk into the first house of a colliery row. "Will you go to work?" the man was asked.

A glance at the wife, the children, the bits of furniture that represented all he owned in the world after years of hard work ... then a grim "No!" The thugs stripped the cottage, and took care that as much as possible should be broken during the process. Under strict orders from the Union the men had to keep their clenched fists by their sides.

Some of the owners took pleasure in watching these scenes. The Marquis of Londonderry got a tremendous thrill out of it ... that curious pleasure which the wealthy man with his Law at his back gets when watching the agony of strong men ... from whose fists he is carefully protected by the police. So pleased with it all was the gallant Marquis that he plastered the district with posters telling how he had superintended the evictions himself ... and meant to do more. Lord Londonderry's field of activity was Seaham, not Jarrow, but parts of the poster are worth quoting as an example of the attitude of the landed coalowner of the period. It is often said that the old families knew how to treat their workers; that the real trouble came from the finance men in London. All the difference the pitmen saw was that the Londonderry type used their position, their appeal to traditional loyalty, as a little oil to make the screw fit tighter.

PITMEN'S STRIKE.
HOLDERNESSE HOUSE,
July 3, 1844.

I once more and for the last time address you. The most deluded and obstinate victims of designing men and crafty Attorneys must now perceive (after twelve weeks' strike) that they cannot become masters and dictate terms to the coalowners. Already 3639 men are employed, principally strangers to the districts of Northumberland and Durham, in hewing coals. And sensible men have left the Union and returned to work. And with this positive fact before your eyes and with more strangers coming forward daily is it possible the old and respect.able wellthinking colliers can he so infatuated as to suppose by still standing out in rebellion that they can conquer their employers?

Pitmen I enjoin! I conjure you! to look upon the ruin you are bringing on your wives your children your county and the country. In twelve weeks more the collieries will be peopled by foreigners and you will have neither shelter protection nor work. While there is yet time ... reflect. I will give you all hitherto in my employment one more trial.

I have been amongst you ... I have reasoned ... I have pointed out to you the folly misery the destruction awaiting you by your stupid and most insane union. I gave you two weeks to consider whether you would return to your work before I proceeded to eject you from your houses. I returned to Pensher and I found you dogged, obstinate, and determined ... indifferent to my really paternal advice and kind feelings to the old families of the Vane and Tempest pitmen who had worked for successive ages in the mines. I was bound to act up to my word *bound by duty to my property, my family and station.*

I superintended many ejectments ... it had no avail. I warned you next I would bring over men from my Irish estates and turn more men out ... you heeded me not. I have now brought forty Irishmen to the pits and I will give you all one more week's notice. And if by the 13th of this month a large body of my pitmen do not return to their labour, I will obtain one hundred more men and proceed to eject that number who now are illegally and unjustly in possession of my houses, and in the following week another one hundred shall follow.

I will be on the spot myself; the civil and military power will be at hand to protect the good men and the strangers; and you may rely upon it the majesty of the law and the rights of property will be protected and prevail.

Believe me, I am your sincere friend,

VANE LONDONDERRY.

Comment would spoil this gem of governing-class hysteria, but it is as well to remember that all the men were fighting for was that they should be paid for the work they did and not be cheated out of their wages by fraudulent means.

Lord Londonderry added a warning to the shopkeepers of Seaham against giving any credit whatever to any of the pitmen on strike

"Because it is neither fair nor equitable that the resident Traders in his own town should combine and assist the Infatuated Workmen and Pitmen in prolonging their own miseries by continuing an Insane Strike and an unjust and senseless warfare against *their Proprietors and Masters.*"

One can but feel that the Marquis of 1844 would feel quite at home either as host to Herr van Ribbentrop or guest to Herr Hitler.

Punch which in those days was not a mere echo of ruling-class opinion made the perfect comment.

"Lord Londonderry has issued another tremendous ukase, warning all the shopkeepers of Seaham against giving credit to his rebellious pitmen. If the inhabitants of Seaham continue to trust the pitmen, Lord Londonderry threatens he will immediately go down, and carrying away the ocean from the place, in some bucket made for the occasion, will ruin the place for ever."

The strike was broken by sheer starvation and exposure. The *Newcastle Courant* even reports cases of men picked up dead from lack of food. They could not face the autumn rains in their temporary encampments. So many blacklegs had been brought in from the South that enough coal was being produced which, sold in London at high prices, enabled even those owners to face a strike indefinitely who were far more dependent on coal-sales than was Lord Londonderry.

The victimization which followed all over Durham was terrible. No leader of the 1844 strike could get a job anywhere. If a young man had been active, then the old parents were turned out of their cottage as well. Some leaders changed their names and tried to get work in distant collieries, always to be dismissed as soon as they were discovered. And yet the indomitable spirit of the men lived on underground. The *Durham Chronicle* of March 15, 1845, records that a secretary and collector were found to have been enrolling members and distributing union cards among the men. They were instantly discharged. "The consequence is that the lodge is left without officials and the organization there nipped in the embryo. Let all collieries act in a similar way and we shall have no more strikes."

In Jarrow that advice was followed. Any of the substituted labour that was any use at all was kept, and only the previous pitmen taken on where their places could not be filled otherwise. The result was disastrous. Inexperienced men were unused to the ways of this difficult pit. On August 21, 1845, an explosion occurred at Jarrow as a result of which thirty-nine lives were lost. The circumstances were so shocking that the miners were able to insist upon a full and complete inquiry into the cause of the accident. James Mather, a mining engineer of great courage and much practical knowledge, with Martin Jude, who had led the 1844 strike, and Mr. Horn, another well-known miner, were chosen by the men as their representatives.

Mather, who had gone down the pit on the day of the explosion, suffered so badly from the effects of after-damp that he was unable to attend the inquest. Though he could have given first-hand evidence on the condition of the pit, the coroner refused to postpone the inquest to enable him to attend. Horn then asked to be allowed to put some questions to the witnesses, which the coroner also refused, saying he knew how to manage his own court and would not allow any cross-questioning there. Horn then said very respectfully that he considered that "the ends of justice demanded that there should be a strict and fair inquiry, and that the pitmen themselves were not acquainted with the forms of the courts." The coroner cut him short by saying that "I cannot allow the time of my court to be taken up with argument". He then went on to ask his own questions, refusing any questions from the miners' representatives.

James Mather, the man the coroner would not wait to hear, though he had been down the Jarrow Pit, had seen the miners shattered and in agony. He records, "Deeds have been done in the darkness of the mine and amidst the most appalling dangers which ennoble our common nature, and which if done in the light of day and before the world would have covered these humble miners with glory," Mather, who had been induced to take an interest in miners' welfare by Martin Jude, went not merely along the main airway, but right into the workings of any colliery he examined. He gave some of his experience in writing

> "It was a general practice [he said] for men to take off their jackets before going into their workplaces and shake them about before they dare take a lighted candle in. The fore-deputy of collieries went early in the morning to examine the working places and when the men went to work they often found when the 'bord' was excessively foul their pan shovel stuck up at the bard with the words 'dad (shake) here' chalked upon it as an indication of danger. When the deputy neglected to give this notice, severe explosions resulted. Another practice was the use of gunpowder for blasting down the coal, a practice which cost hundreds of lives. ... The working places were frequently filled with foul, stagnant air and the smoke which came from the powder hung about them all day."

So much has been made of the Davy safety-lamp, which was invented and first used at Hebburn, that it is grim to realize that the miners regarded it as their worst enemy. It provided the owners with an excuse for not sinking expensive ventilating shafts, and the miners declared that with the consequent neglect of all safety precautions where the lamp was used, their danger was greater than before.

James Mather gave it as his opinion that 60 per cent of the mineral wealth of the mines was being wasted by lack of the most ordinary safety precautions and by the refusal to make compulsory the appointment of mine inspectors. A series of terrible explosions that followed the Jarrow catastrophe, including one at Hebburn where thirty-one lives were lost in 1849, led to an Act making the appointment of inspectors necessary, being passed by Parliament in 1850.

The high-handed action of the coroner was able to hide the causes of the Jarrow tragedy from the public. But the men knew. The mine was got to work again, but in a crippled condition. In 1851, the owners abandoned the pit, and left it as a monument to the waste of brave men and national assets in the interests of a short-sighted get-the-stuff-out-quick policy. The first period of capitalism in Jarrow closed with the pit.

CHAPTER FIVE

The Rise of Palmer's Shipyard

THE CLOSING of the Jarrow Pit hit the little community very hard for a time, but it was not to prove such a disaster as the ruin of its greater industry eighty years later. Tyneside was just entering on a new period in the expanding capitalism of the mid-nineteenth century. But the abandoning of what had been one of the three biggest pits in the county was a symptom of a crisis in the Durham coal-field. Newcastle, with Sunderland, had enjoyed a monopoly of the London market since the sixteenth century, owing to the nearness of the Durham coal seams to the sea. Newcastle had now to meet the competition, not only of other coal going to London, but coal that was being delivered regularly and punctually, and which could, when necessary, quickly take advantage of any sudden demand or price fluctuation. These temporary increases in price and demand were caused by the conditions under which the coal came from the Tyne and the Wear. Sailing vessels were the cheapest form of cargo transport, and had enjoyed a monopoly of such cheapness for two and a half centuries. But these colliers were big, clumsy vessels, built for capacity not speed, and entirely dependent on wind and weather. If one could sail, so could all. All were held up together. When this happened, through storm or contrary winds, there would be a serious shortage of coal on the London market for days at a time. When the Durham colliers arrived, all together, the merchants naturally took advantage of the glut to force down prices. The rapidly growing demand for coal made them equally anxious to find alternative supplies when the ships did not come in. This gave the opportunity to the land-locked coal-fields of the Midlands and Yorkshire, who had to send their coal by the new railways. Their coal cost a lot more to send to London, but it did arrive when required. The coal producers in Durham were equally affected by the irregular sailings of the colliers. They were never sure when the ships would be available. Large heaps of coal had to be deposited at the pit-head, suffering depreciation owing to breakage and weather, or else the pits had to be stopped until news came that the boats were near.

This problem engaged the active brain of a young colliery manager, who in 1847 had become a partner in the great northern coal firm of John Bowes and Partners. This was Charles Mark Palmer, who had been born in 1822 in South Shields, the son of a prosperous merchant and shipowner who had owned a Greenland whaler and was now deep in the Indian trade. Palmer, who had been to school in Newcastle, worked for a time in a Newcastle office. While still in his teens he was sent to work in Marseilles to acquire a business knowledge of French ... a typical early nineteenth-century education for the son of a wealthy middle-class family, far more interested in business than the classics, and unconcerned with acquiring the gloss of an education at Oxford.

Palmer had joined the firm of John Bowes at the age of twenty-three. At twenty-five, he was made a partner, when the firm of John Bowes and Partners was formed to take over the Marley Hill Coal Company, which had gone out of business. Soon after, the firm acquired the collieries of Lord Ravensworth. Thus Palmer was actively interested in the management of what had now become one of the biggest Durham coal concerns.

The problem of the competition from the Midland pits was from the start a very urgent problem for this energetic, restless character, who had had a wider experience of the world than most men working in Durham coal management. When travelling between Newcastle and London he was disagreeably impressed by the amount of coal that was being carried by rail from the Midlands. Similar transport from the Worth would have been prohibitive in price, even if the railways had then been available.

Palmer solved the problem by having an iron steam ship designed for him, screw-driven, to carry a heavy load at a moderate speed with engines that were not expensive to run. Palmer thus became the father of the modern tramp steamer. There was nothing new in the idea of an iron ship. The first sea-going iron vessel was built in 1821. Ten years before that they were in use on canals and rivers. Nor was there anything new in the idea of a screw. But up to 1852, when Palmer's ideas resulted in the launching of the *John Bowes,* screw-propelled iron vessels were a novelty, and a luxury, suitable only for passenger and mail services. To understand how Palmer's idea of using such a ship to carry coal struck contemporary minds, we must remember how surprised and doubtful was public opinion in our day when air liners were first used for cargo.

Palmer stuck to it that steam tramp steamers, while obviously not as cheap in the first instance as the sailing vessels, would more than pay for the extra cost by speed and regularity. What Stephenson did on land, Palmer did on the sea.

Having got the idea. Palmer decided to carry this out himself. He and his brother George formed the private company of Palmer Brothers and Co. They leased from Mr. Carr Ellison ... whose family are still landowners in Jarrow, the old shipbuilding yard that had once been the centre of Simon Temple's ambitious schemes. Their first vessel was an iron tug, the *Northumberland*, launched without any ceremony. Jarrow was then a town of 300 houses. The town of the future was wrapped in the new scheme.

In April 1852, the formation of the General Iron Screw Collier Company was announced with a capital of £250,000. in 50,000 shares of £5. Among the first directors were a director of the London Gas Company, W. Cory, coal merchant of Lambeth, who was later to found a fortune in South Wales coal, and one Thomas Miers, another gas company director. Thus big merchant and coal-using interests were backing the new idea. The prospectus, after detailing the advantages to be gained by a "steady and certain supply of coal", stated, "It is calculated that after allowing for Working Expenses, Management, Wear and Tear and Depreciation of Stock, sufficient still remains to allow a dividend of £10 per cent with a large surplus as a reserve fund for Insurance and Contingencies; and in addition to this a source of profit exists in return freights of Merchandize which has not been taken into account."

Charles Mark Palmer was by instinct a showman and an advertiser on a big scale. He launched this new ship of the big idea, the *John Bowes*, on June 30, 1852, with great ceremony, which became traditional in the firm. There were 300 guests, a special lunch, a dance in the office buildings, great write-ups in all the papers. The *John Bowes* was to have a dramatic career. She did a variety of work. Changed from a collier to a cargo boat, she also changed her nationality, to become Swedish in 1905, then Spanish when her name was changed to *Villa Selgas*. She laid the cable from Dover to Ostend. So long as the *John Bowes* sailed the sea, under whatever name or flag, Palmer's Shipyard still carried on, however great the difficulties. The *John Bowes*, driven on the rocks near Bilbao in a storm, sank off the Spanish coast, just too soon to be a target for Italian aeroplanes. That was in 1933. In that year the great gates of Palmer's Shipyard closed forever. But these events took place long after the congratulatory crowds at that lunch had gone to their graves.

The *John Bowes* cost £10,000, was 167 feet long, had a carrying capacity of 650 tons and could steam at a steady eight to nine knots. These figures caused much head-shaking in the wooden shipyards. Men told each other that the thing could simply not be done. But Palmer had other new ideas. Ballast was one of the big problems of the wooden sailing vessel. Ships that went to London with these enormous, heavy cargoes of coal could not profitably bring back enough goods in return to a North which, though producing great wealth, distributed such small amounts as wages among the men who dug that wealth from the earth that their purchasing power was limited to the barest necessities. All along Tyneside, even yet, there are the great "ballast hills" ... sand and gravel brought back in the empty holds and dumped by the riverside. The *John Bowes* used water ballast which could be pumped out easily and required no expensive unloading.

On July 30, 1852, the *John Bowes* left Jarrow for Sunderland, where she was due to set her compass and pick up her cargo of coal. On August 6th she was ready for the South. A strong north-easter was blowing up the River Wear.

The sailing vessels were immobilized. Their crews stood on the decks to watch the much-talked-of new vessel sail triumphantly out to the North Sea in the teeth of the wind, on her first voyage to London. To quote Charles Mark Palmer's own words, when he described the event to the British Association in 1863, " On her first voyage the *John Bowes* was laden with 650 tons of coal in four hours. In forty-eight hours she arrived in London. In twenty-four hours she discharged her cargo; and in forty-eight hours more she was again in the Tyne. So that *in five days* she had performed successfully an amount of work which would have taken *two average sized sailing colliers upwards of one month to accomplish.*"

Palmer had saved the London market for the coalowners of the North-east and he had laid the foundations of the iron-shipbuilding industry on Tyneside. In 1852 twelve cargoes of coal, amounting to 9482 tons, were carried to London in screw colliers. In 1862, 1427 such cargoes, of 929,825 tons of coal, came thus to London. Further to assist his conquest of the London market, Palmer made special arrangements with the North London Railway Company for the rapid distribution of coal from the docks to a series of London depots.

The success of the *John Bowes* brought many orders for colliers to the expanding shipyard at Jarrow. They were built in such quantities and at such speed that the current joke of the workmen was that at Palmer's they built colliers by the mile and cut them off in the required lengths. The drive behind the yard was this restless, enterprising mind, always seeking the quicker and cheaper method, unimpressed by tradition ... the characteristic industrialist mind of the Britain of the mid-nineteenth century.

During the Crimean War Palmer's secured the contract for building an iron-clad floating battery which it was hoped would reduce the Russian forts at Kronstadt. To get the order, Palmer had promised delivery in three months, and for the sake of the reputation of his Yard he intended to keep to that time. One of Palmer's staff, characteristically anonymous in the shadow of Charles Palmer, had invented the idea of the "iron-clad", armour plates forged four inches thick and hammered on to the wooden side of the vessel. But to get the new battery done in time, it was necessary to find a quicker way to make those four-inch plates than by forging them. Palmer tried out the idea, on the suggestion of MacIntyre, his works' manager, of welding four standard inch plates together, but this was expensive, as the finished plate had to be planed to get an even surface. Palmer worried on this problem, which was met by the suggestion of the manager of Parkgate Ironworks, Rotherham, that four-inch plates could be rolled. They were tried and found to be successful. This was the actual beginning of the British armour-plate industry.

His work on this problem was characteristic of Palmer's method. He was not a technician, he was an organizer. Once having seen the problem, he worried everyone connected with him who would be likely to offer any ideas ... and immediately had them tried out. It was his receptiveness to the ideas of others ... in his posing of problems for them to solve, rather than in any inventiveness of his own, that Charles Palmer's strength lay. Like the other great industrialists of his period, he was never divorced from his plant in the great years of his career. While his organizing brain was actively concerned in it, Jarrow Yard prospered. But the industrialist cannot stop there ... the bigger the enterprise the greater the financial problem. It was when Palmer, the industrial organizer, the builder of ships, tried to become Palmer the builder of financial pyramids, that the trouble started.

The H.M.S. *Terror*, the first ship to be armed by rolled plate, was finished in very little over the three months for which Palmer had contracted. The men worked day and night shifts for weeks to get it finished ... and the job was done to scheduled time. By then, the Crimean War was finished, too, so the *Terror* never went into action against Kronstadt. But it created a great impression in Admiralty quarters, and established the reputation of Palmer's, Jarrow, which was to build many warships in its time.

Charles Mark Palmer's interests were now absorbed by the new possibilities of iron and steel. He conceived the idea of "from ore to finished ship" ... the whole process to be under the control of his firm. Two years after the *Terror* had demonstrated the possibilities of the new armour plate, Palmer had four blast furnaces built at Jarrow. He acquired an extensive lease of ironstone royalties in the district between Whitby and Saltburn at Hinderwell, and formed a company to work it under the name of the Grindle Park Mining Company. But there were no facilities for getting the ore to Jarrow. Palmer met the difficulty by creating Port Mulgrave, north of Whitby, building the harbour there at a cost of £30,000. By the time that was ready he had had constructed at his Jarrow Yard the fleet of steamers necessary to bring the ore from the harbour at Port Mulgrave to the quay alongside his blast furnaces at Jarrow. Rolling mills were added to the blast furnaces as soon as the regular ore supply was established.

A plant of this size could not be kept going on colliers and tramp steamers. Palmer flung himself into the trade for big ships for the Transatlantic and Mediterranean trade. His idea was to form companies for this trade, and thus secure the orders for the ships that his companies needed. He took a prominent part in the establishment of the National Line, which developed a large carrying trade between England and the United States. He helped to promote the Union Line of Transatlantic mail steamers, and became chairman of the Tyne Shipping Company, formed from three smaller firms. The orders for these kept his expanding plant at Jarrow busy. In 1861 Palmer pulled off a contract with the Italian Government to construct and work a line of steamers for the conveyance of mails between the Italian ports and Alexandria. Government orders were coming in, needing Palmer's Rolled Armour Plate. In 1862, the iron-clad frigate *Defence* was launched.

In these formative years, Palmer was working on ideas in advance of his time. While keeping to the tradition of the "family firm" which necessarily was the basis of most concerns in these days before the idea of limited liability made possible the garnering of capital from the small investor, Palmer had the conception of the modern integrated plant ... from raw material to finished product, under one control and as far as possible on one site. To his shipyard, he added blast furnaces, steel works, rolling mills, boiler and engine shops, pig and iron wharves, later even a gas works. His own ships brought in the ore from his own iron mines. Whenever he saw the possibility of further control of needed raw materials, he would form a company to get what was required. Copper is much used in the building and the fittings of ships. Palmer founded the Bede Metal Company for this subsidiary metal work. He was associated with Allhausen in the Tyne Plate Glass Company, so he got his profit there from accessories that could not be made actually on the Jarrow site.

Charles Mark Palmer was the typical "employer" beloved of the nineteenth century economists. He fits nicely into all their theories as the "man of enterprise", who built a hundred ships where one was built before. Starting out with his brother, and the family capital (in their case not inconsiderable for those days), and with the help of a few friends who believed in him, he starts a new business ... becomes the personal controller of a plant which he himself plans and organizes. He gets the orders for the work to be done. He takes the whole responsibility. He gives the orders, whose carrying out is supervised by foremen largely chosen from among the workers themselves.

Following the classic pattern, the firm soon grows too big for this. The actual management of the works is handed over to a manager. The labour force begins to include technical specialists, buyers, agents at home and abroad, the growing "middle class" of the works, with salary and status far above that of the workshop foremen.

Building ships is a costly business, especially when a new plant is growing rapidly. New machinery is wanted, new units have to be added, heavy stocks of material bought. Palmer was determined as far as he could to own or control the sources of the supplies on which his works depended. A heavy wages bill had to be paid before the order was completed. All this expansion needs capital far above the resources of the individual "man of enterprise", and his personal friends.

According to the orthodox economists this is where the "man of abstinence" comes on the scene, making the perfect combination of the man of enterprise who needs money to develop a business and the man who has saved it up for him, so that he can get the reward of his "abstaining" without the bother of being "enterprising".

But in the first half of the nineteenth century considerable risk was involved in thus handing over the nest-egg. The theory of the day was that if you gave to the "man of enterprise" however small a share of your capital, to form even a tiny share of his, then you became an active participant in the concern … and pledged your whole fortune, even to your house and furniture, on the result.

Joint stock companies had existed in the eighteenth century. The East India Company and the Bank of England were the most famous. The wild speculation of the South Sea Bubble days had given joint stock a bad name, and from 1725 the formation of joint stock companies was restrained by law. No new one could be formed unless it obtained a special Act of Parliament. In practice this was only possible for the big public utility undertakings . gas and water companies, canal and turnpike trusts and the railway companies … undertakings that had to have control of land. In over half a century of rapid capitalist development, though joint stock companies were formed, it was not possible to protect the smallest shareholder from being personally liable for the debts of the whole company.

This was inconvenient for the shareholder. It was also difficult for those who desired to trade with the company. Legal actions were made costly and awkward. Shares might change during the period of any action, and the process had to be started from the beginning because of doubt as to who were the actual owners when the action began. There were the obvious legal difficulties of trying to collect debts from an unrecognized body.

All these restrictions kept the typical firm of the earlier days of the Industrial Revolution small enough for partners to run, and a small group of large shareholders to be actively connected with it. There was no room for the small man who could not afford unlimited liability. So many people had been ruined by this that he was shy anyway.

Attempts to get round the position were made. By the Act of 1834 incorporation could be secured by Letters Patent from the Crown ... but these were difficult to get, and only valuable in certain conditions. Recognition of registered joint stock companies as incorporated bodies with legal status was granted. But this did not grant the one thing needful to big capitalist expansion ... the privilege of limited liability.

Palmer started his shipyard in 1851, just at the time when the new capitalist class was growing strong enough to insist on a reform so obviously necessary to their interests. The Act of 1855 gave to the joint stock company limited liability and the full rights of incorporation to all firms which applied for it. There was no spectacular rush to form companies immediately after the passing of the 1855 Act. The smaller investor was still shy of joint stock. But the Act of 1862, amending and consolidating the new system, made possible the great expansion in the heavy industries at this time, and Palmer took full advantage of it. The strain of carrying this expanding company and finding the capital for it for fourteen years had been terrific. Palmer's Shipbuilding and Iron Company registered on July 21, 1865, was formed to acquire the various establishments of Charles Mark Palmer, whose brother had retired from the firm three years earlier. A Manchester firm purchased the Shipyard and floated it as a limited liability company with a capital of £2,000,000. H. D. Pochin, a manufacturing chemist of Manchester, W. H. Newmarch and L. M. Rate of London were the promoters. The nominal capital of £2,000,000 was to be divided into 40,000 shares of £50 each.

The payment to Mr. Palmer was £505,000 for real and personal estate, £200,000 for goodwill and contracts, with a further sum for stocks, etc., to be decided by the valuer. The method of payment agreed upon was that the new company was to issue to Mr. Palmer 12,500 shares in the company to be regarded as having had £16 paid. Palmer was to be paid in cash by the company within one month of valuation for the ships, vessels, engines and stocks. Of the balance, Palmer received £135,000 in cash in July 1865 (that is immediately), and the remainder was to be paid in three yearly instalments. Palmer agreed to remain manager of the company for at least five years at a salary of £3,000 a year, with an additional £300 per annum for every £10,000 profit above £100,000.

The analysis of the investors in the company when it was floated is interesting in view of the new Acts which made possible limited liability for the small shareholder. Reference is made in the *Newcastle Chronicle* to the sale of £50 shares on the flotation of the company. The paper complains that very few shares had been taken up in the North-east.

Despite his shrewd methods of advertising the launching of his ships, and his own picturesque personality, it is curious that Palmer was never able to get in his own district the furore over his shares that George Hudson, the Railway King, twenty years earlier, was able to secure from his fellow citizens of York. But the £2,000,000 capital was actually subscribed ... although, there being no taxation on authorized or issued capital, the fashion of the period was to advertise an amount of authorized capital far in excess of what a company had means of raising or would be able to employ. £1,613,650 of the capital for Palmer's new company was subscribed by seventy-three people each investing £5,000 or over. 80.6 per cent of the capital was thus invested by people wealthy enough to risk £5000. Of these eleven were bankers and financiers who subscribed £266,250, nineteen "gentlemen" fourteen merchants, five manufacturers, while eight engineers subscribed £55,000 between them. The British Consul at Lisbon was one of the £5000 investors.

Evidently the place where money was looking for investment at this time was the Lancashire area. Some of the biggest investors had "cotton" addresses ... Burnley, Rochdale, Darwen. Twenty-three people in London subscribed £374,000 of the total, twenty-two people living in or near Manchester produced £296,000, while nine people living in Newcastle subscribed an average of £10,000 each.

Charles Mark Palmer was to remain chairman of the company for twenty-eight years, until he retired in 1893, but with the floating of the company and the removal of its head office to London Palmer's Shipyard entered a new phase. ... The invention of limited liability provided the urgently required new capital, but the tendency which was to lead to the ruin of Palmer's was implicit in the same transaction. For Charles Palmer the employer, the organizer, the controller of the productive process is replaced on the scene by the financier chiefly concerned with the dexterous handling of monetary values, less and less with the actual production of goods. As G. D. H. Cole points out, in his *Studies in Capital and Investment*, "To regard productive agents merely as instruments for the realization of money values often results in dangerous distortions of view and policy. It lends itself to the ruthless shutting down of competitive undertakings, without regard to the social, or the wider economic consequences of such a policy."

Those two sentences sum up the later history and the tragedy of Palmer's Shipyard.

CHAPTER SIX

"Making" Jarrow

THE GENIUS of Charles Mark Palmer as applied to the great shipyard in Jarrow was essentially that of the industrial organizer. As has been shown, his was the "planning mind". He was one of the first to grasp the idea of making an industrial plant an organized, integrated whole. For his time, and considering the defects of the financial machinery with which he had to work, he made a creditable beginning in industrial organization on his site of 100 acres with nearly a mile of river frontage on the Tyne. Compared, say, with the Ebbw Vale Works of 1938, the Jarrow Works would seem muddled and haphazard. But this was eighty years ago, and viewed relatively to prevailing conditions in the new and rapidly growing industries, Palmer in Jarrow achieved what was then a triumph of industrial planning.

But his planning stopped at the works' gates as far as his men were concerned. Palmer's wanted "hands". The fact had only to be stated, did not even need stating, and the human material was there ... ready to work for any wages ... and, as the terrible hours of overwork on finishing H.M.S. *Terror* showed, for practically any hours that muscle could endure. While all the planning went into the Shipyard, it was assumed that somehow the men and their families would find places to live. The greatest Shipyard on the Tyne was started in a place which had no provision for the labour which would be required. Jarrow was a town of 3500 in 1851 when Palmer started his works. By 1861 the population had doubled to 7000, more than doubled again in the next ten years to 18,000 in 1871, increased to 25,000 in 1881, to 33,000 in 1891, and to reach its maximum of 35,000 at the after-war census of 1921.

In the first seven years, rows of houses were hastily "run up" to add to the colliery rows. In 1860 there were 1005 occupied tenemented houses in Jarrow, where ten years previously there had only been 300. A journalist reporting the launching of the Atlantic steamer, the *Hudson*, from Palmer's, in the *Newcastle Chronicle* in June 1858 tells us, across the years, what the

Jarrow of the rows of white-washed (if insanitary) colliery cottages had become.

> "There is a prevailing blackness about the neighbourhood. The houses are black, the ships are black, the sky is black, and if you go there for an hour or two, reader, you will be black. The architecture of the place has a strong tendency to extreme simplicity – the straight up-and-down brickism common to manufacturing districts – and the atmosphere is of smoke, smoky."

The town adopted the Local Government Act in 1858, and elected their Local Board under it in December of that year. The Board was in existence seventeen years. The best idea of its value to the town can be got from the fact that it was finally laughed out of existence. When, in 1875, the Board gave place to a Town Council, a kindly soul at the meeting moved that "a vote of thanks be passed to every member of the Board as he considered it was deserved". The Report states formally: "The resolution was received with a tumult of laughter and fell to the ground."

One prominent member of the Board, and later of the new Town Council, was a Mr. Handyside. The side door of the County Hotel, used by the clique of speculative builders and other gentleman on the make in this rapidly increasing town, when they wished to meet the local boss, was generally known as "the handy side door".

A Board of this kind was simply an Executive Committee of the local grafters. It had neither the power nor the authority, even if it had had the will, to plan the rapidly growing town. The Big Man, the Great Employer, the Maker of Modern Jarrow could have done it. Jarrow by 1860 was a company town. Charles Palmer, who was to hear in his life-time so many eloquent speeches about his having "made Jarrow", and to receive so many honours for the performance, regarded it as no part of his duty to see that the conditions under which his workmen had to live were either sanitary or tolerable. Simon Temple fifty years earlier, at the turn of the century, showed more concern for his men than Palmer.

A contemporary account says: "Houses are wanted so badly that many are taken before they are finished. Houses already erected are crowded with lodgers". The rateable value increased by over £4000 in one year 1864-65. The number of tenemented houses had increased from the 1005 in 1865 to 2062 in 1869.

Two hundred non-tenement houses were erected by the Jarrow Building Association which was organized by Palmer's Works' officials. It provided one type of house for the rather superior type of skilled workman, and another for the foreman. Tennant's, the new chemical works, was completed in this period, and they wanted a thousand men, who had to find accommodation. The sanitary condition of Jarrow was appalling. A writer in the Newcastle *Daily Chronicle* (May 13, 1865) says:

> "The substratum of society – the very poorest of the lower order of its working population is composed of Irish. These inhabit the old pit houses in the row fronting the old Shields –Newcastle Turnpike – and in the street leading down to the ruins of the once famous pit sunk by Sammy Temple but now an institution of the past, there will be upwards of 100 of cottages of this class inhabited by labouring people. They consist mostly of one room of moderate dimensions with a 'tee-fall' behind and a loft next the tiles. They are low roofed, the ceiling of the larger roof being hardly more than 6 feet from the floor. They are floored with bricks, and the whole, of the rows are about two feet below the level of the turnpike.
>
> "I noticed but 4 conveniences attached to them and as the middens have been removed from the front, upon the site of which new houses have been built, the whole of the ashes and filth from these cottages are thrown upon the ground at the back part of the streets ...
>
> "In these rows there is overcrowding of the most frightful character, and every condition essential to producing a pestilence exists. I visited five or six of these cottages all within one minute's walk of the handsome county police station. The first dwelling I entered contained 5 beds. I asked the woman how many lodgers she had. She replied she had not many, but on interrogating her I ascertained that in this "slack season" even 14 persons slept under the roof of this miserable cottage.
>
> "Many of these cottages lodge from 15 to 19 people in one night. There is no regard to sex. Married people sleep in the same apartment with young men, and young women must either sleep in the same room with married people or with young men, while as to the poor children I do not know how they are stowed away. Many of the beds in these cottages never cool, for as soon as they are vacated by the men who are going on the day shift they are occupied by men who have come off the night shift."

The writer of the article blames the women for dirty floors and bed linen. But no water was laid on until the Shields and Sunderland Water Company extended their main as far as Jarrow in 1864-65. Each tenemented house was charged 1s. 6d. a quarter ... but not for water laid on. The taps were put in the street, but there were so few of them and so remote were these from many of the houses, that women trying to keep house for nineteen lodgers in two rooms would find it difficult to carry in buckets the amount required for washing bed linen.

A protest to the Local Board of Health, which was first elected in 1864, asks that "the large pools of water that impinge upon the main thoroughfare should be cleared away, streets scrapings cleared and drains trapped ... the slops and dirty water thrown from the houses on the Shields and Newcastle Road should not be allowed to remain stagnant in the open gutter as is now the case."

These protests are the answer to the excuses given for the unrestricted capitalism of this period, that people didn't really mind, because they had no experience of anything better. In these mushroom towns of nineteenth-century industrialism, the people living in them had very lively memories of better things, of at least more room. But there was as yet no organized labour movement to force attention on better housing, town planning, or proper sanitation. The Liberal political movement was led by the big employers. Charles Mark Palmer himself was to sit as a Liberal M.P. from 1874 till his death. The workers, followed the Liberal lead in the struggle for the franchise. The vote was a necessary tool for all other reforms they wanted. So they had no political instrument of their own to force the organization of the decencies of life, which were the most prominent feature of all the programmes of their movement when it came into existence later.

Credit must be given to the medical officers of the local Board of Health for the stand they took in the early days against the appalling health conditions in the rapidly growing town. It was not easy in those days (often it is not easy even to-day) for an official to raise a protesting voice against the local bigwigs. But the first medical officers were doctors with their own practices, which made them a little freer. Even so, they did not put the blame where it really lay ... on the men who were putting big industries down without making any provision for housing the workers this would bring to the town and the system of society which allowed this to be done. The doctors and medical officers of health contented themselves with describing the facts.

The immense profits which Palmer derived personally from the Shipyard have been described in a previous chapter. But from a health point of view things got steadily worse in the town from whose workers those profits came. The report of their medical officers in December 1875, commenting on the deaths during the month previous from fever, states:

"There are four cellars situated behind the block of buildings known as the Barracks in Walter Street, which are quite unfit for human habitation. They are built five feet below the level of the ground and they are excessively damp. The openings to the external air are on one side of the road only so that through ventilation is impossible. In front of these only means of ventilation stands in each case a foul privy and ashpit over which every breath of air that enters the room has to pass. As the ashpits and privies, moreover, stand on a higher level, the foul liquid which drains from them may be seen oozing through the bank, and standing in pools immediately outside the doors and windows."

Fevers killed so many the following year, that special reports were made to the new Town Council. One stated:

"The typhoid fever is to be chiefly ascribed to the defective system of refuse removal ... which permits excreta leaving it may be the specific poison of the disease to accumulate for months in close contiguity to the houses, to the doors and windows, poisoning often the sole source of ventilation."

Another report from the medical officers adds to the grim picture:

It is not to be wondered at that the surface water is polluted when the ground around the houses is often saturated with the most foul liquid that drains from a privy midden. In many parts of the town ... notably in those streets where fever has been the most prevalent ... this most foul liquid can be seen oozing through the walls and running according to the level of the ground either into the yards and beneath the houses or into the back streets."

Fever is no respecter of persons. The Town Council felt it had better do something about the appalling housing conditions, and drew up a series of bye-laws. We know of them because of the fierce objections of the building contractors who attended a special meeting of the Council to object to them. These worthy gentry demanded that streets should be only thirty feet wide instead of the forty feet suggested. They wanted the minimum height for the attics to be six feet instead of eight. They wanted to build higher houses along these narrower streets than the Council proposed. They demanded to be allowed thinner walls, smaller privies than those suggested in the Council, and they were particularly furious that the foul earth closets should be prohibited for the future and box types substituted.

The Council received continual complaints about the recurrent outbreaks of fever and by 1877 the medical officer had managed to impress upon them that without an isolation hospital it was impossible to prevent the disease spreading.

He hinted pretty broadly that fever was not confined to the overcrowded streets where it started. "In a house with only two rooms," he reported, "there are at this moment five children seriously ill of scarlet fever. The father leaves his thoroughly infected house to work as a journeyman tailor in a large tailoring establishment in a room where other men, some of them with families, are employed." Difficulties of expense, of site, of co-operation with the sister town of Hebburn were allowed to delay the proposals for a hospital despite the vigorous protests of the medical officer. The cost was to be £3600 for building and site, and another £1000 for furnishing ... not a large sum if its costs had been shared by Palmer, Tennant, and a couple of the other big firms in the town. Yet it was not until 1886 that the foundation stone was actually laid. In his protest at the delay the medical officer pointed out that "while these things are being discussed and plans held up, people are dying month by month of infectious diseases who need not have died if such a hospital had been provided." The hospital might not have been provided even then if in 1883 a smallpox epidemic had not terrified the better-off people in the town. A hastily improvised temporary hospital had soon filled up, and the small-pox patients had had to be left in their crowded tenements and lodgings.

Although there was this long fight lasting over twenty years to get an isolation hospital, one other hospital had been built in the town, the Palmer Memorial Hospital. The story of that dates back to 1865, when a meeting was held in Jarrow to discuss the provision of a memorial to the first wife of Charles Mark Palmer. Collections had already been started to purchase a stained-glass window for the church.

McIntyre, the tough and blunt manager of the Shipyard, suggested that a memorial hospital would be the best tribute. He quoted instances of men injured in the Shipyard who had to suffer agonizing pain en route from the works to the hospital. Of twenty accident cases which were sent to Newcastle Infirmary, eight died on the way. Another speaker said that their lives were jolted out of the injured men. A workman present gave the case of a fellow worker who had his arm severely damaged at 7 a.m., but did not reach the Infirmary till 11 a.m. The pain drove him mad and he died two days later.

The Newcastle *Daily Chronicle* reported that there was considerable opposition to the idea of a hospital from those who wanted a stained-glass window ... and because of the difficulty of financing a hospital. "Eventually the hospital scheme was adopted on the assurance that other firms in the locality would support it."

No one seems to have suggested that as Palmer had been paid that year nearly three-quarters of a million in cash, and shares in the business now capitalized at two millions, the care of their badly injured workmen might have been regarded as a necessary expense by the firm. On the contrary, in gratitude for the contributions Palmer gave to the hospital, the workmen paid for a stained-glass window in the hospital to commemorate the first Mrs. Palmer.

Jarrow, of course, was not the only town where insanitary conditions prevailed during this pirate period of nineteenth century capitalism ... where the health of the workers was not even considered where profit was to be made. The description in the sanitary reports of the period for any of the quickly growing towns – Manchester, Leeds, Liverpool, London – were as bad, or worse. What made the problem so terrible in Jarrow was the sudden rush of workers to what was little more than a village. It is no wonder that men like Palmer were Liberals believing in "free trade", "free labour", "freedom of the subject" when these doctrines relieved them of any consideration for the welfare, even the elementary needs of housing, sanitation and medical care, of their "free workers".

But even in the later part of the century, when public sanitation had improved generally throughout the country, the deaths from zymotic disease (small-pox, scarlet and enteric fever and the like) were much higher in Jarrow than in towns of a similar size. In 1883 these deaths were 51 per ten thousand as against 24.6, the average of fifty other towns.

The compulsory notification of these diseases led to a reduction to 38.2 the following year, as some attempt was made at isolation. It was still ten points above the average. The next year it had risen again to 44, nearly double the average figure for other towns, and the medical officer writes despairingly that "social conditions in Jarrow are exceptionally favourable to the spread of the disease". In the following year an epidemic of infant diarrhoea caused forty-eight deaths ... of which not one was among infants who had been fed from the breast ... a sufficient guide to the conditions of milk and milk-keeping facilities in the town.

The effect of the Notification of Infectious Diseases Act, which enabled something to be done regarding infection, made such a considerable difference in the average figures over a period as to indicate how easily preventable the unduly high death rates were.

DEATHS IN JARROW BEFORE AND AFTER NOTIFICATION OF INFECTIOUS DISEASE MADE COMPULSORY.

	1871-78	1879-88
Mean death rate (per 1000)	25.19	20.81
Small-pox death rate (per 10,000)	15.31	0.36
Scarlet fever death rate (per 10,000)	17.87	11.15
Other fevers death rate (per 10,000)	7.81	2.65

The birth rate in Jarrow during all these years was, and still is, higher than average, but the infantile mortality at this period was usually about the same, sometimes lower than the average (average in these figures always means the average for fifty towns of the same size). The health history of Jarrow during the whole history of the Palmer Works was closely linked with the work available. In 1884, after two years of high death rates from infectious disease, the medical officer reports: "I believe the lamentable depression in trade in the borough with the consequent distress amongst the working classes has had an appreciable effect upon the mortality statistics of the year." A few years later the M.O.H. is lamenting the effect of still more overcrowding to save house rents in a period of bad trade. At the end of the next cycle in 1892 the Health report says grimly:

> "The year that has passed has been marked by great distress in the town and the result of this was apparent by an outbreak of typhoid fever due, no doubt, to the lowered vitality and lessened resisting power to disease induced by want of proper food and other necessaries together with the neglect of cleanliness which usually accompanied such a condition."

In a leading article commenting, in February 1894, on the just-issued *Medical Officer of Health's Report* for the previous year, the local Jarrow paper calls attention to the fact that the death rate from zymotic disease was 5.24, while in England and Wales the average was 2.46. "And in the face of that alarming fact", says the editor indignantly, "we still have leading men who treat it as of no consequence!" The editor goes on to say: "Jarrow is not an unhealthy town. One great advantage of Tyneside is that twice every day the river is well-washed out. The vast body of water which rushes up from the sea at every tide is undoubtedly health-giving.... Notwithstanding this we have an abnormally high death rate. Is not the whole question a startling one, and one that demands an immediate and thorough enquiry?" The editor did not get his inquiry, and people continued to die at an alarmingly high rate in an area which nature had made healthy, but which had been converted by over-rapid and unplanned industrialization into what the local editor called "a veritable death-trap".

CHAPTER SEVEN
Labour Fights Palmer

THE FIRST twenty years of Palmer's Shipyard were the peak years of almost unhampered exploitation of the workers of Britain by their employers. The trade-union activity of the 'thirties and 'forties had sunk very low under the burdens of a period of bad trade. As always, at such times, the thoughts of such workers as had time to think had turned to political channels. The vigorous pioneer types had thrown themselves into the fight for the Charter, and when that failed, they joined in the struggle for extending the franchise. Politics were more exciting. There was the help of the middle class who had their own interest in the political struggle. The trade-union road was terribly hard. The laws regulating the relations of Masters and Servants (1824), administered by Magistrates' Benches packed with the employers and their friends discriminated sharply against the worker. Hours were long, and wages terribly low.

The grim pictures drawn from Government reports by Marx and Engels of the England of this period show a whole working class exploited to the limit, its strength sucked by long hours, and by wages which kept most workers at a level of deadly malnutrition. "The cotton trade has existed for three generations of the English race. During that time it has destroyed nine generations of factory operatives." Marx gives this quotation from a speech in the House of Commons in 1863. Enormous profits were made. In the steel and shipbuilding trades, as we shall see later, dividends of 50 per cent were boasted of on Tyneside. Such profits only whetted the appetite for yet more advantage from the wonderful new inventions. The machine was placed on the altar of the age. The orthodox political economists, priests as always of the gods of profit-making, stood around in subservient attitudes anxious to produce appropriate creeds. Not the least of the services of Marx to the workers was the biting fun he made of these pompous lackeys.

Around the time when Palmer was starting his Works in Jarrow, it is computed that there were probably not more than a hundred thousand trade-unionists in Britain. Apart from the miners, these were mostly in the craft unions of the time – small friendly societies in type among the building, carpenters and the skilled workers in the iron industries.

But trade-unionism lives not only in organizations but in the hearts of men. Then as now, conditions were worst in the areas where there was no trade-union tradition. The great fights in the coalfields in the 'thirties and 'forties, the miners beaten back bleeding and broken to their knees by starvation and coercion, yet stubbornly keeping the spirit of unionism alive, had created an atmosphere favourable to trade unions among other workers in such districts as Durham and Tyneside and South Wales. It was in such areas that the new iron and steel and shipbuilding trades had to be located, because of their nearness to the coal-fields, much as the employers disliked the trade-union tradition of these areas.

The sharply marked differences among the skilled trades in the iron and steel industries naturally tended to develop the craft idea of trade-unionism, as the conditions of mining encouraged mass organization. There was the further difficulty of the trade-unionist employer. The puddler, for example, was paid by the ton, and tried in his turn to pay his underhands on the same basis. This they strenuously resisted, demanding a time wage. Owing to the inequality of the law, the early unions had had to stress the friendly society side of their work. This was to prove a great encumbrance in the fierce battles that lay just ahead. For with the general upward trend of trade at this period, and the need of the United States of America for skilled men for their new industries, British labour in the iron and steel trades was in a position which, had it been able to use its advantage, might have won for itself a very different position than it has to hold when the century closed ... or, for that matter, holds now. Unfortunately the lack of solidarity with the unskilled men weakened the fighting power of the skilled unions. Even such "new-model" unions as the Amalgamated Society of Engineers were so concerned with friendly society benefits that they kept out of vital trade disputes. The upward swing of British capitalism gave them the chance of effective fighting. Instead the best officials of the period were mainly concerned with conserving the sick and death benefits.

The oldest union in the iron trades was the Friendly Society of Ironfounders. Founded in 1809, it had about 7000 members in the 'fifties, with a good branch in Newcastle. Its members belonged to the very oldest section of the trade. The rapid extensions of the steel-making and -using industries led to the forming of the Associated Iron and Steel Workers in 1864 on the basis of an existing union. This had a somewhat wider appeal, among the skilled men only of course. It was controlled by two committees, one meeting in Gateshead and the other at Brierley Hill, in

North Staffordshire. Its main strength lay among the puddlers, who were themselves sub-contractors.

The ironmasters themselves were fairly well organized, even at this early date. In January 1865, in consequence, as they claimed, of trade depression, they proposed a 10 per cent reduction on puddlers' rates. This was rather surprisingly accepted everywhere, but not in North Staffordshire, where the puddlers claimed their work was harder, and where, in fact, they felt themselves strong enough to resist the cut. The puddlers elsewhere, who had accepted the reduction, supported the North Staffordshire men.

The owners were determined to break the Union in Staffordshire, as they knew they could not keep the 10 per cent cut otherwise. In February, representatives of seventy-six firms met in Birmingham, and decided to close their own works if the Staffordshire puddlers did not give way. A curious decision, as in fact it would give the striking ironworkers of Staffordshire what the Durham miners had been seeking in vain to secure, a general stoppage when one area was on strike. But what the employers were after was to prevent the growth of national unions in the steel industry. It was a period when the employers in all the big industries were using the lock-out freely in an attempt to check unionization.

Unfortunately the union branches on Tyneside were not as yet such seasoned fighters as the miners. The craft nature of what organization there was did not produce the same sense of class-solidarity. The unions on Tyneside therefore passed resolutions deciding to do nothing more to support the Staffordshire men.

The way Charles Mark Palmer handled the situation at Jarrow was characteristic of the type of "benevolent employer" of the period. As anxious for profit as the others, but anxious to keep in with all sides as long as possible, he was certain at the moment of crisis to come down against the worker, but always in a welter of moral protestations. Not present at the Birmingham meeting, and unsure how things would go, Palmer promised to the men at Jarrow that he would not close the works so long as they did not send any money to help the Staffordshire men.

Shortly after this promise, the ironmasters of the Northeast coast met in Newcastle on March 9, 1865. They concurred with the Birmingham decision and decided to close all works belonging to the Association on March 11th. Charles Mark Palmer accepted a seat on the committee set up by the masters to implement this resolution. The decision astonished Tyneside. The men had already agreed not to continue their support of the Staffordshire dispute, yet in spite of that they were to be penalized for the militancy of the Staffordshire strikers.

Public opinion was clearly against the masters. Even the *Newcastle Chronicle,* always inclined to take Palmer on his public valuation as a great philanthropist "providing work for his men and building up Jarrow", had to take account of the wrath of the shopkeepers on Tyneside at the prospect of the purchasing power of thousands of their customers being stopped. The pained surprise expressed by the *Chronicle's* leading articles corresponded to local feeling. The owners, however, were concerned to break trade-unionism in the steel trades while it seemed weak enough. Nearly all of them had been or were then connected with the coal trade. Many of them had taken part in the fierce battles in the mining industry. They were out on the same union-smashing game in steel.

On March 11, 1865, 70,000 men were locked out in the iron and steel works of the country. To Jarrow, so dependent even in this short time on Palmer's, the lock-out would mean ruin if it continued any time. The last fortnightly pay at Palmer's had totalled £20,000. For a time, the Shipyard could continue working, though the supply of plates available when the mill stopped was clearly limited. But the iron works alone employed 1500 men. Their purchasing power was wiped out. The craft unions could distribute a little strike pay, but the unorganized labourers had no resources at all. It was a vicious decision to condemn the men and their wives and families, at least 5000 souls according to a contemporary calculation, to starve, when the men had already accepted the owners' terms.

But Jarrow had militant traditions. There was a strong left wing among the younger men in the steel mill. They saw that the too ready acceptance of the owners' terms had been treated as a sign of weakness. Palmer had flagrantly broken his own pledged word to his own men not to lock-out if they did not support the Staffordshire men. The only way to deal with this situation was to hit back.

The lock-out had been on five days, when, at a meeting of the Jarrow Lodge of the Iron and Steel Workers, this more militant section got a resolution passed that before Palmer's Ironworks could re-open it would have to be 100 per cent union. Bladen, the manager of the works, had to deal direct with the men and was not too pleased about the lock-out.

He took this information to Palmer, who met the situation at once by ordering that all the men engaged in building extensions to the Palmer Works should be laid off.

It was an obvious try-on. Palmer would be glad enough to continue his extensions the moment the lock-out ended, despite the elaborate pretence he always maintained that all his concern was not for profit but to keep his men in employment. His action, however, scared the older men, as it was meant to do. An emergency meeting of the Lodge that same afternoon withdrew the resolution.

Palmer now felt that he had the situation well in hand and could afford to teach the men a lesson. A meeting between the committee of masters and the men was called for York on March 18. Charles Mark Palmer was in the Chair. He made a great fuss because one of his workers, a man from Staffordshire, who was a member of the Jarrow Lodge, had said bluntly at the Union meeting that neither Palmer nor anyone else would stop him sending money home to help his mother and younger brothers who were suffering because his father had been out on strike since January.

"How do you consider," said Palmer, striking an attitude, "that negotiations are possible if such speeches are made?" A curious sentiment from a man who delighted to pose publicly as a great defender of the home and the family. That the capitalist has no use for the family relationship when it interferes with profit-making has been sufficiently demonstrated by now ... but the Palmers of the Victorian Age were used to making great speeches about the responsibility of children for parents whenever anyone dared to hint that any other provision should be made for the aged.

As the ironmasters did not feel that the strength of the Union was broken yet, Palmer used this incident and the fact that some of the Staffordshire men had not arrived, to break off negotiations. The fight was to go on. Nevertheless Palmer had his own difficulties. The story of that loyal Staffordshire son when reported back to Jarrow did not improve the personal feeling towards Mr. Palmer. Plates began to be urgently needed for the Shipyard. Bladen did his best to persuade some of the millmen to come back and get some plates through. The terms offered were attractive, but the millmen stood firm. Palmer had locked them out in breach of his own pledged work, and he could take back all or none. Palmer thereupon announced haughtily that he had made arrangements for sufficient plates for some time to come. The millmen, who knew enough about what was going on elsewhere to know that the great man was lying, told him in effect to get on with it, and held out.

Someone among the local union leaders thought of a bright scheme of counter-pressure. The skilled man always had a back door open at this period. The U.S.A. wanted British craftsmen badly, and were prepared to pay good prices to get them. The Union therefore, with all the publicity they could get, put up in the Union offices details of prospects in the U.S.A., and outlined a scheme to assist passages across the Atlantic. A hundred of the most skilled men on a wink from the Union Secretary promptly signed up to go ... a fact duly published in the local papers. The owners of house property in Jarrow, and all the other interests dependent on the pay of Palmer's men, grew alarmed. By private letter, by influence, and by every other means anyone could think of, urgent representations were made to Mr. Palmer to bring "this disastrous and unwanted lock-out to a close."

The plates about which Palmer had boasted did not appear. Men had to be laid off in the shipbuilding yard, and orders were held up. The unhappy Bladen was ordered to get some millmen back to work at any cost. The men held firm. By this time tempers were rising. In the old tradition of coal-strike days Palmer had had extra police imported into the town, some of whom were armed. The men complained hotly of the conduct of these police. The concentration of some 2000 men with the sympathy of the town behind them was a very different proposition to the much smaller groups of miners, helpless in tied cottages, whom Palmer in his younger days had seen evicted from their homes and hunted by the police in the 1844 strike. Just because Jarrow had become Palmer's, the whole town was heart and soul with the men.

Bladen's efforts to entice some men back to work were by now hopeless. The locked-out men would have ended the career in Jarrow, police or no police, of any blackleg from among themselves. Palmer realized he dare not import any, even if he could find any skilled men to come. Bladen himself donned workmen's clothes and caused his staff to do likewise to try to get some plates rolled, to the great joy of the mill workers who hailed the white-collar men as they went home with sympathetic questions as to how they liked doing a bit of real work for a change.

Charles Palmer was now in a position new to him. The ironmasters had pushed this vain and vigorous man into the limelight as chairman of their lock-out committee, where he rather than they would collect most of the unpopularity. The Press, following overwhelming public opinion, was against the lock-out, and Palmer's fall from grace was severely criticized.

By the time the lock-out had lasted a fortnight Palmer was ready to call it off, provided he could do so with due moral parade. In a letter to the Press he suggested that the lockout in the North could be ended if the men would agree to sever all connection with the men in Staffordshire. To save his face from the obvious retort that the men had done this before the lock-out was imposed, he pompously declared that " the men should hold meetings and pass resolutions free from restriction and reservation in favour of the course suggested and that they should empower the delegates to speak in their name fairly, honestly, and without reservation".

All of which meant that Palmer was beaten. The *pro forma* resolutions were duly passed, but the Jarrow men were not in the mood to be too obliging to Mr. Palmer. At the meeting in Darlington on March 27, at which it was decided to open all the works on the 30th, Mr. Palmer created a scene, pettishly declaring that the resolution of the Jarrow men was not sufficiently definite. However, he had to be content with it. The Palmer legend had received somewhat of a shock from the incidents of the lock-out. What was more important, the spirit of trade-unionism had been given considerable impetus. When he had had time to cool down, Palmer realized that his role of the "local lad who had made good", the employer who was always ready to listen to his own men, was the strongest card he had in his hands. He was to play it with great cleverness in the big dispute that followed. This card has been used with success all through the capitalist period in Britain by certain firms. From George Robert Stephenson, the great locomotive engineer who was to keep his Newcastle men at work with it, as we shall see in the study of the Nine Hours' Movement, down to the Cadburys and Nuffields of our own day, the benevolent capitalist has been an interesting feature of the British industrial landscape. His benevolence has not been allowed to interfere with profit. In fact, the resulting increased profit has been an argument for the benevolence. But the belief that disinterested capitalists do exist; the fact that if any employer shows the least tendency that way his men are prepared to give him credit far in excess of any virtue he actually possesses, has played a not inconsiderable part in the development of the more conservative aspects of British trade-unionism. The end of the lockout left the Jarrow men with a new and exciting sense of solidarity. The Amalgamated Society of Engineers, founded the same year as Palmer's Shipyard, and which had had a branch there for some time, grew rapidly. There was no organization as yet among steel labourers anywhere, but the general wave of enthusiasm drew every kind of worker at Palmer's into the new Nine Hours' Movement which was sweeping the North-east. A vigorous personality, Andrew Gourlay, a Jarrow worker who had been the active spirit in getting the 100 per cent trade-union resolution carried during the lock-out, the resolution which had so infuriated Palmer, was the leader in the new movement.

At this period, excessive hours were the rule in British industry. The machine and its needs filled the mind of the go public and absorbed the employer. They were expensive. Experiments and new inventions made it necessary to keep them up to date ... though as a trade-unionist of the time remarked, he had heard a lot about inventions and new machines, and had seen plenty of new machines bought, but he had not yet seen an old one scrapped. It was the firm conviction of the employers that only by the extreme lengthening of the working day could they make profit upon their outlay.

The dictum of Nassau Senior in his *Letters on the Factory Acts*, though made in 1837, was still quoted as the last word on the subject whenever the excessive length of the working day and the disastrous effect upon health were discussed in Parliament, or between workmen and employers. Senior, of whom Marx remarked that he first taught economics in Oxford and then went to learn them in Manchester, solemnly asserted that "if the hours of working were reduced by one hour per day (prices remaining the same), the net profit would be destroyed. If they were reduced by one hour and a half, even the gross profit would be destroyed."

Whatever other economics the manufacturers neglected, that sentence they learned off pat. It was in vain that the men, when they could get anyone to listen to them, pleaded that even a machine could get exhausted as well as a man. As a delegate urged when the Nine Hours' League was interviewing the Mayor of Newcastle: "As anyone knows there is a great difference between a man and a Wylam Dilly, and even a Wylam Dilly gets exhausted, much less a man". A Wylam Dilly was a heavy-type colliery locomotive ... and what these men knew from their own experience, researches into the fatigue of metals was to confirm years later. All the employers of the period would look at was, to them, the obvious fact – that the longer hours the machine and the men worked the greater profit they would make.

The Fourth Report of the Children's Employment Commission gives particulars of fantastically long hours worked by children, and therefore by adults, particularly in the completely unorganized and unregulated trades of the period. Marx, from a careful study of factory inspectors' reports, as well as the Children's Employment Commission, showed that even in the staple male trades, where there was a certain amount of resistance to the worst exploitation, and where the employers' talked much about "the normal day", terribly long hours were worked over and above the boasted norm.

The steel mills at this period generally worked two twelve-hour shifts, and other engineering works from 6 a.m. to 5.30 p.m. At one rolling mill, three hours' overtime four nights a week was regularly worked, even by boys of nine. A boy of nine is quoted by the Commission's report as having worked three twelve-hour shifts running. Boys of ten were worked from 6 a.m. till midnight three nights in the week, and until 9 the other nights. A boy of thirteen had worked from 6 a.m. till midnight every night for a fortnight. When Mr. Palmer spoke, with pride, of the excessive overtime worked by his men for three months to get H.M.S. *Terror* built in time to reduce the Kronstadt forts ... this is the sort of thing that in practice was what happened.

In the decade 1860 to 1870, there were a number of strikes for the nine-hour day ... though not among the factory workers. The quarrymen fought a twenty-two weeks' strike and were the first to win it. The masons' strike in Newcastle after eleven months won the boon for Tyneside.

Andrew Gourlay was determined to use the feeling left after the lock-out, to get nine hours in Palmer's, if necessary by a strike. On a Thursday evening in February 1866, a huge meeting of over 2000 of Palmer's men adopted a requisition which was sent to Mr. Palmer signed by a very large number of the men themselves.

"We, The undersigned, beg to acquaint you that an association has been formed on Tyneside for the reduction of the hours of labour from ten to nine hours per day and also to inform you that we have identified ourselves with this movement believing that the period has arrived when such reductions may reasonably be expected.

"We submit the following reasons as the grounds for our request:

"By the introduction of improved machinery into the various departments of labour the profits of the employers have been considerably increased while no corresponding benefits have accrued to the working classes, though in most instances such improvements in machinery are mainly attributable to the increased intelligence and application of the artisans themselves.

"No suggestion is required to prove that machinery, however complicated or simple, is safer in the charge of intelligent and moral workmen, than men without education and rectitude; and as the shortening of the hours of labour will afford opportunities for mental and moral training, thereby a mutual advantage could not but be realized by both employer and employed.

"We could advance other reasons equally powerful for a reduction of hours of labour but we trust those already given will be sufficient.

"We submit this memorial for your careful consideration and respectfully request your answer on or before March 1st 1866."

On receiving this respectful but firm letter, Palmer could be under no illusions that the separation of his puddlers from the Staffordshire union men, for which he had fought a fortnight's expensive lock-out, had had much effect on their militancy. A similar document seems to have been sent to other engineering firms in the area.

A meeting of directors of these firms was held and decided of course to resist the demand, and also looked round for a little help, considering that a "general committee of the trades engaged in the manufacturing industry should be appointed to consider the best means of resisting the Nine Hour Movement".

Palmer had, meantime, to deal with his own men, and he wasn't having them out this time if he could help it. He met his men in a large mass meeting and argued with them that wage increases were impossible owing to the fact that Tyne wages were already higher than wages on Clyde, Mersey and Thames. In a long conciliatory speech he closed by pleading:

"I hope and trust that you in this locality will not be made the tools of *men* in other localities and be the first to stand out for a concession which will end in ... what? ... the desolation of your homes, the driving of trade from this locality, the bringing of misery to yourselves and misfortune to your employers."

Alderman Pochin, that £25,000 share-holding director from Manchester who had initiated the turning of Palmer's into a limited liability company, addressed the meeting in a speech from which the following is worth quotation as being a characteristic gem of the employers' oratory of that period ...

"I wish from the bottom of my heart that the workmen not only in this country but everywhere throughout the world were able to obtain a decent subsistence working only nine hours per day. I am sure this is a sentiment which animates us all; but when I declare that the rate of wages does not depend upon the individual will of anyone of us I am only stating a truism. The only legitimate means of raising wages is this ... that there should be two masters competing for one man's work; then the men could fairly demand an increase in wages; the only legitimate means of reducing wages is when there are two men competing for one master's work."

One could hardly expect the workmen of that time to reply to this bright piece of economic nonsense that the only times when actually there had been two masters competing for one man's work in Britain, Parliament had promptly passed measures making it a penal offence for the worker to use this advantage.

The men were not impressed by these arguments. A man who had worked in other districts challenged Palmer's statement that other wages were lower on Tyneside and instanced that much higher wages were paid on the Thames. Palmer neatly countered that by admitting it, and saying that that was why they were getting work in Jarrow which was formerly done on the Thames.

Palmer left economic arguments and pleaded that Jarrow should not be the thin edge of the wedge ... and why not twelve of the men meet twelve of the employers and just talk the whole thing over. Of course if any one class of men left work he would have to close the whole works ... and he knew what some men were up to ... but why go to extremes. He would always give conditions that were general in the district. The men were unconvinced, but hesitant. A man who to please Palmer proposed a motion against the nine hour day was received with hisses. Their real difficulty was that though they spoke of a " movement", it was a matter of sentiment rather than organization. It weighed with the more cautious that if the other firms won the nine-hour day, they would get it ... so why be the first? John Burnett, the man who five years later was to lead and win the great Nine Hours' Strike in Newcastle, remarks of this meeting in his pamphlet on the Nine Hours' Movement: "It cannot fail to be a source of great gratification to that gentleman [Mr. Palmer] to think that by his tact and cleverness he was then able to avert from Jarrow the misfortune of becoming the battlefield of a movement which has now been fought out elsewhere." Far more than the Palmer tact and cleverness, two causes helped the movement to die down for the time being at Jarrow. There was a sudden depression in trade, consequent upon a money panic that year, which halted the movement generally. And Palmer took advantage of the moment to dismiss Andrew Gourlay, thus getting rid of the forceful personality who had been the centre of resistance to him in Jarrow. Andrew Gourlay seems to have been a remarkable man, though his character has to be judged by his achievement, for there are few other records left by him. Dismissed from Jarrow he had a spell of unemployment, when it was difficult to get work owing to the depression. But he was a highly skilled workman, and got work in Sunderland as soon as trade revived. He was quietly determined to start the Nine Hours' Movement ... and to do that in the best practical way by showing that it could be won. A member of the

A.S.E. himself, he knew the difficulties of craft jealousies and the problem of the unorganized labourer. His idea was to get them all keen on the one thing, and then the requisite organization could be formed, even if it had to be on an *ad hoc* basis, so as not to rouse the jealousy of the skilled unions. In a "small quiet meeting" he gathered round him a number of his workmates, and started the demand for the nine-hour day. Under his skilled leadership, the other sections were brought in, and by April 1871, as President of the Sunderland Strike Committee, he was able to run a strike at all the engineering works in Sunderland for a nine-hour day. As a piece of organization it was really remarkable, and showed what could be done to get round inter-union difficulties by an agitation for something that every man wanted. In three weeks, the largest firm gave way, the Sunderland Engineering Employers' Association broke under the strain, and after another week, under Gourlay's clever leadership, the rest gave in, and the nine-hour day was won in Sunderland. As things turned out, Gourlay had won it for the whole engineering trade of the country as well. After that, Gourlay drops out of history. John Burnett, perhaps a little jealous, says of him: "The chances are that had Gourlay been allowed to remain at Jarrow, he might very possibly have got a house through the medium of the Factory Building Society; the possession of the house would have kept him quiet at Jarrow (the possession of a house having that effect upon a man, a fact which Mr. Palmer had not failed to note), he would never have originated the Sunderland Strike, and the Nine Hours' Movement would still have been left in the limbo of unfulfilled aspirations." Still, the tribute, though a trifle catty, is a handsome one from his chief rival to fame, the man who was to become the General Secretary of the A.S.E. From the little one knows of Andrew Gourlay it would have taken more than the possession of a house on instalment payments to keep him passive. Like many of the real heroes of the working-class movement, he comes into the picture doing a good job of work in the struggle, shows high qualities of courage and leadership ... then the work done, goes back to his bench if the masters will let him work; and probably starves quietly like Hepburn and Macintosh of the Miners if they won't. The little we know of such men throws light on the fine human material, that, despite long hours, low wages, crowded home conditions, the working classes of each country are able to produce for an emergency.

John Burnett was the young and active secretary of one of the Newcastle branches of the A.S.E. He had organized the meeting with the Newcastle men for the strike delegates sent by Gourlay to state their case for help. The Sunderland men said frankly that the best help the Newcastle men could give would be to bring the Newcastle firms into line. Otherwise it would be impossible to keep the nine-hour day in Sunderland if they won it. Meetings were held by the men in the various engineering works, but the national unions stood aloof. They had just come through a period of bad trade, and were anxious about their funds. In any case, as they organized only the skilled trades, the unskilled labour in the steelworks and shipyards was unorganized.

This problem had to be faced. Burnett was a moderate man. He had moved the resolution for arbitration after the strike resolution had been passed at the first general meeting on the Nine Hours' Issue. But in the circumstances he saw that the only thing to be done was to organize an *ad hoc* Nine Hours' League to run the agitation. Such a League could raise funds, and at least give some support to each striker. But it was a bold decision for Burnett to take. The craft unions, though still small, were well entrenched, and jealous of any newcomers on their ground.

On April 29, 1872, a historic meeting was held at the Westgate Inn, Newcastle, consisting of delegates sent by practically every engineering shop of any size on the Tyne. The business was to form a Nine Hours' League. John Burnett was elected its President, and a committee was formed to send a letter to the employer asking for the fiftyfour-hour week. The employers promptly refused, through their solicitors. The next question was therefore ... the strike. Was it to be a general strike on Tyneside, or were a selected list of firms to come out, while the others remained at work pledged to support the strikers? Clark, Gurney, and Watson's men put themselves on the list by coming out at once. Palmer's was not included in the list. Whether they would have been had Andrew Gourlay still been at Jarrow is not clear. That they were heart and soul in the movement is shown by the fact that their delegates attended all the meetings, and heavy subscriptions for the strikers were raised in Jarrow. Throughout the strike Mr. Palmer walked warily. He did not put himself at the head of the employers this time. He carefully confined himself to offering his services as mediator when occasion offered. The strike lasted from May to October, and was fought with bitterness and determination on both sides. It is not necessary here to follow the details of the struggle, but a few facts that emerge throw a light on conditions in Jarrow and Tyneside at the time. The Mayor of Newcastle received a deputation of the men before the strike started. In the course of the discussion a delegate told the Mayor that:

> "Messrs. Palmers had often built boats for Government and yet the engines had invariably been put in by Penn of Greenwich or Messrs. Maudsley of London or some other distant firm. These men not only had to obtain their coal and iron from long distances but they sent down men to fit the engines and their heavy travelling expenses had to be met. When additional local men had to be employed then they bad the anomaly of Palmer's men receiving 26s. or 27s. per week, and Maudsleys 6s. or 7s. more."

27s. for a fifty-nine-hour week of highly skilled labour should be noted in connection with the amount of money Palmer had received for the goodwill of Jarrow Shipyard. Another part of this discussion as reported in the *Newcastle Chronicle* is worth quoting.

A delegate (who seems to have been John Burnett himself) said:
"The steam shipping trade had been largely developed of late and the demand for engines was now very great. Every commercial man knew and the working men also knew of steam shipping companies boasting in their circulars inviting capitalists to take up shares that they were able to pay from 30 to 50 per cent."
The Mayor: "You think you ought to have some share of the 30 or 50 per cent?"
The delegate said that he did not wish to be misunderstood nor that it should be thought he was a leveller.
The Mayor: "You think, if those ships when built can pay 30 to 50 per cent. the builders might get more money for the ships and if greater prices are obtained more wages can be paid to those who build them."
The delegate: "Why don't they put bigger prices on the engines?"
The Mayor said it was known that the shipowners made a great deal of money, though 30 or 50 per cent was probably a little exaggeration.
The delegate: "They say it themselves."
The Mayor: "I have heard it and seen it stated."

It is interesting that the Mayor of Newcastle did not laugh at the suggestion of 30 to 50 per cent profits, but merely thought it "probably a little exaggerated".

Note that Burnett used the old Cromwellian term "leveller", in the days when the Socialist Movement had hardly touched the workers of the North.

Some idea of the force which the Nine Hours' Movement had gathered behind it can be seen from John Burnett's statement. While protesting, as was true enough, that he had been a moderate man all through, he said, in reply to a request for postponement by the Mayor that "he would not dare to go into the committee room that night and advocate an extension of time. The delegates had not agitated at all. The men had pushed the delegates forward. It was like running downhill with a force behind which could not be resisted."

The pamphlet written by John Burnett soon after the strike ended shows what it meant to come out on strike without union backing in 1872. Some men were described as having resources in the co-operative society, and they did not come on to the funds. The first strike pay amounted to 1s. 9d. per man. The second division in the third week of the strike 3200 men received 3s. each. At the next pay, each man received 2s. 9d. with 6d. for each child. Not until late July was it possible to pay as much as 4s. per striker with 1s. for each child. This was due to the number of men who left the district and got work elsewhere. As the flour millers and bread retailers of Newcastle and district had passed a resolution the week the strike commenced to give no credit to strikers, the depth of the distress among the strikers and their families must have been terrible. On this pay they stood firm for just over seventeen weeks.

Another interesting feature of the strike was the help given by the International Working Men's Association. The employers, led by Sir William Armstrong, were beginning to import workers in quantities from Germany and Belgium. Burnett went down in August to London to meet the Council of the International. The Council gave every help in their power. They undertook to advertise in continental journals, and sent their Danish secretary, Mr. Cohn, to Belgium to warn Belgian workers by posters and public meetings against taking jobs on Tyneside during the strike. When Cohn got to Brussels he found English agents there trying to get men, and the town covered with bills offering inducements to men to take work in England.

Curiously it was the cigar-workers who gave Cohn the most help. A large party of workers was to be sent to Newcastle by ship, but the cigar-workers' secretary held them back. Cohn held meetings at Verviers, Liege and Seraing. A great mass meeting in Brussels, then at Antwerp and Ghent, all agreed to influence workers not to go. A meeting with the "smiths" led to a resolution not only to refuse all offers, but to start a trade society among themselves. Cohn was so successful that the English agents complained to the Belgian authorities, who promptly ordered him to leave Belgium. The A.S.E. the next month, at their own expense, sent him to Newcastle, where his knowledge of languages enabled him to induce numbers of imported men to accept the offer to send them home at the expense of the strike funds.

Though the strike had started at the end of May it was not until July 22nd, that the Amalgamated Society of Engineers, in the words of its loyal member, Burnett, "began to stir itself in earnest". In a circular issued on that date, the General Secretary, William Allan, blandly began by saying that the Council had remained silent to the society upon the great conflict between the Newcastle workmen and their employers not because of indifference, but owing to the position as regards a levy. The circular went on to ask for voluntary subscription lists to be opened in every branch and workshop, and to bespeak their advocacy and aid. As the request was only for a voluntary levy anyway, it is difficult to see why the A.S.E. should not have showed some interest earlier in a fight which was to improve the position of every one of their members.

The men at Jarrow, who had been working hard raising funds to keep the strike going, sent a specially strong contingent to the vast Nine Hours' Demonstration held late in September. When the strike unexpectedly succeeded in October, by the Newcastle employers agreeing to the Nine Hours as from January 1, 1873, the issue was won in fact for the whole industry. George Stephenson and Charles Palmer agreed that it should apply in their respective works from the settled date, and Burnett closes his pamphlet with the statement that "since the Newcastle strike was settled, not a day has gone over without some firm, first in this district and then over different parts of the country, conceding the Nine Hour system to their men". The fifty-four hour week thus won remained in force generally until January 1919, when the forty-seven hour week was conceded.

CHAPTER EIGHT

Fifty Years of Palmerstown

WITH THE growth of England's industrial power Palmer's marched on. British industries were best fitted to exploit the developing overseas markets. The increasing international trade necessitated more and more ships. Raw materials and foodstuffs had to be brought to England, and our manufactured goods had to be shipped to the ever expanding markets overseas.

The increased financial resources resulting from the flotation of the limited liability company had led to a much increased output. Whereas the average annual output of new tonnage amounted to only 6027 tons per year during the first ten years of the firm's existence, the second ten-year period saw the average annual tonnage launched jump to 20,096. For the decade 1872-81 the output increased to a yearly average of 24,700 tons and for 1882-91 it reached an average of 37,104 tons.

New improvements in the construction of ships took place. Steel ousted iron. And the demand for ships led to great activity in Palmer's. Skilled men came from Sheffield and from the Midlands to work in the iron and steel works. The problem of the unskilled labourer was solved by immigration from Ireland. Strong men, yet willing to work for a very low wage, were needed in the iron works for the arduous job of carrying the "pigs" of iron, weighing about one hundredweight each, from the moulds to the wagons waiting to carry them to the next process. Irishmen excelled in this work, and soon a large number arrived in Jarrow from Ireland, to take up this particular job. They constituted a separate group in Jarrow's social, political and religious life.

Although the latter half of the nineteenth century were years of industrial progress it was not a continuous age of golden years. In Jarrow the rhythm of shipbuilding activity became most noticeable. All the technical terms which the modern economists employ to discuss trade cycles were known to the Jarrow of the 'eighties and 'nineties as "good times" and "bad times". Shipbuilding as an industry is extremely susceptible to changing trade conditions. When freight rates fall, and shipowners find little profit in running their ships, new orders fall off. But as soon as the demand for shipping space revives, shipowners rush to order new vessels. Therefore shipbuilding output follows a cycle, almost corresponding to an international trade index.

Remarkable variations exist in the yearly output of Palmer's. In 1874 the firm launched 25,057 tons, but by 1876 the yearly output had fallen to 8635 tons. For the next seven years output increased steadily each year, until in 1883 61,113 tons were launched. Next year the launchings fell suddenly to 28,911 tons, and declined until 1887, when only 19,324 tons were launched. These cyclical variations are one of the most serious problems of the shipbuilding industry as it is now organized. In a few years Palmer's have ranged from working at full capacity to almost complete idleness. In 1901 Palmer's yard launched 61,016 tons, in 1909 the yard launched only 1620 tons – the lowest annual output which the firm had experienced since its first year. Yet in 1912 the firm built 58,902 tons.

Business men denounce the very idea of planned socialism as inefficient and wasteful. But under capitalism shipbuilding seems to be as wasteful as it could be. Productive capacity in one great yard has to be maintained to handle an output of 60,000 tons per year, and yet there are times when only 1620 tons are launched. To ensure ability to deal with the highest possible demand, men and productive resources are left lying idle during the greater part of the trade cycle. For the men the industry accepts no responsibility. It seeks however to compensate the owners of the capital by charging such prices during the good years as will make it possible to pay a fair average return to its investors.

Before the war the "bad times" in Jarrow meant hardships to the workmen and their families which are difficult for us to realize. As a shipbuilding programme was completed, and if no further work was ready, men were discharged from the yard. Their number increasing as the slump developed, and unable to find work elsewhere, they had to prepare to exist until the "good times", and of course without any unemployment benefit. The whole town lost its purchasing power when the gates of Palmer's closed. The march of the trade cycle seemed as inevitable as the plague. There is a grim fatalism about the way in which the workmen prepared for the bad time. With little or no resources to fall back on the first move was to effect an economy in rent. Two, three, or more families would move together into one house. Rent was halved or even further reduced, but the overcrowding was appalling. Large families were herded into one room. At the same time some streets of houses would almost be empty. This overcrowding and the inadequate nourishment led to effects which are continually bewailed by the medical officer of health. In 1884 the local officer prefaced his report with: "The lamentable depression of trade in the borough, with the consequent distress among the working classes, has had an appreciable effect upon the mortality statistics of the year". In 1892 the town was badly hit and when recovery seemed to be on the way the medical officer wrote: "The depressed state of trade during the past few years, and its accompanying hardships seem to be now passing away, and no doubt, with brighter prospects and regular employment, the health of the town will improve considerably. The overcrowding in tenement houses that necessarily exists in times of want and depression will diminish, and that means more sanitary and better ventilated dwellings with less exposure to disease and infection".

When Palmer's closed down, it meant that the shipyards on the river were closed too. But though no work was available anywhere within miles – the full deterrent clauses of the Poor Law were applied to the workers, skilled and unskilled alike, of the stricken town. No relief could be given to an ablebodied man without "task-work". The Poor Law Guardians had to provide this. Men walked to the workhouse, and in return for a day's stone-breaking received 1s. 6d. That they were treated exactly like criminals is clear from the records of the time.

The wife of Canon Liddell in her life of her husband, who was rector of Jarrow in 1876, gives a vivid description of what their parishioners had to endure when Palmer's was closed. "Our hearts were made sick by the sight of groups of able-bodied men standing round a heap of stones, waiting for their turn to begin stone-breaking – the hardest and worst paid of all occupations. At that time a stone-breaker earned ordinarily from 9d. to a shilling a day. It was 'piecework' and for a skilled workman it was almost a hopeless task. 'He's at stone-breaking', said a wife, speaking of her husband, 'But it's very few stones a joiner can break'".

Of the following winter she writes: "Whose heart would not ache to see what was seen that winter of sad memory, on a day of intense frost – a man struggling with the miserable task, afraid to stop for an instant, lest the cold should compel him to desist, while on her knees beside him his wife was scratching out the stones for him with her benumbed hands?" As is usual the men themselves rallied to assist their neighbours in distress. Distress committees were formed and subscriptions were solicited throughout the town. Each week the committee would meet on a Thursday evening to allocate the money, and they would commence their collections for the next week.

The "bad times" were hard. And yet in the "good times", too, poverty was everywhere. Wages were low, especially among the labourers. Shipyard work is intermittent. A labourer's wage was about £1 per week. A mechanic would get about 27s. Some idea of the general wage level of Palmer's can be gauged from the weekly wage bill. In 1883, one of the best years experienced by the company, the average total wages paid to 7000-8000 workers was just over £10,000 – an average of about 25s. each per week per man.

The veterans recall what a struggle life was in the "good days". During Newcastle Race Week, the famous Tyneside holiday, the works were idle. This respite was used for certain overhauls of machinery. A holiday for most of the men meant a week without pay. The usual practice was to pay a little each week to the landlord in excess of the rent in order to cover this wageless week. Similarly with the grocer. Otherwise they had to be dependent on the landlord and grocer allowing them credit in the hope that it would be paid off, little by little.

Only gradually did Jarrow build up some social amenities. The first result of the expansion of the town, which employed so many men on arduous work, was an increase in the number of public-houses. In 1860 there were nine "pubs" in Jarrow. Five years later there were thirty-one. Drunkenness became a serious problem, but new social opportunities were created which acted as counter attractions. In the early morning the "pubs" adjacent to Palmer's did quite a good trade. The gates of the Shipyard were only opened at 6 a.m. Men arriving early had to wait outside. And the prospect of a wait on Tyneside, on a chilly November morning about 5.30 a.m., was not over pleasant. The alternative was the shelter and cheer of the nearby public houses. As one of the earliest social workers in Jarrow, Canon Liddell recognized the danger, and tried to meet the needs of the men by providing a travelling coffee-stall. Every morning he set up his stall at the workers' gates from 5.30. It was gruelling work, and helped to smash the health of this fine scholar and Christian. But he hoped by his example to shame the works' management into doing something more adequate for their men. It took more than that to shame Palmer's. Not till thirty years later did the company recognize any responsibility towards the crowds of men gathered round the works' gates each morning, numbers of whom had had to come in by train. In 1904 the company turned some tenement property near the works into refreshment rooms, which were opened from 5.30.

It is one of the significant factors about heavy industry company towns, whether in Britain or in West Virginia, that social amenities and social organizations for health and hygiene come late. While the big money is being made, the firm can't be bothered to spend time or money in planning to make the life of its "hands" tolerable. At the same time, it presses with its whole weight against any attempt to do these things communally, through the municipality, lest that might cause a rise in the rates.

Throughout the nineteenth century, but particularly in the three last more prosperous decades of that period, social life in Jarrow centred round the churches and chapels of the various denominations. The Roman Catholic Church, of course, mainly worked among the Irish and their descendants. Among the skilled workmen in the Shipyard, nonconformity was very strong. The large nonconformist churches in Jarrow, of a size much too big for the modern needs of Jarrow, bear witness to the large part these played in the life of a town where the church and the "pub" provided the only social alternatives. In this thriving, jostling, overcrowded town, both sections were well organized for political purposes.

Jarrow's charter as a municipal borough was granted, and its first town council elected in 1875. Charles Mark Palmer headed the poll, and was its Charter Mayor. He held the office for a few weeks, and then handed it over, retaining a seat as alderman. He used to pay the Council an annual visit to give them an address "on the state of trade and allied matters" ... a pontifical pronouncement which set the tone of the Council's work. The first council was composed of builders, tradesmen, and a few professional people, but the guiding hand came from Palmer's. Malcolm Dillon, general manager, and later a director, made clear the relation of the firm to the local authority, and the Palmer view about municipal efforts, when he said, in a speech, to a Secretaries Association:

> "The alarming and constant increase in local taxation will come within the scope of our considerations. A very large part of the cost of keeping up our towns falls on limited companies, who have practically no voice in the expenditure for which they are made responsible and no representatives, as such, on local Boards or Councils. On the other hand a number of members of spending authorities are ratepayers only in theory ... that is to say they pay rent in which the rates are included. I may perhaps be permitted as a typical case to instance Palmer's Company. We pay over one-sixth of the rates of Jarrow. Every time the Council, or the Education Authority, or the Board of Guardians spends £1, we pay three-sevenths of it. I mention this to show how largely interested we are in local expenditure, and how necessary it is that we should have *a greater control over it.*"

This speech was made, not in the "dark ages" of the 1870s, but in 1905. Lest we should think that "of course things have changed" it is as well to remember that precisely those ideas were at the back of the de-rating of industry in the 1929 Act, when the companies were relieved of three-quarters of their rates.

There was no need for the legislature to provide the Mr. Dillons with "greater control". When the company had the general manager, the secretary and the chief cashier on the Town Council, victory for the works view could be safely left in such hands. A works employee who made himself conspicuous in any opposition to the works "interests" on the Council, would not be long employed at the works ... he would follow the road of Andrew Gourlay and other outspoken men. At a time when it was imperative in the interest of health ... even of life ... that Jarrow should be provided with drainage, health services, and some diminution of the appalling overcrowding, the interest of Palmer's Company, and the builders and traders controlling the Council demanded lower rates.

As with health, so with social amenities. None were provided by the Council, who did best in education owing to the work of the first chairman of the education committee. In 1864 a Mechanics' Institute was opened for the benefit of the men at the Shipyard. Weekly lectures were organized, rooms were available for recreation, and a small library was started for the members. But Jarrow had no free public library until 1937, when, after much agitation, the scheme was carried through by Jarrow's first Labour Council.

To the gods of the works, and on the altar of low rates, a heavy toll of human sacrifice was paid yearly by the Jarrow workers.

Each year the town was swept by diseases that were as much by-products of Jarrow's industrialism as the pall of smoke that hung over the town and could be seen out at sea. For years the councillors decided to save the £4000 needed for a hospital for infectious diseases. It took fifteen years hard campaigning by the medical officer of health to get his hospital, although a small-pox epidemic was almost a yearly feature. After one bad outbreak of small-pox the Council were forced to provide a temporary wooden hut to do service as an isolation hospital. But it was a very temporary building, for when there were "severe gales of wind and rain, the rain came in rather freely and the ventilation was somewhat excessive". On occasions when small-pox seemed to slacken in virulence this hut was hastily disinfected and prepared for typhoid cases.

Against a council of small traders anxious to keep down the rates the medical officials had a difficult task to force the Council to take action against some of the anti-social nuisances. Diseases like scarlet fever, typhoid, diphtheria and measles were much too prevalent, and Jarrow's death rate from these diseases was much higher than the average for the country. Particularly fatal was an annual plague of diarrhoea, which killed a large number of young children. The medical officer came to the conclusion that much of the disease was due to the privy midden. "A privy midden is always foul and generally contains water so that the ground underneath and for a considerable distance around is saturated with the filthy oozing which has been going on for years, and where there are 'privy middens' the yards for the most part are paved with bricks, which become rotten and sodden from the same cause, so that under suitable atmospheric conditions the specific disease organisms which may have been latent in the ground an indefinite period are given off in the foul emanations from the polluted soil, and if a susceptible person is exposed to the infection the result is Enteric Fever or Diphtheria, as the case may be." For years successive medical officers stated the case against privy middens. Their official reports vividly describe the revolting conditions and the mortality figures revealed the price which was being needlessly paid. The Council protected the interests of its members. A council consisting of property owners is hardly likely to take compulsory measures against property owners. A council of tradesmen is more interested in keeping the rates down instead of providing services for its citizens. In spite of the evidence brought against this midden nuisance Jarrow Council took no vigorous action. It was not possible to get the magistrates to condemn these middens. They lingered on for twenty-two years more. Each year a few were replaced by box closets. After twelve years the medical officer of health reported hopefully that "At our present rate of decrease we shall in a very few years have got rid entirely of this very fertile means of breeding and spreading disease." Long before the substitution was complete the sanitary officials had condemned the box closets and were demanding water-carriage systems as the only effective method likely to safeguard the health of the people.

Delays of this sort and the havoc they wrought in their own families caused it to dawn on the more enterprising workmen that if they did not protect their own interest nobody else would. In the industrial field the workers were organizing to protect themselves. The skilled men had long been organized and about 1890 attempts were begun to organize the labourers. Jarrow was always a good union town for the skilled men. The skilled Shipyard men were organized largely in the Boiler Makers' Society, while the skilled workers in the iron and steel works were members of the Steel Smelters' Union or the Iron and Steel Workers' Union. They were always ready to insist on the essential principles of their Union and to fight for their rights.

Strikes of varying length and amongst different groups were common. With so many different unions concerned at the same works there were awkward problems of demarcation as well as the more usual causes which led to labour disputes. For the union members a strike meant serious hardship. Strike pay was inadequate and was strictly limited. A strike amongst the blast furnacemen which established the principle of seniority lasted seventeen weeks. For the first ten weeks a strike allowance of l0S. per week was paid, but after that the allowance had to be reduced to 5S. per week. Other strikers were not so fortunate, as they had no union funds behind them and they had to depend on the support of those who remained at work in other trades not involved in the dispute. It was these men, who by their sacrifices and by their hard work gained the privileges which are taken for granted to-day. What happened to the'women trying to feed children on these pitiful allowances has to be imagined. Of their trials no record remainsonly the increase in the death statistics for mother and child.

Jarrow suffered severely in the first years of the 'nineties. The yearly output fell from 64,000 tons in 1889 to 30,279 tons in ,89', and in 1893 only '9,543 tons of shipping were launched. Palmer's was, of course, affected by this depression in trade, but serious as was this general decline, the position of Palmer's was made much worse by special features affecting the firm.

In 1889 the Naval Defence Act authorized the construction of eight new battleships. Four of these were let out on contract to private yards, and Palmer's, anxious to secure the work when trade seemed bad, submitted very low estimates. When work was commenced on the two ships, H.M.S. *Resolution* and H.M.S. *Revenge,* Palmer's estimates were found to be much too low and the company lost heavily.

To add to the problem, 1892 was the year of the serious Durham coal strike. This led to the closing of the blast furnaces at Palmer's. The Shipyard had to carry the overheads of the iron and steel works during this difficult period. And another new venture of the company, an Ordnance Works, had proved unsuccessful.

In 1890 there was a loss of £ 11,000 and in 1891 the loss was £22,000. Rumours developed as to the weakness of the company. When in 1893 the directors produced no accounts for submission to the shareholders at the Annual General Meeting the future of the company seemed in the balance. Charles Mark Palmer fought hard for his company. He threw his personal prestige into the balance ... assured the shareholders that all was well ... appeared everywhere in apparently the highest spirits. Accustomed as he was to the rigours of private business he was not ready to accept defeat. When a colleague suggested that he might have to file a petition of bankruptcy, Palmer retorted, "Bankruptcy. You don't know what you are talking about. Why, if I went bankrupt I should have to resign from my clubs and from the House of Commons". Instead he resigned from the company. The shareholders were not content with his assurances and a special Consultative Committee was set up. There was some disagreement and the man who had founded the company resigned. A local man, James Milburn of Newcastle, joined the Board to help the company through its difficult years. A mortgage of £650,000 was raised and in 1896 there was a further reduction of capital, the £35 shares being written down by £20.

The suffering and the uncertainty of these difficult years gave an impetus to the local political and trade-union movements. In 1891 the Jarrow Trades Council was set up to co-ordinate local trade-union activity. And with the increasing union activity came the movement towards political work. Shortly after the formation of the Trades Council a large meeting was held in the Co-operative Hall, and a resolution was carried "That Jarrow being an essentially labour constituency should send a labour representative to the British House of Commons". Consequently, when the General Election of 1892 was fought Jarrow had a labour candidate. A London solicitor, Mr. E. Dillon Lewis, came to Jarrow to oppose the "creator" of the town. His support came largely from the Hebburn miners. In Jarrow opinion was divided, because the Palmer hold was so strong. Robert Knight, the secretary of the Boiler Makers' Society hastened to the support of the employer. "I cannot think", he wrote, "that any working men who have the least idea of what Sir Charles Palmer has done will ever vote against him. It will be a most deplorable mistake for my fellow workers to vote for a perfect stranger who knows nothing of the wants of the toiling masses, in preference to an honoured and tried friend."

Electioneering in that campaign was vigorous and vociferous. Hebburn supported Lewis, while the workers of Jarrow lined up behind their employer. Lewis was severely heckled in Jarrow, Palmer had difficulty in getting a hearing in Hebburn. Cunningham Graham, who came up to support Lewis at Hebburn, had a lively time at some of the meetings. The intervention of the Irish, who were told that it was their plain duty to support Charles Mark Palmer, heightened the excitement of the election. The Palmer hold was too strong to loosen at the first challenge. At the eve-of-the-poll meeting Palmer characteristically told the audience that the prosperity of Jarrow was due more to the workers than to him – which was received with the expected applause ... and no one asked why the share in the results had been so unequal.

On polling day most Shipyard workers had the afternoon off and they assembled in the centre of the town near the Ben Lomond Hotel where the Labour candidate was staying. When Lewis with his supporters made a tour of the town they were showered with flour, eggs, and anything handy. There are workers in the Labour movement on Tyneside today who can recall the suits they had damaged in that election. Even the children joined in. "Charlie" Palmer was popular with them. He used to throw pennies to them from his cab as he drove through the streets of Jarrow. They carried effigies of Dillon Lewis through the street. Defeat was inevitable, Lewis getting 2400 votes out of a total poll of 9700.

In 1895 and 1900 Charles Mark Palmer was returned unopposed. But the strength of organized labour was increasing. In 1892 Keir Hardie had been elected for West Ham as a Labour representative. The feeling was growing that the workers should have their own representatives in the House of Commons. The President of the T.U.C. in 1898 urged a scheme of political organization for the workers, and in the following year a Special Conference was held out of which the Labour Representative Committee developed.

At Jarrow everything depended on whether the "old man" would fight another election. A small group of the more active workers decided that Labour must fight the next election in any case. As candidate they selected Pete Curran, an organizer of the Gas Workers' Union. He had been in the division during the 1892 election to assist Dillon Lewis. He was an excellent speaker and an experienced candidate – having fought Barrow-in-Furness and Barnsley in previous elections – and a typical Irish working-man.

When the 1906 election was imminent Palmer announced his intention of standing again. The usual section rallied to his support. There were "boss's men" in the Union movement. Robert Knight of the Boiler Makers' Society again supported Palmer. Some of the Irish, though nominally Labour, were urged to vote for Palmer by their various national organizations. In this early day, the important thing was to get out of the workers' heads the idea that big Liberal employers were any better than the old Tories. In spite of these difficulties Curran gained a great deal of support. He resolutely opposed Liberals as enemies of the working class posing as sympathizers. His battle cry was "The Tories would, at least, give the workers promises, but the Liberals would give them nothing." Lady Warwick and Cunningham Graham both came to support Pete Curran, who polled 5000 votes as opposed to Palmer's 8000.

It was a heartening result. Pete Curran, with his striking appearance and his racy speeches, had gained much support in the division. Even Charles Mark Palmer was impressed by the calibre of his opponent. Encouraged by their success the local Labour Representative Committee soon met to consider the choice of their candidate. Curran was again selected, but among the list of possible candidates were the most famous names of early Labour Party history – James Sexton, Bruce Glasier, Stanton Coit, and George Lansbury. The death of Charles Mark Palmer gave Curran a byeelection. Against a Tory, a Liberal, Spencer Leigh Hughes, and an Irish candidate he was successful. Jarrow had its first Labour M.P. It was not for Liberalism but for Palmer that the workers had voted. Realizing their mistake the Liberals, at the next election, brought forward a candidate with the magic name of Palmer. He was successful and held the seat until the post-war years, when it was won for Labour.

Charles Mark Palmer's death in 1907 was the end of an epoch for Jarrow. Already the signs of a decline in the Shipyard were present. The average annual tonnage launched over a ten-year period reached a maximum in the years 1882-91, when it was 39,900 tons. For the next ten years it fell just a little, but for the period 1902-11 it was to fall as low as 26,740 tons. Charles Mark Palmer had seen the years of development and he died at the time when England was having to meet competition from other nations. The town he had developed was his memorial. The Town Hall, with its Palmer commemoration tablet, the Palmer portrait in the Council Chamber, and the Palmer Works photographs on the corridor walls, appeared to be an adjunct of the company's offices, as in fact it was. The hospital is the Palmer Memorial Hospital, with a bronze statue of the man in the gardens. The only libraries were in the Palmer Mechanics' Institute. The streets of Jarrow are named after the early managers and directors of the companies. If Palmerstown be a memorial to the capitalist system it reveals the social cost of this system of private ownership.

Although wages were low one senses in these opening years of the present century a feeling of solidity, at least in the lives of the skilled men. The future of the shipbuilding yard seemed safe beyond all possible doubt. And there was hope in the hearts of the workers as they strengthened the Unions and developed their political work. Their town had few amenities, but they were starting the battles in local political life by which these were won. Their local newspaper reflected the interest of its readers when it published a series of articles by Ramsay Macdonald and George Barnes. E. D. Morel came to widen their view by addressing a town's meeting on the Belgian Congo atrocities. The religious life of the town was developed and strengthened as the new churches and chapels were built. For entertainment there was a theatre, and in 1906 moving pictures came to Jarrow.

These feelings of security were given a severe jolt by the slump in shipbuilding during 1907. All English districts were affected and Palmer's suffered seriously. 1908 was a worse year, during which the Jarrow firm launched only three ships. With the distress came an attempt of the owners to reduce wages which led to a strike amongst various groups of shipyard workers. Bad trade and industrial disputes caused Palmer's a loss of £58,000 in 1908. The company's future was in jeopardy, and special measures had to be adopted to save it. To help the company through this period a mortgage was raised. No dividend was to be paid on either the preference shares or the debentures until the mortgage had been paid off. In addition there was some reorganization of the management. A new manager, A. B. Gowan, was appointed.

In an attempt to obtain some work, a campaign developed on Tyneside to persuade the Admiralty to order a floating dock for the River Tyne. Jarrow men were greatly interested and were largely responsible for the campaign, since the dock was to be anchored in Jarrow Slake. A deputation went to the Admiralty to see the First Lord. Mr. McKenna was impressed by the argument that there was no dry dock on the East Coast capable of accommodating a dreadnought, and he promised that an expert would investigate the scheme. They visited Jarrow and pronounced the Slake unsuitable for the purpose. A dock was built, but it was anchored in the Medway, which was thought by the experts to be the best place. Shortly after the war broke out, this dock was towed up to Jarrow and anchored in the Slake. Its useful service in the Great War was a bitter comment on the judgement of the experts who had declared Jarrow unsuitable for such a dock, and its story curiously prophetic of the steelworks' scheme twenty years later.

The main task before the company was now the repayment of the mortgage, and to settle the company on a sound financial basis. Under the new manager, certain modernizations were carried out and the nearby yards of Robert Stephenson and Company of Hebburn were purchased. For three years the debt was reduced, but in 1912 there was a further increase, when the debit balance reached £128,413. This uncertain progress was causing anxiety. But all the cracks were hidden by the outbreak of war.

For Jarrow the war meant a period of intense activity. Warships and merchant tonnage were urgently needed. A shipyard so near the North Sea had to be ready to deal with the repair jobs resulting from torpedo attacks, damage by mines, or naval battles. Combined with great activity in their shipyard, Palmer's ventured into shell-manufacturing, and a large number of women were employed in this work.

There were difficulties in the way of their increased activity. In the rush to volunteer for active service a number of the skilled men from the Shipyard dropped their tools and joined up. Enlistment in the industrial districts, especially those districts associated with engineering, was high. By the end of the first year of war Mr. Lloyd George notes that 19.5 per cent of the men in the engineering trade had enlisted. When the need for new tonnage became apparent as the months went by efforts were made to obtain from the army the skilled men who had enlisted.

Very soon it was demonstrated that the inefficiencies of the individual capitalist firms, each working for its own profit, were too wasteful and too slow for war. The first stage was the appointment of a Shipping Control Committee to survey the situation as a whole. But it did very little. By early November 1916, Mr. Runciman, the President of the Board of Trade, in his typically negative fashion, was forecasting a complete breakdown of the shipping services before the summer of next year, without suggesting that anything might be done to prevent this. The building of merchant shipping had been reduced owing to the demand for naval vessels and now there was a shortage of steel for shipbuilding purposes. With the appointment of Lloyd George as Prime Minister a more vigorous policy was pursued. Sir Joseph Maclay was appointed Shipping Controller, and his first task was to arrange for immediate discussions with shipbuilders as to the best way to increase their output. Control of shipbuilding passed to the Ministry of Shipping, and later to Sir Eric Geddes, when he took over the appointment of Controller of the Navy.

The war, with its period of rising prices and rising profits, brought some wage increases for the men. From June 1914 to May 1920 the Boiler Makers' Society were able to gain a total wage advance of 37s. 6d. per week, most of it to meet the rapid rise in the cost of living. The capitalists, who protested so vigorously against increases for the men, were able to make very handsome profits. By the end of the financial year of 1914-15 Palmer's were able to report that the debit balance which in 1913 had amounted to £126,146 had been wiped out and the company had now a credit of £42,772. Profits continued at the same high rate. In one year they were able to pay off the arrears of preference dividend to the extent of 10s. 6d. for each share held. The weakness of Palmer's lay in the fact that such a high proportion of the windfall profits of the war years had to be devoted to paying off the debts due to the earlier weaknesses. During the war, other companies were able to accumulate large reserves, but Palmer's had to meet their debts incurred in 1908. This was the first cause of the financial trouble which brought the company into the hands of the receiver.

But during the war years the future was hidden in the hectic activity. More and more men were wanted in Jarrow to keep the shipyard and the steelworks going. Many came from the South of England. Their arrival taxed the accommodation in Jarrow. Lodging-houses were packed full and many private houses were overcrowded. It took some time before the directors of Palmer's recognized that this was any concern of theirs. Not until it became clear that the shortage of accommodation was likely to restrict the number of men working for the firm did the directors of Palmer's decide to build their own hostel near the works. It was finished too late to be of much use during the war. Now, when the industry has left Jarrow, part of the hostel is adapted as a lodging-house.

The new arrivals in the town settled down well to their jobs, but occasionally there was friction. Owing to the wartime restrictions on labour it was not possible for a man to change his job without the agreement of his foreman. And foremen never seemed ready to allow one of their best men to go to another department, or to another group of men. The result was that some of the experienced men lost their chance of promotion or transfer during the war. New men came in, and, in some cases, were able to secure better jobs than the more experienced locals, which led to great resentment among the Jarrow workers. Limitation of labour tended to encourage the works management to take on more men than were actually required in order to have sufficient reserve, and this increased the already desperate state of overcrowding in the town.

As in every other town Jarrow had the usual food queues and other difficulties associated with rationing. Its war experience was grimmer than some, for it suffered an air raid in 1915. Bombs were dropped on the works, and men in the machine and engine shops were killed. When the Yard was closed and the machinery sold for scrap there were still on the walls discoloured and corroding tablets commemorating the sacrifice of these men. On other tablets were the names of the men who left the Shipyard and were killed in the war.

In November 1918 Jarrow was working at full pressure. With the peace the reason for its war output passed. But to those who had worked so vigorously in the war, for all that was promised by the peace, there seemed to be a new future ahead. Trade seemed safe because Britain had won, and because ships would be needed to replace the war losses. It was with hope and confidence in the future that Jarrow celebrated the Armistice.

CHAPTER NINE

Palmer's After the War

THE OUTSTANDING fact of 1939 in the shipping world is that the proud and once pre-eminent British shipbuilding industry, one of the most individual and competitive of our industries, has pressed for and has successfully obtained a subsidy. The industry which in 1892-94 built 81.6 per cent of the tonnage of the world, and maintained a preeminent position up to 1913, was in 1938 building only 31.6 per cent. of the world's tonnage.

When 1939 dawned the outlook was worse. Then the tonnage of merchant shipping under construction amounted to only 780,000 tons, occupying about one-third of the capacity even of those yards which remained effective after the most drastic pruning of a severe rationalization scheme.

This compared very badly with the 1,125,000 tons in hand in January 1938.

For the first time since steel and steam superseded wood and sail, it was not a British shipyard which held first place in the world in tonnage launched in 1938. That position was taken by a German yard, the Deutsche Werft A.G. Hambourg. Nearly half of the work of that yard was done for foreign shipowners. Many ships were being built in Germany for British and other foreign owners. Germany's problem in the five years of Hitlerism has been to secure sufficient foreign exchange to finance her purchase of munitions and raw materials. One very successful way of securing foreign currency has been by selling ships to foreign shipowners. When unemployment in the shipbuilding trades was increasing rapidly at the end of 1938, a deputation of trade-unionists came to interview M.P.s of all parties sitting for shipbuilding constituencies at the House. I remember the union leaders telling us that 80,000 tons of shipping were being built in Germany then at a cost of £1,500,000. While British shipowners were campaigning for a subsidy some of them were ordering ships from abroad. When Germany's threat to the British Empire was increasing, some shipbuilders were supplying Hitler with the foreign exchange with which to buy more munitions. We were told that during 1935 and 1936 Germany had built for one large British combine ships to the value of £4,500,000. Foreign purchasing power to that amount would be very welcome in Germany.

Other European companies were also building vessels for British owners. Denmark had ships on order to the value of £2,750,000, while Sweden was building 17,000 tons of shipping for us. Other vessels were being built for British owners in the Far East. Altogether, at the end of 1938 there were eighty British ships, worth £8,000,000, being built abroad.

When foreign competitors were strong enough to obtain orders from Britain's "patriotic" shipowners they were more than ready to compete with us for international orders. The Italians, who once bought many ships from British yards, had developed their own industry to cater for their own needs and to accept orders from abroad. The Japanese used to buy their ships from Great Britain. Their craftsmen and their students studied the theory and practice of shipbuilding in our yards, our technical schools, and our universities. Today Japanese ships are built in Japan. These countries, coming new to shipbuilding, are already attracting foreign orders. In doing this they are aided by the growth of barter systems of exchange – which are adopted so readily by the totalitarian states. A mail boat for the North Sea crossing was ordered from Italy because Italy was prepared to accept payment in herrings. Two large vessels for Poland were ordered from Italy because the Italian Government was prepared to accept Polish coal in return.

As the shipbuilding industry was growing so was the mercantile marine. Since 1914 all the nations but two have increased their merchant navy. Germany owns less tonnage today because many of her vessels were seized after the war. With Great Britain it has been a gradual decline. By comparison with 1914, ships on the register of the United Kingdom show a deficit of 2000 ocean-going ships, or 2,000,000 gross tons of tonnage. Ten years ago our export of ships was worth £19,000,000. In 1938 shipping showed an adverse balance of £3,000,000 ... a serious situation for an island dependent on sea-borne and foreign-purchased food for the people, and sea-borne and foreign-purchased raw material for its factories.

Sir James Lithgow, who was responsible for the rationalization in shipbuilding, and whose activities will be detailed later, made a speech at the engineering congress in Glasgow in June 1938 which started the agitation for a shipbuilding subsidy. He said British prices could not be above the level of world prices, therefore a subsidy must come from somewhere. The shipowners could not subsidize the shipbuilders, hence the need for state assistance.

"It is comparatively easy for some countries with a relatively small number of their people engaged in shipbuilding to afford a large subsidy to that small section, but in our country shipbuilding is so extensive that a direct subsidy to our operatives would call for a substantial sacrifice from other sections of the community.

"Our National Exchequer does pay such a subsidy to the builders of houses for the working classes. By a process of thought typical of the times that burden on the community is justified by better and cheaper housing accommodation. To me the distinction between houses for the health and comfort of our workers and ships for the preservation of our life and Empire is not clear."

And in order that too great a burden should not fall on his fellow super-tax payers, he proposed that the sum should be provided by the unemployed, the sick, and the old-age pensioners. Of course, he did not put it quite like that. He pointed out that the "expenditure on social services which in 1900 stood at 33.5 millions had risen to 421.5 millions in 1936". He believed that "some judicious pruning of these services which have outstripped the bounds of healthy growth to be an obviously preliminary step to a sound foundation of our competitive trades" ... which is just rather a more tactful way of saying "make the poor pay the subsidy to the shipbuilder".

In these days of depression it is easy to make out a case for a subsidy for any industry. Even armament manufacturers have managed it. When it is for an industry so obviously important to an island people the case may not be easy to answer on immediate figures. But with the demand for a subsidy, the shipbuilders made it clear that they will brook no supervision. Their leading trade paper remarked (December 1938): "The root of the problem is whether they can get relief without such a measure of control as would interfere with the efficient management of the industry."

The Chairman of the Liverpool Steamship Owners' Association, in an article demanding the appointment of a Minister of Shipping, says: "This does not mean Government control of management and operation, all experience having markedly demonstrated the unwisdom, to say the least, of State-owned or controlled shipping."

Has the industry been efficiently managed? Would it be wise statesmanship to leave shipping and shipbuilding in the hands of those who have brought it to its present plight ... still less grant large sums of public money in order to keep the industry in private hands? The story of Palmer's Shipyard after the war is an object lesson in the mismanagement of a great national asset of high technical efficiency, by men whose whole interest lay in the amount of profit that could be squeezed out rapidly with little regard to national interests, to the ultimate interest of the concern, or of those whose whole livelihood and interest depended on it.

Shipowners and shipbuilders alike point proudly to their war record as evidence of their national service and their claim on the taxpayers' support. Of all industries, the directors of shipping and shipbuilding companies as a body had least to be proud of. While their staffs worked terrific health-destroying hours of overtime, the demands of the owners brought this country to the verge of defeat. The rate of coal from Cardiff to Port Said, which was 7s. 9d. on an average in 1913, rose to 80s. in 1916. Freight rates for grain that had been 12s. 6d. in 1913 had risen to the fantastic height of 145s. by the end of 1916. Freights which were immediately reflected in the cost of commodities to the people. That the Government in fact bore the cost of all the risks at sea made no difference. Any owner who could escape requisition on any pretext charged these outrageous figures. When the Government extended requisitioning, no feelings of patriotism prevented something like a strike of shipowners ... though working men on strike in wartime against the rises in the cost of living which this policy produced, were raged at as traitors in the newspapers in which the striking shipowners held considerable shares. Mr. Lloyd George, who faced a situation where the sinkings by mine and submarine had outstripped construction wrote in his war memoirs, about this period :

"With the extension of government requisitioning the owners ceased to have the same interest in their business. They did not appear to realize that now if ever was the time when their utmost efforts should be put forth to get their ships round quickly. They were still working as in peace time, each company with its private berths, and no one working for the common good to help his neighbours either by offering the use of an empty berth or by turning over a supply of bunkers which were not immediately required ... this difficulty had to be dealt with by bringing government pressure to bear on shipowners who were disposed to take too narrow a view of their responsibilities in a national emergency."

As the experience of Jarrow during the war plainly shows, the technical direction was in the hands of experts who could just as well have been employed by the State. The orders, directions, priorities for supplies and the like were in the hands of the officials of the Shipping Control. The main work of the directors of the companies seemed to be to obstruct the Shipping Controller's work until they got the financial terms they wanted and repeated assurances that shipping control would be taken off after the war.

With the requisitioning in 1917, rates were settled by the Admiralty Committees consisting of shipowners who, as an official of the Ministry of Shipping drily remarked, "dealt not too cruelly with their industry". During the first twenty-six months of the war the total net profits were estimated to amount to £262 millions. British tonnage increased in value during that period from £175 millions to £500 millions. No statistics are available as to total profits. A considerable proportion of British shipping has always been in the hands of private companies who are not bound to publish their figures. Even in the case of the public companies large amounts were placed to all kinds of special reserve funds before the actual rate of admitted profit was published.

Even allowing for war taxation and Excess Profits Duty, the legal ways of evading the latter were for a large concern many and various. The shipping industry, whether owners or builders, ended the war with huge reserves at their disposal.

It was clear to anyone able to look at the question unblinded by considerations of private personal profit that the shipping industry as a whole would have to face an extremely difficult time in the changeover to peace conditions. Naval orders stopped abruptly. True, there were arrears of trade to be made up, but the volume of British imports, exports and re-exports was considerably below that of 1913 and remained so for the first four years after the Armistice. Despite the sinkings tonnage was greater. Customers who had gone to the neutral countries would take time to win back. All this was present to the minds of those who had had experience of shipping control. Lord Maclay, the Minister for Shipping, himself one of the greatest shipowners and personally anxious to get back to the good old days and ways of high private profits, admitted that the policy of nationalizing shipping had "many advocates in high places". But he refused to wind up the Ministry of Shipping until he had personally made sure that this policy would not be carried through.

An advocate of the shipowners stated the case against nationalization which they then put forward, in words that sound curious now in view of the present position of British shipping.

"Shipowners generally held that any such step, apart from their personal interests, would mean the complete disorganization of the industry. ... They pointed out that shipping was our most valuable export industry, providing employment for thousands of workers. Healthy competition was, they claimed, its life blood. So long as British shipowners were spurred by domestic competition, such a standard of efficiency would be maintained as would guarantee a measure of success in the competition with foreign shipping on the trade routes that could not be obtained under bureaucratic control."

What of course they could not have envisaged then, but what they recognize only too anxiously now, is the enormous lever in international competition supplied to certain of their competitors by that national control they deride as "bureaucratic".

Instead, therefore, of a wise conservation of their huge reserves to meet what was obviously going to be a difficult period, the companies with few exceptions embarked on policies so reckless that the reserves were dissipated and the industry laid on its back within two years.

Orders for new tonnage were placed on the assumption that international trade was going to continue to increase and that Britain's share of the carrying trade would remain the same as in 1914. High freight rates stimulated a rush of orders. Because urgent cargoes had to be carried to meet shortage left by the war, rates were charged by British companies to Italy and other European countries so fantastic that the export of British coal was injured in those markets, never to recover. The United States were able thus to get markets for coal they had never had before. Coal, for example, carried from South Wales to River Plate at a rate of 21s. 9d. in 1913 was charged 60s. in 1919, 58s. 9d. in 1920. From South Wales to Barcelona in 1913 the highest rates were 11s. 9d. In 1919 85s., and the lowest rates on certain classes of coal were 52s. 6d. Average rates from Bombay, deadweight, were 21s. 2½d. in 1913. In 1919 they were 137s. Rice from Saigon to the United Kingdom which had been charged 37s. in 1913, had to pay as high as 220s. in 1919, the lowest charges being 145s. True rates were lowered in 1920, but that came too late to save certain trade which has never been recovered since those days of unconscionable profiteering.

Thus to strangle markets so soon to be badly needed was stupid enough. More serious was the dissipation of reserves, the lack of which was to cause widespread unemployment in the industry only a few months later. Companies had issued huge quantities of bonus shares during the war, on which interest had to be paid. The Leyland Line, for example, in 1917 had issued bonus shares of 700 per cent. In August 1919 Furness Withy issued £2,000,000 in bonus shares out of undisclosed reserves, their open reserves being £1,800,000. The White Star Line increased its ordinary share capital by bonus shares of 400 per cent. The Cunard, which had issued bonus shares twice during the war, added a gift of 100 per cent bonus shares to its ordinary shareholders in 1919. The *Economist* estimates that of eighteen leading shipping companies, their paid-up capital in 1922 included about 60 per cent "water" in the form of bonus shares. This meant that the dividends earned in the immediate post-war period had to be paid on greatly inflated capital. Deep depression settled on the shipping industry as early as 1921, and that and the following year were periods of acute depression. Yet even in that time dividends of over 9 per cent were paid on this watered capital.

The Government paid for the loss of requisitioned ships during the war. By the end of it, they had paid £104,000,000 for the loss of ships which had cost in all just over £50,000,000 to build. The companies had paid huge sums to insurance companies formed among themselves far in excess of real risks. These formed reserves of cash which were distributed after the war. Like the other funds these were soon dissipated. The rush to buy tonnage on which quick profits could be earned as soon as it was again possible to get merchant ships built, brought a flush of hectic prosperity to the shipyards, soon to fade away in the general depression, for such rates as were being charged strangled trade.

The price per ton of a new, ready cargo steamer of 7500 tons according to figures given in the trade paper *Fairplay* was:

		£.	s.	d.
In December	1913	7	2	0
"	1914	8	0	0
"	1915	16	13	0
"	1916	25	0	0
"	1917-1918	22	0	0
"	1919	31	0	0
"	1920	34	10	0

The rush to give orders for tonnage at such prices could only be justified on the assumption that the preposterous freight rates to meet the abnormal situation left by the war scarcity were likely to last, to become the new norm. The men whose appetites were so whetted by war profits that their judgement was clouded to that extent would seem the last people to be able to say so confidently that "all experience has demonstrated the unwisdom of State owned or controlled shipping".

To give orders for ships at these prices, ships which could not be delivered until the following year, used up cash resources and involved the companies in heavy liabilities for which there was no reasonable prospect of earnings to justify. But in the rosy glow of optimism induced by the great days of war profits, schemes were undertaken of buying up at inflated prices whole fleets of ships and even of industrial concerns.

Before the war the Cunard Line had paid 4½ per cent on its £1.4 millions of debentures. In 1921, after the reckless dissipation of its reserves left by the war, and mainly owing to its expansion policy, it had to issue £4 debentures at the rate of 7 per cent. The effect of the buying of whole fleets at high prices is illustrated by the sad case of the Moor Line. The Western Counties bought up the Moor Line from Mr. Walter Runciman (father of the present Lord Runciman) and his directors at the rate of £22 per ton for 82,000 tons in 1920. The following year they had to sell eight of these ships at £4 per ton. Such transactions hardly demonstrate "the wisdom of privately owned and controlled shipping". Such speculative transactions, the dissipation of cash reserves, and the handicap of the increased interest liabilities consequent on the issue of bonus shares and the heavy watering of shipping capital, left the British shipping and shipbuilding industry without the reserves necessary to meet the post-war problems. Those problems were foreseen by experts at the time and shipping directors were warned without avail ... the appetite for big and immediate profits was too keen. The desperate demands for shipping during the war years and the submarine campaign had induced such an expansion in building capacity throughout the world that England's position as shipbuilder to the whole world was ended forever.

In technique Britain was necessarily behind. In the urgent demand to build, and build, there had been no time or energy to spare for experimental work. But the Continental yards, particularly Norway, had been devoting much time and money to the improvement of Diesel engines and the construction of new types of motor vessels generally. Post-war vessels tended to be larger and faster than pre-war. The "cargo liner" meant fewer vessels but needed larger berths. Money was needed for re-building and widening berths ... the money that had been dissipated in a joyous profit-taking orgy. There was the whole problem of readjustment from coal to oil. This technical work had to be done under the handicap of the new financial liabilities, and debentures at high rates of interest had to be raised, for which, when the war ended, companies had the cash in their coffers.

This general background of the shipping position is necessary in order to understand what happened at Palmer's. During the war Palmer's had built the battleship *Resolution,* the cruiser *Dauntless,* three monitors and eighteen destroyers. When Palmer's Report was presented in 1919 for the previous year the directors announced a profit on the year's trading of £221,000.

With this they were able to pay off arrears on the preference shares which had haunted them since 1908. On the assumption that profits were to continue at the same rate for some years, they proposed to provide further capital of £1,000,000, mortgage stock at 5 per cent. Twenty-five thousand pounds of this stock was offered to the workmen at par. So confident were the workmen in the future of their industry that they applied for £74,000 worth. On this they only actually received dividends in 1920 and 1921.

With the money thus provided by mortgage, improvements were made at the steelworks, and extensions foreshadowed at the Hebburn Shipyard. The shipbuilding berths, which had to be enlarged to meet the demand for bigger ships, created a serious problem. Houses had been built close up to the Shipyard, and at the high prices for houses then ruling the cost of demolishing this property was prohibitive. It was impossible to put the boiler shop near to the fitting-out basin. The result of having to build it some distance away was that the boilers had to be brought to the basin over a network of lines. Delays took place. Often an entire night shift would be employed in getting the bogey carrying the great boiler back on to the lines. This meant delay and additional expense.

Yet, technically, the staff at Palmer's faced these difficulties with such success that in 1919 Palmer's output was the third largest on the Tyne. They launched 44,480 tons and repaired sixty-three other vessels at the Hebburn Yard. On that year, after paying debenture interest, the total amount available for distribution was £354,866, and this on a capital of approximately £1,500,000. The directors put £100,000 into reserve account, and paid out the rest by 10 per cent on preference shares (this included some arrears) and 10 per cent on their ordinary shares. There was the useful sum of £350,000 standing to the credit of reserve account. How was this to be used? At first the Board thought of using it to raise fresh capital by the attraction of a payment of 10s. per share on £700,000 ordinary shares, to be created and issued to shareholders. Eventually, however, it was distributed by giving a £1 bonus share for every £2 share held, thus adding to interest liabilities. With all this money to give away, Palmer's did not forget education. They provided one scholarship of £250 per year for nine years at the Jarrow Secondary School.

The shipping boom still held the following year. Palmer's were still third on the river. Their trading profit was £317,000. After paying debenture interest and other charges the new profit was £247,895. This they used to pay a dividend of 12 per cent. But this was paid on a capital that had been watered by the issue of £1 for every £2 shares held. So that for every £200 invested, the shareholder received not £25 but £37 10s. Palmer's shares rose to 27s. 6d.

Prosperity seemed to be eternal. At times like these some of our capitalists seem incapable of restraining their appetite for more profits. There were signs of the coming storm which were even then clear on the horizon. Palmer's directors thought the time opportune to build up a gigantic combine. They began to buy up subsidiary companies.

They bought up a small shipbuilding yard at Amble. Built during the war it had been used for the construction of concrete vessels. It was thought that this yard could be used for the building of the smaller vessels ordered from the company. The first steel ship launched was the Jarrow ferryboat. To provide coal for the blast furnaces the South Pelaw Colliery was bought up. The coal was well suited for coking. A separate company, the Hebburn Transport Company, was set up to buy and operate the ships engaged in carrying iron ore from Port Mulgrave. Not content with those purchases the directors rushed to acquire shares in the Ransome Machinery Company, a Midland engineering firm, in the belief that engineering was the coming thing. Shares were purchased in ore-mining companies in Spain in order to ensure future supplies of ore. And to cap these dreams for future development 200 acres of land were purchased in order that they would be ready for development when the time was ripe.

Lord Aberconway, discussing the difficulties of the Tyne at this period, writes: "The losses of Vickers and Armstrongs arose mainly from speculative undertakings unconnected with shipbuilding. Palmer's had made no outside investments foreign to its real objects ... but it suffered from the locking up of its working capital caused by heavy overhead charges." Their purchases of Amble Shipyard, the colliery company, the shipping company, and the shares in the ore mines were all designed to acquire holdings auxiliary to shipbuilding. But it was doubted at the time whether these purchases were well advised. Experience has shown that the policy was the height of folly.

When the purchases were made prices were at their highest. In 1925 the directors had to write off some of their losses incurred on these subsidiaries and they explained that the losses resulted from the assets being acquired "at abnormal prices under war and post-war conditions". And even when the boom was at its height there were signs of the slump ahead. It was not as though the slump came out of the blue. The signs of the coming storm were clearly visible in the shipping returns, in the world trade statistics and in the warnings of the experts that trade was being strangled by the preposterous freight rates and the cost of new tonnage. Normal experience of the cycle of shipbuilding construction should have urged caution upon the directors. Profits should have been saved from the boom to build up reserves for the depression that lay ahead and was inevitable. Instead, on the brink of the slump, the directors dissipated their reserves in unjustified dividends, in boom shares, and in the purchase of subsidiary companies.

Two new factors to those already discussed helped to make the position worse. The new yards which had been planned, and their construction started, in the last months of the war to meet the submarine menace were only coming into production in this period. But their capacity was known. They shared in the hectic ordering after the war. Production rose from 1,348,120 tons in 1918, to 1,620,442 tons in 1919, and reached the peak of 2,055,624 tons in 1920. Shipyard capacity in Britain had increased from 580 berths in 1914 to 806 berths by 1920. And this was in a world where every industrial country, that had bought ships from Britain, was now building for itself.

As though this were not serious enough in itself, the shipping industry threw itself joyously into the demand "for squeezing Germany till the pips squeaked". Every ship over 1600 tons was taken from Germany to replace the Allied shipping sunk. As those ships would have joined in the scramble for orders anyway, the shipowners might claim that they were justified ... though from the shipbuilders' point of view, Allied countries which might have come to Britain for shipping to replace the losses of the war, would get these reparations ships free. What was quite mad from the point of view of the British industry was the insistence, in Part VIII, Annex III, clause 5, of the Treaty of Versailles, that the German Government must cause merchant shipping not exceeding 200,000 gross tons to be laid in German yards to the account of the Allied and Associated Powers, every year for five years. This order put the ruined German shipping industry on its feet. Did no one among the shipping magnates who so enthusiastically flung themselves into the campaign of bringing the utmost pressure on Mr. Lloyd George at the Peace Conference to turn the screw tighter and yet tighter, ever stop to think of what their action might mean ... or even to heed the warnings sent from the Peace Conference itself? But no warning and no expert could shake that invincible optimism, based on the wild greed for immediate profits and immediate dividends whatever might be the consequences.

Like a hangover after a joyous night, the year 1921 opened dismally for Tyneside, and for Palmer's. Shipowners, faced with the high prices for new tonnage being demanded by the shipbuilders, and with the figures of the falling freight market at last beginning to impress them ... for there had really been nothing in the world trade figures of 1919 and 1920 to justify the shipping boom, cancelled contracts or had work on ships suspended.

When the shipping employers at last realized that the prosperity was not going to last forever they prepared to face the crisis by an attack on wage rates. Before the year 1921 was a month old the managing director of Palmer's was using the launching of a ship as the occasion to tell the workmen that ships were being constructed at a very high cost, and that therefore it was time that some agreement should be reached to readjust wages at such a level as would provide both employer and employee with a living. There was no suggestion, in the previous year, when the war profits were available for distribution, that the wages should be increased.

1921 was a year in which the wages of workers in all groups were attacked. Shipbuilding, engineering, coal, and the railways all suffered. In December 1920 the shipyard joiners came out on strike against proposed reductions. Ships were lying in the fitting-out basins with their woodwork not completed. Some vessels were taken into French ports to have this work done. The joiners' strike lasted right through the summer, but eventually after a long fight work was resumed in August. A wage reduction of 6s. per week was to take place immediately, there was to be a further reduction of 3s. in October, and the possibility of another 3s. a week reduction in December. The wages of the other workers in the industry were attacked in March. After a conference in Newcastle on March 10th the Shipbuilding Employers' Federation gave notice of a reduction of 6s. per week or of 15 per cent on piece rates. Eventually, though with some opposition from the skilled trades, this reduction was carried out in two instalments. Negotiations about the reduction on the engineers' wages lasted longer before similar reductions were forced on to them. While the shipping trades were preoccupied with their own disputes the coalminers came out on strike. The shortage of coal and coke affected the iron and steel industry. Palmer's newly acquired South Pelaw colliery was affected. The shortage of coke was used as the reason for the closing of the ironworks at Jarrow. For most of the men the closing down was wholly unexpected. Work was going on steadily and about two thousand men were employed there. Then suddenly at the beginning of April the works shut down completely. Its effect on the town was moderated by the fact that the Shipyard continued at work. The men from the ironworks hoped that the end of the miners' strike would soon see them all back at work. To maintain the plant in good order a special squad of men were employed. Careful attention was paid to the machinery. Cranes were operated and oiled each week. But the changed conditions of the English iron and steel industry had killed Palmer's ironworks. Developments on the Continent immediately after the war had led to a more efficient and modernized industry being set up there. When at the beginning of 1921 North-east steel firms were quoting shipbuilders £24

10s. 0d. per ton for steel plates, Continental producers were offering similar plates for £18 per ton. The iron and steel works remained closed all through 1921 and 1922. In 1923 there was work for three months, but then the furnaces closed down until 1927, when two furnaces were lit up for nearly a year. There was another spell of work in the boom of 1929. But when they closed after that boom the maintenance men were dismissed as well as the ordinary workers. During the earlier years there had been a gradual movement of men from Jarrow. But there were many who hoped that the steelworks would soon be back in production and who waited, hoping that the day would soon come when they could return to work.

1921 was a bitter experience for the Palmer company. Their Shipyard workings were affected by the general depression in shipping and by their losses as a result of their efforts to force wage reductions on the Shipyard workers. All the shipbuilding companies suffered in the same way. But Palmer's was vulnerable in other directions. Their balance sheet reveals the weakness of the colossal firm in modern capitalism. Having purchased a colliery at the top of the market they suddenly found themselves faced with a coal strike. Maintenance costs and the heavy overhead charges had to be met, and funds allocated to cover these expenses. Then, when the iron and steel works closed another extra burden of maintenance costs and overhead charges had to be borne. Yet in 1921 the company managed to pay a dividend. On the year's trading – which included, of course, the good months of 1920 – a gross profit of nearly £200,000 was made. But interest on debentures and loans swallowed up £113,000. In order to pay the 5 per cent interest on the preference shares and the modest 2½ per cent on the ordinary shares, the working reserves, so badly needed for working capital, were raided for £30,000.

There was a great difference between this small interest payment and the previous year, when the directors had hastened to issue bonus shares. This payment of 2½ per cent was the last the shareholders were to receive. When the blank years are considered it cannot be said the average dividends paid by Palmer's were excessive. During boom years – like the war – high profits were made and were promptly distributed to the shareholders. When the bad days came the shareholders in the know were able to pass the burden to others. A nationalized industry, conserving its reserves, and paying a modest but certain return on the actual capital would have been much better for the average shareholder.

Financial complications prevented the issue of a report in 1922, but when the directors' report for 1923 was published it revealed the difficulties with which the firm had to struggle. According to the trading account a gross profit of £88,555 was made in the two years. But debenture and loan charges amounted to £159,084 and other debt services called for £39,035. Even after calling on the remaining money in the reserves there was a total debit balance for the year of £75,208. That balance sheet was the forerunner of many similar dismal reports for the shareholders. Technically the Shipyard was holding its own. It was doing as well as most shipyards. In 1923 and 1924 its output was the second highest of all the firms on Tyneside. But firms like Swan, Hunter, and Wigham Richardson of Wallsend, or Hawthorn Leslie's of Hebburn, were not hampered by having an idle steelworks on their hands. The Shipyard at Jarrow was able to compete favourably both as regards price and quality with any firm. Yet out of the profits from the operations of the Shipyard the losses and overhead charges on the idle plant of the iron and steel works had to be paid. It was a heavy financial burden for the Shipyard to carry. Even though the directors could see that losses had resulted from their efforts to extend the range of the company they did not cease. Feeling that profits were to be made somewhere the directorate of Palmer's turned their attention to the western seaboard. They came to the conclusion that the repairing facilities there were inadequate. So a subsidiary company was formed to construct a graving dock and ship-repairing works at Swansea. It was an excellent dock, and the facilities offered were the most up to date in the country ... if only there had been a need for it. This adventure led to a further drain on the company's capital resources. There was a serious housing shortage in Swansea. Consequently, in order to provide accommodation for their workers the company had to embark on a building scheme.

Swansea was not a success. And on Tyneside conditions were worsening. Trade was so bad in 1925 that men said it could not be worse. Armstrong Whitworth's had only one slip out of twelve occupied. The yards of the Tyne Iron Shipbuilding Company were closed. The Newcastle Shipbuilding Company at Hebburn – a modern yard from which only two ships were launched – was sold up. These conditions were representative of the depressed state of shipbuilding in Great Britain. In thirty out of the ninety-six shipyards of the country there was, by October, not a vessel on the stocks. In fifteen other yards work on the remaining orders was nearing completion and there were no signs of any further orders. The remaining yards had some work in hand, but they were only occupied to one-quarter of their capacity.

Palmer's only built three small ships. Their repairing yard dealt with sixty-eight vessels. On that limited turnover it was impossible to provide for the heavy loan charges and the overheads of the idle plant. On the one year a loss of £206,946 was incurred. By now the total debit balance of the company had reached £462,000. The chairman admitted that "though some orders were obtained the volume of work was not sufficient to absorb the heavy standing charges". It was a black year for Jarrow. Thousands of men were out of work and a reduction of the skilled staff was effected.

The wastefulness of shipbuilding under capitalism is well illustrated by the activities of Palmer's during the closing years of their existence. In 1925 only three ships with a total tonnage of 11,000 tons were launched from the yard. Men and machinery were idle ... waiting for orders. By the next year production had increased to 50,000 tons. By 1927 the launchings increased to 61,112 tons and an even busier year was recorded in 1930. Owing to orders placed in the boom year of 1929 launching in 1930 totalled 65,896 tons. Yet in the next year production had collapsed completely. Only one complete ship was launched. The total tonnage was only 15,478 tons. Such variations within so short a period as six years reveal the wasteful results of the uncoordinated and essential individualistic shipping and shipbuilding industries. For a year shipyards are idle. Capital and the manpower is wasted. Gradually activity increases, there are perhaps two good years, and then a gradual decline to idleness again. Government reports have condemned, in general terms, the lack of planning in the industry. But the conditions under which capitalism operates do not offer opportunities for successful planning. As long as our industries are organized for private profit we can expect to suffer the waste of unco-ordination.

Although, after 1925, Palmer's production improved, shipbuilding activity was not sufficiently high to enable the Shipyard to discharge the whole obligations of the company. By the end of 1926 the company was facing a crisis. The debit balance had increased on the year's operation by another £211,000, making a total loss of £669,712. And there were certain capital losses amounting to £482,000 which had to be written off. With, therefore, a total indebtedness of nearly one million pounds the future of the company was in jeopardy. The only alternative to bankruptcy was a scheme of financial reorganization. Such a plan was prepared and accepted by the shareholders. The capital of the company was written down by reducing the nominal value of £1 shares to 5s., arrears of preference interest were cancelled, interest rates were revised, and further debentures were issued. Two new directors were appointed and the chairman of the company resigned.

Such cuts as these in the share capital of a company are used, curiously enough, as excuses for the capitalist system. The shareholder has his good times, but he has his bad times as well. Taking the good with the bad – does he get more than his share? In financial operations the men who get the advantages of the bonus shares and the increased dividends, the men who make the real profit, are the men who know when to get out. For them gambling in shares is a profession. The quick profits and bonus shares distributed to please the profit-makers are often, as in the case of Palmer's and many other big companies at this period, the causes of industrial collapse. The experts know when to buy or sell. But the workmen and the other small investors rarely sell. They are not versed in the intricacies of finance. The smaller conservative investors tend to keep their money in, and it is they who are ruined, often after they have bought the stock at prices inflated by the bonus shares. So often they are induced to buy shares upon the past dividends of a company rather than the prospects of future earnings.

That was the case with Palmer's. Not all the workmen and foremen gambled or drank their high wages of the war years away, as is usually said. The rise in bank balances, in co-operative shares, and in war savings shows that. They trusted the firm on which their own town depended, and many of them put all their savings into the stocks offered them. Their shipyard was real. They could see the travelling cranes which towered over the river, they knew the skill of the men who worked there, and they knew the fine ships that had been launched from the Yard. That was security. From their investments they may have received two years' dividends before payments ceased. Some of them who had been on the staff lost their jobs as Palmer's sank deeper into the financial quagmire. The savings which might have helped them over that bad patch went down with Palmer's. There are men in dire poverty today in Jarrow who still speak as though they could not believe that the £200 or £300 which represented their whole savings and which they entrusted to Palmer's can really be lost to them forever ... not till in 1938 they saw the great travelling crane dismantled. Then they knew.

Experience of the post-war years stressed the growth of foreign shipbuilding. Even the smaller countries like Holland were able to secure, by competitive tender, orders for British vessels. In this period capitalism turned to "rationalization" as the apparent solution of its industrial difficulties. Germany led the way and the reorganization of the German shipbuilding industry led to the development of similar ideas in England. But the industry was still too individualistic and too optimistic to consider a large-scale reorganization. There were too many small firms to be placated. However there was a tendency for the bigger firms to get together. If the lambs would not lie down with the lions, the lions were ready to co-operate together to make certain of their victims later. Vickers and Armstrong

Whitworth's came together. There was a fusion of interests which allied Swan, Hunter, and Wigham Richardson with Barclay Tube. Another combination of these years was the co-operation between Workman Clark of Belfast, the Fairfield Shipbuilding Company of the Clyde, William Doxford's of Sunderland, and the Northumberland Shipbuilding Company on the Tyne. After having suffered such a reduction in capital and still having the derelict steelworks bound to the Shipyard Palmer's was not a sufficiently attractive proposition to come into this stream.

But the reputation and ability of the firm were high enough to enable them to get their share of the trade. Their output was amongst the highest on Tyneside. They got their share of Admiralty work. In 1931 the Duchess of York came to Jarrow to launch the cruiser *York,* which was the last cruiser ever launched by the great yard. The next time she came there the Duchess was to see Jarrow under very different conditions.

Jarrow's swan song was the last rush of orders in the 1929 boom. Rising freight rates brought shipowners again into the market. There were a few weeks of ordering and then shipowners tightened their purse strings. In that rush of ordering Palmer's obtained a goodly proportion of the work available. Their output in 1929 was 65,896 tons – the second highest output of the Tyneside firms. As a result the trading account of the company showed a profit of £25,000. It is interesting to note that £6,332 – or a quarter of that sum – went to the directors as fees. Lord Aberconway, the chairman, was also a director of twenty-two other companies. His son served on the Boards of sixteen companies, as well as being a director of Palmer's. Another director was associated with eleven other companies. Whether directors are worth such a remuneration in view of their widespread connections, and their inability therefore to give much time to anyone company's affairs, is a question that is considered to be almost treason to ask these days.

This boom brought life back to Jarrow. The Shipyard was well occupied and the steelworks were back in production. There was hope in the town and the feeling that industrial recovery was on its way. Settled conditions and the development of international trade would increase the demand for ships, said the conscientious joy-boys on the local newspapers. Palmer's craftsmen were good enough to get their share of the orders. Such dismal croakings as were heard about the financial dangers ahead did not reach Jarrow.

CHAPTER TEN
N.S.S. Cuts Jarrow's Lifeline

ALTHOUGH THE short-lived boom of 1929 brought a flow of orders to the shipyards, there was much anxiety amongst shipbuilders in the early days of 1930. There were few indications of any further orders. The tonnage under construction was about 1,500,000 tons. Yet only one-half of the productive capacity of the industry was engaged. Many shipbuilders were complaining that they were only able to keep their yards occupied by accepting contracts at unprofitable prices. Out of that discontent came rumours of an attempt to re-organize the industry.

Obviously in such circumstances some measure of reorganization was desirable. When there was such a margin between the capacity of the industry and the work on hand it was intolerable that affairs should be allowed to drift. But if organization was necessary, who ought to do the job?

For us in Britain shipbuilding is a vital industry. We are dependent for the greater part of our foodstuffs on our merchant shipping. Much of our industrial prosperity is based on raw materials brought from overseas. If, for any reason, the safe passage of these ships were interrupted, England would be in a desperate plight. With the breakdown of the rule of law in international affairs, and with the increasing menace of fascism, the importance of our merchant navy is paramount. We must have sufficient shipping for our needs, and behind our shipping we must have an adequate shipbuilding industry. Without that we should be incapable of building the vessels on which our security depends. It is therefore vital to the nation that we should have an efficient shipbuilding industry. Any form of re-organization therefore is of grave concern to the nation as a whole. It is not a mere matter of private interest to a financial group.

Equally, the interests of the industrial workers ought to be considered in any scheme for re-organizing the industry. In 1930 there were 204,000 workers directly concerned with the shipbuilding industry. The industrial centres of Clydeside, Tyneside and Barrow-in-Furness owed a great deal of their prosperity to their shipyards. In many cases whole communities were based on shipbuilding. Around that one industry, as in Jarrow, the social and economic life of a town had developed. Any measure of re-organization was therefore a concern of the workpeople and of the local authorities.

But the driving power of capitalism is private profit. Neither national interests nor workers' interests are a concern of the capitalist. Sentiment, they say, does not enter into business. What concerns a capitalist is the return on his money invested. Ships are not built because the safety of our nation depends on an adequate merchant navy. They are built because an investor can make a profit out of lending his money for that purpose. When the profit goes out of the industry, or when other industries offer greater profits to the investor, shipbuilding activity tends to decline.

Besides the individual investors the banks were widely interested in the shipbuilding industry. Much of the day-to-day capital of the industry is provided by the banks, who advance money to the shipbuilder until payment for the finished vessel is made. During the pre-war slumps the banks loaned money in the confident hope that they would soon have their money repaid. But post-war conditions continued "abnormal". Shipbuilding slumped and many firms were unable to secure orders. The banks were in an awkward position, for they had made loans with an eye on the capital assets of the company rather than on the earning capacity. Consequently, when it became clear that certain markets for ships had gone forever there seemed little chance of the loans being repaid. To sell up the companies could only result in the return of a small fraction of the loan. With large credits" frozen" in this way the banks were invariably interested in any scheme of re-organization.

During this period of the late 'twenties the idea of "nationalization" became fashionable. When the fears for the future increased in the early months of 1930, there was some talk of a nationalization scheme for the shipbuilding industry. To counter this idea, considerable interest began to be shown in the rationalization of the big Continental firms, by the British shipowners. In Sir James Lithgow, the shipbuilders found a man strong enough and sufficiently determined to lead them to accept a plan for a rationalized industry as more likely to suit their interests than the hated nationalization.

Sir James Lithgow is not a seeker of publicity. He has none of the modern urge for hitting the headlines. But he is today one of the most powerful figures of the industrial world. His firm, Lithgow's of Port Glasgow, is among the largest shipbuilding companies in Great Britain. He is also chairman of three other large shipbuilding companies: Ayrshire Dockyard Company, Fairfield Shipbuilding Company and David Rowan and Company Ltd. Not content with dominating the shipbuilding industry he has more or less brought the iron and steel industry of Scotland under his control. He is a director of Colvilles Ltd. With an issued capital of nearly £6,000,000, this company is the most important iron and steel firm in Scotland. Altogether Sir James is chairman of seven important companies and a director of seven others.

When he set out to rationalize the shipbuilding industry he was only forty-seven, but he had behind him a wide range of business experience. He came of a shipbuilding family, his father having been associated with Russell's of Port Glasgow. During the war James Lithgow raised an artillery battery from the workpeople of his father's firm and commanded the unit in France. He was wounded in action and was awarded the M.C. before his service career was cut short by Mr. Lloyd George recalling him to England. He was asked by the Prime Minister to be Director of Merchant Shipping when the Ministry of Shipping was formed in 1917. About this time, he and his brother Henry purchased the firm of Russell's and changed it into a private company with the family name. When his government post came to an end Lithgow was able to concentrate upon his own business. He has been elected to high office in the different employers' organizations. Twice he has been President of the Federation of British Industries; he has also been President of the Shipbuilding Employers' Federation and has represented the employers' interests at the meetings of the International Labour Office.

James Lithgow is as typical a capitalist of the British decline as was the optimistic "Charlie" Palmer of its ascending period. He prides himself on being a realist. Lithgow stands for capitalism, and for the maintenance of private profit-making, with no apology for the results. To him the man who can make profit is the only factor really worth considering in national life. "Healthy growth and development can only follow the maintenance of an adequate profit standard" is a typical quotation from one of his speeches. The economic ideas of this very powerful British industrialist are an indication of how the outlook on life that we have come to call "fascist" works in the higher ranks of British Big Business. Hitler at least claims to regulate the lives of the working people in the interest of the nation. Lithgow considers that they should be regulated for the benefit of industry. He dislikes regulation by government departments which "regard industry as a suitable field for the exercise of their inspectorates who on various pretexts added to the cost of production" – presumably by demanding fencing of machinery, ventilation, and other provisions of the factory acts. He adds:

"It ought to be clear that no nation can stand a sudden sprouting even of social amelioration without demoralizing influences setting in to destroy the healthy growth which has taken place."

He asks:

"Are we getting value for the vast sums provided from the fruits of industry for the universal education of our people? ... some consideration should be given to the question whether industry can provide suitable jobs for the great majority of those to whom higher education is given at great cost."

Sir James suggests that

"the true solution is to return to something nearer the standard which we set ourselves, on which we were a contented people, in 1901";

or otherwise

"we must wait for the time when the real productive capacity of our people may by gradual growth catch up with social standards which have for the present outstripped the international value of those who enjoy them."

It would be difficult to think of a neater way of expressing the demand for a return to the coolie standard for British Labour. And with no unemployment allowances, of course. For, asks Sir James,

"who can truly assert that the various forms of payment of allowances during unemployment have had the effect of bringing back into employment many of the recipients so much fitter and happier than was customary when such allowances were not so general and uncontrolled."

These remarks cannot be dismissed as the "typical nonsense of an industrial Bourbon". The quotations are taken from an address by Sir James Lithgow to the International Engineering Congress of 1938, when he launched his public campaign for a subsidy to the shipping industry. That campaign he has won, as he won the more difficult struggle to cut down the shipbuilding capacity of his country ... continuing the closures even in the face of a growing war danger. In February 1939 Lithgow launched his third big campaign – his attack on the skilled unions and for the abolition of skilled grades for shipyard labour.

From his presidential address to the Institute of Welding in February of this year the following quotations are taken as indicating his line in this campaign. If I quote his own printed words, I cannot be accused of misrepresenting this astute and powerful capitalist.

"Other nations have entered the field unhampered by demarcation arrangements and systems of grading which required of certain operators a particular degree of skill, and consequently a special remuneration."

"We are greatly concerned to maintain democracy, but we do not hesitate to elevate into a superior position, persons who happen to belong to a craft guild from which in the past, after long years of apprenticeship, special skill of hand, eye and brain combined are required, even though the functions which the individual may now be called on to perform are of a very much more limited character."

"The wider skill associated with the older forms of craftsmen is therefore not only not required but becomes a definite disadvantage if it finds its way in the form of false values into the cost of the finished product."

"Opportunity should be taken to fix the type of operator and the scale of pay appropriate to the particular job, without reference to the peculiarities of the job which is displaced."

Sir James's quick brain has chosen the perfect moment for launching this difficult attack on the skilled unions. With the assistance of a government which has proved so amenable to his other campaigns, the supply of a sufficient number of trainees from the Unemployed Training centres could and would be put in hand as soon as any form, however disguised, of " industrial conscription" is imposed. The day after Mr. Chamberlain announced conscription for the army, the City Editor of the *Evening Standard* demanded the lengthening of hours of work.

The skilled unions, of course, will resist. But in this present crisis they may soon find themselves up against emergency legislation, "in the national interests". The engineering and shipbuilding employers would thus avoid the awkward position in which they were placed in the last war, of having to give promises to restore trade-union conditions in return for the unions relaxing their rules. Sir James, however, is not basing his campaign on the war emergency. He made the demand some time before the Prime Minister announced that we were in a state of neither peace nor war. But, of course, the general war neurosis is as useful to him in the fight against the wage rates of the skilled workman as it was to get a subsidy out of the taxpayer for an industry which had so shamefully wasted its huge war profits.

This, then, is the position of Sir James Lithgow after nine years of successfully aggressive capitalist leadership. Let us now go back to where he was in 1930. Having determined that ruthless measures must be taken if capitalism in Britain was to be kept on its feet, he had come to the conclusion that there were too many firms competing for orders, the rapidly dwindling orders, for new ships. He considered that the way out lay in reducing capacity in a way which would concentrate production, minimize overheads and make possible a suitable increase in prices. That is how James Lithgow came to be the moving spirit behind the formation of National Shipbuilders' Security, Ltd., the company which has bought and scrapped one-third of the British shipbuilding industry. In some towns shipbuilding has been completely wiped out. In others large firms have been closed down. Shipyards with an annual production capacity of over one million tons have been scrapped in an effort to safeguard the profits of the remaining firms.

On February 28, 1930, the first public statement was made regarding National Shipbuilders' Security, Ltd. Its purpose was defined as being to assist the shipbuilding industry by the purchase of redundant or obsolete yards. To ensure that the productive capacity of the industry was definitely reduced the shipbuilding equipment was to be scrapped and the site of the yard was to be restricted against further use for shipbuilding. Furthermore, the company was empowered to make payments to other firms to contract not to build ships. By concentrating production in this way the promotors felt that they would be able to effect substantial reductions in overhead charges.

Gradually more details of the new company became public. Its original list of directors – one shipbuilder, two solicitors and two clerks – gave little clue to the support it had received. Its first published accounts showed the issue of only seven shares of £1 each to seven subscribers. But within a few weeks the backing of the company was revealed. Each of forty-four shipbuilding companies in Great Britain held 100 shares of £1. By the next month the total number of holding companies had increased to forty-seven. Although the nominal capital of the company is £10,000, since its formation there has been no increase on the £4700 issued capital. Some of the firms originally holding shares have closed down. Their holdings have been transferred to employees of N.S.S. The list of directors reveals the impressive support of the company. During the years since 1930, there have been one or two slight changes in personnel on the Board of Directors, but in that time most of the more important shipbuilding firms have been represented. Sir James Lithgow is chairman. Next in importance to him on National Shipbuilders' Security, Ltd., is Sir Charles Craven, leading industrialist on Tyneside, managing director of Vickers Armstrong and of the English Steel Corporation. He is chairman of Gresham and Craven's, and the Gresham Engineering Group, and on the Board of Guest, Keen and Baldwin's. His nineteen directorates include leading companies in shipbuilding, iron and steel, armaments, and shipping insurance. All the other directors are from these interests. Both Sir Amos Ayre and Mr. John Barr are Armstrong Whitworth's directors. F. C. Pyman of West Hartlepool of Pyman Bros., is iron, shipping, dry docks. A. Stephens (Clyde) is Clyde Electrics, steel, shipping. R. N. Thompson of Sunderland is also a director of Armstrong Whitworth's. John Brown and Co. had a director in George Brown, who died shortly afterwards. Joseph Batey was appointed to the Board while still a director of Hawthorn Leslie's. F. E. Rebbeck represents the link-up of Colville's with Harland and Wolff's, the great Belfast firm, and is also a director of the L.M.S. Mr. Thirlaway represents the most financially successful Tyneside firm, Swan, Hunter, and Wigham Richardson, Ltd.

The directors' list shows the strength of the interests that had come in behind the Lithgow scheme. The omissions were also significant. Though Palmer's was among the Big Six of British shipbuilding firms, none of its directors sat on the Board of N.S.S. Three of its directors, however, were also linked with John Brown's, who for a short time held one director's seat.

Behind these men were Mr. Montagu Norman and the banks. They were interested in the re-organization of industry because they saw some chance of securing a return on their frozen loans. They realized that if schemes of rationalization were to be carried through, more money would be required. So early in 1930 the Bankers' Industrial Development Company was formed. It had a nominal capital of £6,000,000 divided into only sixty shares of £100,000 each. Half the voting power rests with an offshoot of the Bank of England and the other half is shared by the various banks and issuing houses of importance.

Mr. Montagu Norman is chairman of the Board. The purpose of the company is to assist in the rationalization of industries. If a scheme for the rationalization of a complete industry is approved, the Bankers' Industrial Development Company will see that the financial support necessary to carry the plan through will be forthcoming. Because of the way in which the shares of the B.I.D. are held, their approval of a rationalization scheme puts the biggest financial powers of the country behind it. Actually the shipbuilding industry was the first one to be "rationalized" with the assistance of the Bankers' Industrial Development Company.

How was the money to be raised to buy up the condemned shipyards? As the yards were to be purchased at a price somewhat above the scrap prices, because they were to be purchased on terms which would not permit of their being used as shipbuilding yards for forty years, the business was obviously not an ordinary commercial proposition. It was therefore decided to raise the money by a levy from all shipbuilders. By joining National Shipbuilders' Security, Ltd., a shipbuilding firm undertook to pay the company a levy each year amounting to 1 per cent of the contract price of all vessels built over a length of 300 feet. It was estimated that on the basis of the tonnage launched in previous years, this would bring in about £300,000 a year.

Until this money was available the new company had to borrow money for its purposes. In November 1930 a £300,000 mortgage was raised from the Bank of England. Later, in February 1931, a public issue of £1,000,000 5 per cent First Mortgage Stock was made under the auspices of the Bankers' Industrial Development Company.

There was one element of public control over the activities of National Shipbuilders' Security, Ltd. As long as it was a limited liability company, and as long as its mortgage stock was held publicly, it had to return an account of its yearly activities and publish a balance sheet. Thus, year by year an interested member of the public could get some idea of the progress of the company. It was the only information which the M.P.s for these towns, for example, could obtain of the activities of this company, which was deciding the future of whole communities of working people. After eight years, during which the company have had to face criticism from all quarters, they have managed to find a way to withdraw their activities out of the light of publicity. In March 1938 an Extraordinary General Meeting of National Shipbuilders' Security, Ltd., was held at which it was agreed to convert the company into a private company with not more than fifty shareholders other than past or present employees. According to Section 26 of the Companies Act of 1929 a private company need not send a balance sheet to Somerset House so long as there are not more than fifty shareholders. Since 1938 the finance of the company has been brought under private control also. The £1,000,000 5 per cent mortgage stock has been repaid and arrangements have been made for a nominee firm, the Birchin Lane Nominees, Ltd., to cover all moneys "due or to become due by the company to Williams Deacon's Bank, Ltd.". For this transaction the annual levies from the shipbuilders were to be the security. By complying with these legal technicalities, a group of industrialists and bankers, engaged in closing down the shipbuilding industry of this country to maintain their own profits, are able to carry out their work in secrecy without any evidence of their transactions being made public. And that at a period when the capacity of these yards might decide the issue of a war. While perfectly legal, the fact that a company engaged on work of such vital moment to the nation can conduct its operations without public control is obviously not in the public interest.

Palmer's were not the earliest of the new company's victims. During 1929 they had received a fair number of orders which kept them busy during 1930. Although Palmer's launched ten ships during the year each successive launch caused much anxiety, for it was difficult to find any new work. In fact, during the whole of 1930 Palmer's had no new vessels ordered. This decline was repeated in other shipbuilding areas. As the year progressed it became clearer and clearer that the industry was facing a difficult period. When men were worrying about their jobs, N.S.S. made their first purchases. They acquired three shipbuilding yards in Scotland, William Beardmore's Dalmuir shipyard, a yard at Old Kilpatrick and the South Yard at Ardrossan Dockyard were bought up, and also the firm of John Chambers of Newcastle. Their purchase by N.S.S. meant the end of shipbuilding in each yard for the lifetime of the men who had worked there. Closed for shipbuilding the plant was demolished and sold for use elsewhere or as scrap. As shipyards the sites cannot be used for forty years. Men saw the possibility of work being taken from them for a lifetime. There was growing resentment, and on Clydeside there was a feeling that they were being the special victims of the new rationalization scheme.

The next year's purchases equalized the balance. Eight yards were acquired on the North-east coast. At Whitby the only shipbuilding company was bought up. Three firms in the Middlesbrough and Stockton area were closed. Also during this year agreements were entered into with two companies by which, in return for grants from N.S.S., they would discontinue shipbuilding. Some of the best sites in the world for shipbuilding were being sterilized. Some of the most skilled craftsmen in the industry saw the source of their livelihood fall into the hands of the scrap merchant. For it is not as if these yards, though closed, were still available. Their machinery is scrapped and sold to make it impossible to use the sites again for the building of ships. Both the shipowners and the workmen began to express their anxiety about the activities of the new company. Speaking early in February 1931, Mr. John Greig, the President of the Clyde Steamship Owners' Association, said that shipowners "must view with concern the prospect of having in future a greatly restricted competitive market in which to negotiate their orders, and at the same time find that they had to pay 1 per cent on the cost price of new ships to enable that policy to be carried through. ... Shipowners do not want to see turnips growing where they now build turbines". Their anxiety about the welfare of the men took second place to the danger of their having to pay a higher price for the ships. Better prices for the shipbuilders meant higher capital costs for the shipowners. For the men the situation was very serious. Shipbuilding involves various groups of men who have to serve long periods of apprenticeship. If the yards were scrapped it would mean that many skilled men would lose permanently the prospect of following their trades. Skilled men would be forced to take unskilled jobs if they were to keep off the dole. At the end of 1930 there were 92,000 shipbuilding workers out of a job. By 1931 this number had increased to 117,000. Sixty per cent of the insured workers in the industry were unemployed. In the North-eastern Division seventy-two per cent of the shipyard workers were without a job. For every three able to find work seven men were left idle.

In Jarrow conditions were worsening. As no orders were received in 1930, 1931 was a bad year. Only one ship was launched, but a little additional work was ensured by the building of the centre section of the oil tanker *Saranac*. By June 1931 there were 6700 unemployed in Jarrow, just double the number of a year before. Nearly three-quarters of the working population of the town were out of work. By the summer of 1932 over 7000 were on the dole. Eighty per cent of the insured population were without work.

Anxious about the future of their members the trade unions approached the Shipbuilding Employers' Federation and the National Shipbuilders' Security, Ltd., for an opportunity to discuss the activities of the latter company. With the scrapping of the shipyards the trade unions were anxious to secure for their unemployed members either some compensation or alternative employment without loss of status or income. Will Sherwood, then President of the Federation of Shipbuilding Trade Unions, led the Union delegates. In reply to their request for either compensation or alternative jobs for the men whose industrial lives were doomed when the shipyards were closed for forty years, Sir James Lithgow produced as soothing syrup the optimistic claim that no men would be displaced. For, argued Sir James, the improved efficiency of the industry resulting from concentration would enable more work to be obtained when trade improved, since the work available would have to bear the charges of smaller capacity and would thus be produced at more economical prices. Having thus blocked any discussion of the real problem by a piece of wish fantasy the conference was then led on to a discussion of subsidies as a way out of the depression.

The conference was adjourned to give the Unions an opportunity of discussing policy. When it re-assembled at Edinburgh in February 1933, the union leaders again stressed the case for compensation to the men. Employers were being compensated for setting the yards for sterilization. Why not the men? And with this demand the Unions stressed the case for the opening up of new industries, in connection with shipbuilding, on the sites of the old yards. Such factories could manufacture furniture for the ships, or could prepare some of the materials, the plywood or paint, used in shipbuilding. Once again the employers refused to venture into any discussion of the problem of displaced labour, because they argued that the increased efficiency of the industry would lead to more jobs.

What is the employment record of the industry since N.S.S. started operations? In 1930 when the company was formed there were 204,720 insured workers attached to the industry. Until 1935 that number fell each year until it reached 157,230. With the subsequent improvement in trade the number of shipbuilding workers increased, until in 1938 there were 175,050 workers. Thus, in the best year that the shipbuilding industry has experienced in this decade there are 30,000 less workers in the industry than there were when National Shipbuilding Security was formed. Of the 175,050 workers attached to the industry there were, at the end of the year, 39,393 without jobs. Not even Sir James Lithgow would still claim that N.S.S. can buy up yards and scrap them without displacing men, but his statements at the time made it possible to explain away the awkward position that the employer who lost the opportunity for continuing work would be compensated, whilst nothing at all would be done for workers who had spent a lifetime in the industry. Sir James, as shown in a previous quotation, has even complained about their unemployment benefit.

On the point of attracting new industries to the cleared sites Sir James Lithgow assured the union leaders that the N.S.S. directors were of course anxious to do this. Empty shipyards meant heavy maintenance charges. Therefore they were trying to attract industrialists to take over the shipyard sites for other purposes. There was little comfort for the men in this, as such industries might be long in starting, and in any case were unlikely to employ the displaced men. The only act of the conference was a general agreement to press for the abolition of shipbuilding subsidies at the forthcoming World Economic Conference, a vague general conclusion which was hardly likely to lead to any practical result. It does appear however that Sir James felt a little bitter about the actions of his fellow capitalists. Germany was increasing her shipbuilding industry and was tempting some overseas orders to her yards because they were able to offer four years credit to the purchaser. The money for this extended credit, suggested the chairman of N.S.S., was being provided by the City of London.

As the months went by, the depression developed and the situation in Jarrow became more and more acute. Between December 1929 and December 1930, unemployment on the river doubled as the pace of shipbuilding at Palmer's and on Tyneside slowed down. By the end of 1931 unemployment in Jarrow reached a total of 6572 persons. Only one vessel, an oil tanker, was launched from the shipbuilding yard. New orders were difficult to obtain. Political pressure probably led to orders for two new destroyers being placed with the company. This was their only source of work in 1932. Only a small number of men were engaged on this work. On July 19th they launched H.M.S. *Duchess,* the 109th warship built by Palmer's. It was the last ship the yard launched.

Earlier in 1932 a meeting of the unsecured creditors of the Palmer's Shipbuilding and Iron Company was held in London. Owing to the absence of any contracts Palmer's directors were not able to meet their liabilities. Either a receiver had to be appointed, or else the moratorium had to be extended. The latter alternative was more acceptable. Interest on the debts at 6 per cent was to be paid, and the "standstill" agreement was extended until January 15, 1933. The shadow fell deeply over Palmer's. They had a six months reprieve in which to save the Yard. Was there a worse time in which they could have been placed in this position? The Great Depression had brought the wheels of trade almost to a standstill. Shipping was laid up in the ports and inlets around the English coast. At the end of June there were in the River Tyne 163 idle vessels. This was repeated in other ports. Holiday-makers in Devonshire were surprised to see rows of apparently derelict ships, rusting in idleness, in the various inlets. With their existing tonnage idle there was little hope of persuading owners to order new vessels.

Almost the whole of Jarrow was workless. During the autumn men chafed at their enforced leisure. By December 1932 there were 7248 unemployed. And for the staff, striving with the threat of extinction held over their heads, autumn was a difficult time. Commercial orders seemed impossible to obtain. But there was a chance of obtaining an Admiralty order for the 1932 naval programme. It was the hope of this that gave the company a reprieve. When the moratorium expired in January of 1933 the officials were able to apply for, and obtain, a further extension of six months. They were able to explain that 1932 was a year of exceptional distress. Total launchings on the Tyne were only 29,224 tons, 118,130 tons less than 1931, and there was hope of a Government contract.

That Admiralty order failed to materialize. It has been suggested that the Admiralty, realizing the financial weakness of the company, did not wish to place an order because there was a danger that the company would not be able to complete it. That may be the real reason, or it may be that a hint was given in Admiralty quarters that B.L.D. saw no reason to save Palmer's, and that it would be better not to prolong the life of the Yard, but allow it to be used for rationalization. For whatever reason, Palmer's were passed over and the failure to gain an Admiralty contract precipitated the end.

The moratorium was due to expire at the end of June. There were no new orders on the books of the company. There was no hope of an Admiralty contract. The banks were interested in the N.S.S. scheme and saw a means of liquidating some of the assets. A further extension of time was refused. And so, in a dull court-room in London on the last day of June 1933, the fate of Jarrow was decided. On the application, in formal phrases, of the counsel for Branch Nominees, Ltd., an order was made appointing a receiver to the company. An unknown company, its real backers hidden, cut Jarrow's lifeline.

There was hope that the company might be reorganized if some additional capital were forthcoming. As a shipbuilding yard Palmer's was as efficient and as capable as any in the industry. For years the shipbuilding yard had had to meet the heavy overhead charges of the derelict steelworks. Yet when ships were being ordered Palmer's, on their record and ability, got a fair share of the orders. As a firm they had a technical reputation second to none. They had maintained their position as a pioneer firm which Charles Mark Palmer had gained for them at the outset. In the late years of their life they had built the first tanker on the Isherwood bracketless system. Almost their last mercantile contract was for a feat of ship's surgery which required the highest technical ability. Owing to the fact that the oil-carrying tanks of a tanker have to be steamed out at the end of each voyage these vessels suffer from corrosion. At the end of ten years the tanks are usually worn out while the engines of the ship are in good condition. The owners, therefore, have to decide either to scrap the ship or to place it in dry dock for lengthy repairs. The Anglo-American Oil Company, in conjunction with Palmer's, tried an experiment in rejuvenation on their 17,000-ton tanker the *Saronac*. Instead of scrapping the ship it was decided to build a new centre section. For six months the *Saronac* continued in operation and then, when the new centre section was built, she was brought to the Tyne. She was docked, cut into three pieces, and the centre section of the ship was replaced. To carry out an operation like this on a 17,000-ton vessel requires technical ability of a high order. In 1930 Palmer's were able to carry this operation through successfully. A special film was made by the Shell-Mex Company, which records the feat of the Palmer workers as "Wonderful Ship Surgery". As a better testimonial to their efficiency as shipbuilders is the performance of their vessels. Palmer-built ships are still in operation over the seven seas, and are giving good service wherever they sail. Amongst the officers and men of our navy a Palmer-built warship has a high place.

The company had survived "bad years" many times in the past. Every firm, in an industry so liable to cyclical fluctuations as shipbuilding, had to survive lean years when the orders for new ships fell off. And although a receiver had been appointed, there was no reason why Palmer's should not continue as a shipbuilding company. A receiver could do what the Board of Directors, had it been a strong board, should have done. The iron and steelworks, with no industrial future ahead, could be scrapped and the shipyard set up on its own. There was every reason why the shipyard should continue. It was technically efficient and up to date. It was a compact and well-designed economical yard. Its ships had a reputation throughout the world, and in the eighty years of its life the company had established an international connection. Built up around the firm was the town of Jarrow, with its industrial population almost entirely dependent on shipbuilding. To the quality of the workmen repeated tributes were paid. Jarrow men were recognized as being in the front rank of the craft.

In offering an "inducement to those who wish to get out" National Shipbuilders' Security claims that it does not buy up the companies concerned. It merely provides a market for those firms who no longer wish to continue. The distinction is somewhat fine! Hitler does not conquer a country. He takes control in response to invitation. A combine organized as closely as the shipbuilders are organized now can soon bring an individual firm into line. Once a shipbuilding firm becomes involved in financial difficulties it is almost impossible for that firm to raise the additional capital needed to restore their fortunes, without the agreement of the controllers of the shipbuilding rationalization scheme.

By offering the highest price to the directors or receivers of shipyards in low financial water National Shipbuilders' Security have been able to gain control of some of the best shipbuilding sites in England. This is very important when we consider the trend towards monopoly. Co-operation with the banks has made it difficult for new capital to be found for any proposition not approved by National Shipbuilders' Security. But in case a company with the available capital did try to crash the shipbuilders' ring it would be faced with the grave difficulty of securing a suitable site. All the finest sites for the development of shipbuilding have already been developed. Normally a newcomer would take over a derelict yard and redevelop it. By acquiring sites and sterilizing them for forty years National Shipbuilders' Security prevents newcomers starting in the industry and assists in the tendency towards monopoly.

Had National Shipbuilders' Security, Ltd., not been in existence there would have been little anxiety about the ultimate future of Palmer's. There would have been a period of re-organization and then, when trade improved, orders would come in again and work would commence. That was just what N.S.S. wished to prevent. In a speech in 1933 Mr. F. C. Pyman, one of the Directors of N.S.S., said: "By offering a price substantially above the scrapping value of the yard, the company offers an inducement to those who are tired of the struggle to get out, and it prevents such yards from falling into the hands of bargain hunters who have no stake in the industry and who do not understand it at all." Palmer's workers were not tired of the struggle. The managers and technicians tried their hardest to keep the firm in existence. The crisis which forced Palmer's into bankruptcy came from the financiers and the banks who wished to liquefy their frozen assets. If left to itself the company could have been re-organized. Substantially the same staff would have remained – shipbuilding is hardly an industry for" bargain hunters". There were plenty of far less efficient yards to be dealt with, had efficiency rather than finance been the criterion.

During the closing months of 1933 there were rumours of negotiations between N.S.S. and Palmer's. Anxiously the staff and the men waited for some definite news. Schemes for re-organizing the company were prepared, but they came to nothing. In the early summer of 1934 it was announced that Palmer's had been sold to N.S.S. The death warrant of Palmer's was signed. The reason for Jarrow's existence had vanished overnight.

Why was Palmer's Yard sold? It certainly was not an obsolete yard. One of the biggest firms in the industry and one which had invariably secured a fair share on competitive tenders cannot be classed as obsolete. It had one of the finest sites in the country. Was it redundant? And what factors were taken into consideration? Was it in the national interest that a first-class shipyard should be scrapped? National Shipbuilding Security, Ltd., were able, by the financial weakness of a company which had chained a derelict steelworks to an efficient shipyard, to buy one of the six largest firms in the industry at scrap prices, and thus close down one of their strongest competitive firms. For the directors of N.S.S. the closing of Palmer's meant that the wide connection of the firm would have to turn elsewhere for their orders. Financial weakness, and not technical inefficiency, decided the fate of the company. The rationalization of the shipbuilding industry has been carried through in that way – with an eye on the balance sheet rather than on the efficiency of the particular companies. Writing in the *Industrial Survey of the North-east Coast Area,* which was made for the Board of Trade in 1932,

Professor H. M. Hallsworth remarks: "It may well happen that a firm with a relatively well-equipped yard may get into financial difficulties, and have to close down, whilst a less efficiently equipped yard may weather the storm. Under the scheme as it stands, it is difficult to see how the possibility of this can be avoided. This does not affect the merits of the scheme so far as the members of the company are concerned, in fact it rather enhances their position. But from a wider point, the result is, of course, undesirable." N.S.S. has the interests of its members at heart – not "the wider interests". Palmer's was scrapped to safeguard the profits of some of the firms remaining in the industry. Who benefited by the sale? It was the receiver's job to make as much money as possible by the sale of the assets of the company. It may have been that those who were anxious to raise sufficient funds to carry out the re-organization of the company found that their way to raising the million pounds needed was blocked. For the banks and financial houses were backing the rationalization scheme. It would not have been to their advantage to make money available for Palmer's to continue. And as the offer made by N.S.S. was in excess of scrapping value of the yard, the receiver had no alternative but to accept it. With the money received the receiver was able to make a distribution of 5*s*. 8*d*. in the pound to holders of the first mortgage stock. Of the £650,000 of this stock which had been issued £356,840 of stock was held by the National Provincial Bank, Ltd. Therefore more than half of the money received from the sale of Palmer's to N.S.S. went to the banks.

Holders of the ordinary shares or of the debentures received nothing. The workmen, who in the better days of the company had invested their savings, were left with worthless script. Share certificates, which had represented hard-earned money, were worthless. For many of them, forced on to the dole by the closing of the company, it was a terrible shock.

Protests were made, but nothing effective could be done unless the Government were prepared to act. In reply to a question in the House, Mr. Runciman coldly said: "Nothing is to be gained by giving Jarrow the impression that its shipyard can be revived. The best thing is to make a clean sweep of the premises, and throw open to purchase one of the best sites in the world for the establishment of prosperous new industries." That phrase "one of the best sites in the world" is to recur with tragic irony in the next chapter of Jarrow's sorrow. Runciman's words sealed Palmer's fate as later he was to seal Prague's. Sold by National Shipbuilding Security to a demolition firm, work was commenced to clear the site. Oxy-acetylene burners made short work of steel girders. Cranes crashed to the ground, the machine shops were emptied, the blast furnaces and their numerous chimneys were demolished. The familiar overhead cranes vanished. For forty years, shipbuilding is exiled from Jarrow. The irony was that in a shortage of tramp shipping eighteen months later, British orders were undertaken by Belgian yards at cut prices, because they had bought first-class machinery at Palmer's sale for the price of scrap.

In spite of the outcry raised by the scrapping of Palmer's, N.S.S. continued undisturbed. Protests were made by trade unions and by local authorities. But the supporters of rationalization were too powerful for democratic criticism. Sunderland Town Council protested against their activities on the Wear. Newcastle Town Council fought them when they tried to sterilize the site of the Tyne Iron Shipbuilding Yard. When the fate of Jarrow became apparent, ten local authorities joined together to protest to the Government and to try to get the Prime Minister to see a deputation. But Downing Street replied that "the Government had no power to interfere in the activities of the company". A few months earlier another Government spokesman had said, when discussing the activities of N.S.S., that he did not see any grounds on which the Government could properly take action. Was it of more interest to Mr. Baldwin that the profits of a few companies should be safeguarded than that the shipbuilding capacity of Jarrow should have been saved for the nation, which he had realized must rearm?

The Government have not interfered with the task of N.S.S. In their short existence the company has scrapped shipbuilding yards with a capacity of 1,350,000 tons per annum. Some of the best shipbuilding sites in this country have been cleared of all the equipment essential to their purpose. Workman Clark of Belfast, the Egis Shipyard, Robert Thompson and Sons of Sunderland, William Beardmore of Glasgow are only a few of the famous firms which have been bought up. With the experience of the last war behind us was it not folly to allow a private company to scrap yards and sell their equipment? In 1939 when we have a mercantile marine 2000 vessels below '9'4 in strength, when Germany has four times as many submarines as in 1914, when a hostile Italy has assisted in the conquest of Spain and has established submarine bases there, we have been bereft of one-third of our capacity to build ships. When the shipping boom was at its height, shipowners were finding it difficult to get orders placed for delivery at a reasonable date. To scrap these yards N.S.S. have spent over £1,750,000. What benefits have they gained?

Throughout the career of N.S.S. there have been protests from shipowners about the prices of new tonnage. At the outset, while he was soothing down the Unions, Sir James Lithgow endeavoured to persuade the shipowners that the economies resulting from the concentration of production would enable the shipbuilders to pay the 1 per cent levy without increasing the price of the ships. But once a movement to rationalization gets under weigh, there is a grave tendency towards the setting up of a price ring. If a number of companies get together and with the support of the banks agree to close down certain firms it is more than likely that they will make some agreement amongst themselves about price-fixing. Unless there were some such price agreement there is a danger that the benefits of rationalization would be offset by increased competition amongst themselves. As far back as 1930 there was talk of a shipping ring, although a director of one of the bigger firms suggested that the name of "Shipping Conference" would sound much sweeter. In 1933 Mr. F. C. Pyman was saying, "I suppose that true Rationalization would not stop at the adjustment of capacity to demand. There is room for improvement in the organization of every industry and shipbuilding is no exception. The work of rationalizing the shipbuilding industry is not finished, and it is the last turns of the screw which hurt." As the process of buying up the yards continued, machinery was being devised to continue the rationalization. In May 1936 it was announced that Mr. A. L. Ayre of the Burntisland Shipping Company had been invited to accept "an important appointment in connection with the fuller development of co-ordination and unification within the organization of the shipbuilding industry on the commercial and economic side". It was later revealed that this was the post of permanent chairman of the Shipbuilding Conference. Evidence from people in the industry indicates that the Shipbuilding Conference is in reality a price ring.

Speaking in Glasgow on February 11, 1938, Mr. S. Cranford Hogarth, a prominent local shipowner, said, Trade rings were the order of the day.... It was well known that their friends the shipbuilders had succumbed to the prevailing tendency, and had a very close and efficiently run corporation. It was obvious that every ship turned out of a British shipyard must carry in her first cost a percentage to maintain this organization. It was even whispered that, in cases where a number of builders had been asked to quote, they had a system to provide a solatium to the unsuccessful. This was known by the euphemistic term of rationalization. Of course it was quite legitimate, and they all knew that shipbuilders – like steelmakers, and incidentally shipowners came through a very desperate time a few years ago, but all these extra costs, he contended, went to explain why a shipowner today was being asked 100 per cent increase in price for a new vessel. It also explained why even the boom months of last year hardly induced even an inquiry for new tonnage, and why shipbuilders not engaged in naval construction were now beginning to look anxiously for new orders.

Four months later Mr. Wilfrid Ayre, the brother of the chairman of the Shipping Conference, spoke at the Annual General Meeting of the Burntisland Shipping Company. "During the depression", he is reported as saying, "the prices which builders were forced to offer for new vessels sank to levels which would never have been permitted if any sensible scheme of industrial co-operation had been in existence. It was significant that all important industries were becoming interested in schemes of commercial Rationalization which were designed to prevent the selling prices of their products being forced down below a reasonable level of remuneration. Shipping and shipbuilding were not lagging behind in this respect, and it was hoped that they would each in future enjoy some of the benefits which close industrial unification could give."

Could there be any clearer indication of the drift of the shipbuilding industry? If the plan was originally designed to reduce the capacity of the industry only, as the scheme developed there would be a temptation for it to be carried a little further towards monopoly than was originally intended. During this period shipowners have constantly spoken of the rising prices of new tonnage. Lord Craigmyle had explained that the "high cost of constructing new tonnage had been responsible for the delay in placing orders for the two new ships which are required by the Canadian-Australasian Line.... It had been a terrible disappointment to those who had for many years been fighting the battle of British shipping all over the world that just at the time these years of struggle had matured into an agreement with all the governments concerned ... they found that the price of the two essential ships was well over £1,000,000 in excess of the highest figures previously tendered." Yet with even their policy of scrapping and their price ring British shipbuilders have failed to safeguard their position. A policy of scrapping shipyards did not result in fresh orders for new tonnage. With falling freight rates after the shipping boom which reached its peak in the late summer of 1937 orders for new tonnage declined and more and more ships were laid up. By the end of 1938 it became apparent that unless a great number of new orders were forthcoming only one-quarter of the shipbuilding capacity of the country would be in use during 1939.

The shipbuilding statistics demonstrating this point were used with great effect to buttress the campaign which Sir James Lithgow had launched for a subsidy at the International Engineering Congress in Glasgow in June 1938. It is interesting in the House of Commons to watch a campaign of this nature develop. Each member usually receives a shower of memoranda, reprints and articles outlining the case for special assistance. A few members working very closely with the interests concerned are provided with more elaborate information on which questions can be asked and speeches made. Little of this publicity comes into the public eye. Perhaps when the situation is deemed to be suitable efforts are made to obtain good publicity in the Press. But generally a subsidy campaign is carried on out of sight of the general public. Propaganda is directed towards a chosen few. Wires are pulled at dinner parties. And the result quite often is far more successful than the protests of the Left however well organized. A government composed of industrialists and men representing one class is all too ready to listen to requests for assistance from their friends.

The subsidy campaign was developed in the columns of the trade papers. It extended, a little, in 1939 to the general Press. Shipbuilders can only benefit if shipowners are assured of a profit and are prepared to order their ships from British builders. The subsidy campaign developed along two lines. The Chamber of Shipping put forward demands for subsidies to guarantee the profits of the shipowners. They demanded a subsidy of £2,500,000 per annum for five years for owners of deep sea tramp steamers, a subsidy of £5,000,000 per year for five years for the liner companies, a subsidy of £500,000 per year for five years for the tramp owners in the Near Continental trades, and a subsidy of £500,000 a year for five years for the coasting trade. For the shipbuilders a plea was made for a subsidy which would make their prices more attractive to the shipping owners. The *Shipowners' Report* said: "It will be essential for British shipowners to be able to acquire new tonnage at competitive world prices."

Eventually, on March 28th in the House of Commons, Mr. Oliver Stanley outlined the money which the Government were prepared to give the shipowners. For the tramp shipping companies a dole of £2,750,000 for five years was granted. £500,000 a year for five years was set aside for a subsidy to shipowners ordering new merchant tonnage in England, and to assist in the finance of these orders a special loan fund of £10,000,000 was announced on which capital would be lent to owners for two years on favourable terms. Finally £2,000,000 was earmarked for the purchase of British vessels for use as an emergency reserve. The claim of the liner companies for £5,000,000 a year was not immediately granted. Instead an Advisory Committee was to consider separately each claim for assistance and if it were granted Parliamentary approval would be sought for the money. The demand for a subsidy during the years 1938-39 was being pressed on the grounds that it was necessary that Britain should have an ample shipping reserve in time of war. Yet in that period from January 1st to April 1939, 210 ships with a gross tonnage of 539,000 were sold abroad, a large number of them to Germany. In response to Labour questions all the Parliamentary Secretary to the Board of Trade could say was that "The Board of Trade have no powers to oppose or prohibit the sales of these ships to foreigners." Later, under continued pressure, the President of the Board of Trade agreed to acquire such powers by legislation.

Their original demand was for £8,500,000 per year for five years, or a total of £42,500,000. Some authorities estimated that if the sea power of the country were to be retained the total cost would be near £100,000,000. Already a grant has been made of £16,500,000, as well as the loan fund of £10,000,000 and the reserve purchase price of £2,000,000, while the liner authorities will get their subsidy individually. Public money will therefore guarantee the profits of the shipowners during the next five years. Experience in the U.S.A. has revealed that the taxpayer gets little benefit from a subsidy to the Merchant Marine. Mr. Maxwell Zies, in his book *American Shipping Policy,* reaches the conclusion that the various American shipping subsidies, amounting to the colossal sum of four billion dollars, have gone into the pockets of private individuals without giving the taxpayer any substantial advantage in return. There are no indications of the advantage that the British taxpayer is to get from this large subsidy.

Instead, the change in British policy has been regarded as another step in the war between nations to retain control of the trade of the world. England's traditional doctrine of the freedom of seas in the commercial sense has been disowned. Our shipping lines are now subsidized, and a strong campaign is being waged for even worse restrictive measures. The outcome will be to intensify the fight. Subsidies do nothing constructive. They merely guarantee the profit of the interests concerned. A wider organization of our merchant navy is desirable – a reorganization which can involve adequate planning for the purpose which our fleet serves. Sea transport is more a subject for careful planning than for the haphazard operations of private capitalism. Instead of reorganizing the industry and bringing it under public control the Government has chosen to finance it out of public funds. The *Shipping World* says: "There is not a shipowner in this country today who will receive the Government subsidy without embarrassment and regret." – This deserves quotation as the perfect example of the crocodile tear!

As soon as the President of the Board of Trade made his statement at the end of March, 1939, orders poured into the shipyards. In two weeks 250,000 tons of shipping were ordered. In one week contracts for twenty-three tramp ships and cargo liners were placed. Not since the height of the 1929 boom had orders flowed in at such a rate. The shipowners had won their "hold-back" strike.

Experience of the earlier assistance given by the Government to shipbuilders has shown the way in which they seek their own advantage. To encourage the modernization of our tramp-shipping fleet and to stimulate new orders for the shipyards the British Shipping (Assistance) Act of 1935 set up the "scrap and build" scheme. The Board of Trade was empowered to lend up to a total of £10,000,000 in advances to shipowners for twelve years at 3 per cent to enable them to build new vessels. It was laid down that two tons of shipping must be scrapped for every ton built. Eventually when the scheme came to an end fifty new vessels had been ordered for twenty-two different firms. Ninety-seven vessels had been scrapped, ninety-one of which were purchased by the firms to enable them to qualify for the subsidy. Forty-eight of the vessels were bought from foreign owners. At one stage the tonnage which was being suggested for demolition by the owners anxious to obtain the subsidy was so useless as to be banned by the Board of Trade. Nearly half of the ships were later sold abroad for scrapping. So the net result was a neat little ramp at the expense of the patient taxpayer.

Shipbuilding has passed through the same phase as many other industries under capitalism. Originally strictly individualistic, the wastage of severe competition during the depression has encouraged the industry to "organize". It has been compelled to plan its future. But under capitalism the restricted purpose for which planning is undertaken limits the results. Planning is undertaken to maintain or to maximize private profit. Its first step is generally either to fix prices, or to restrict production in such a way as to maintain, or even to force up prices. And re-organization in modern industry has normally implied an effort to reduce the weekly wage bill and to increase the output per man by mechanization. Our exporting industries, we are told, have to be as efficient as their competitors in the world market. So we concentrate our production, mechanize our steelworks, mechanize our collieries ... and behind each step in mechanization lies a derelict community. Men skilled in jobs for which there is no demand are scrapped. The industry pays no compensation to the workers it throws aside. They are left for the State to maintain. A bare allowance is made to cover their limited material needs, but no regard is made for their personality. They are left to drag on through empty day after day, without purpose and without usefulness.

Charles Mark Palmer started Jarrow as a shipbuilding centre without considering the needs of his workers. They crowded into a small colliery village which was hurriedly extended to receive them. They packed into insanitary houses. They lived without any social amenities. They paid with their lives for the absence of any preparation for the growth of such a town. And in 1933 another group of capitalists decided the fate of Jarrow without reference to the workers. A society in which the decisive decisions are invariably taken by one group, and in which those decisions are reached only by considerations of their own welfare; is not a just society. And in the modern age of machine production it is not an efficient society. Everywhere private profit is a restriction on economic progress. The changed conditions under which British capitalism has had to work in post-war years calls for reorganization on socialist lines.

CHAPTER ELEVEN

The Fight for the Steelworks

THE GREAT shipyard of Jarrow was dead ... killed because it was a powerful competitor ... rooted out, not because it was inefficient, but because it stood in the way of a group of big financial interests, who wished to consolidate their grip on the shipping industry and get control of shipping prices. In the doing of this, as we have seen, this group have crippled the British shipbuilding industry.

At Jarrow, where the shops were closing, men drifting away, and grim despair was in the hearts of the masses of unemployed in the town, there came news – the possibility of a vast new industry. A catalogue of the sale of Palmer's machinery and fittings and of the Yard generally came into the hands of T. Vosper Salt, a man of wide experience in steel, particularly in America. He had come to the conclusion that a world boom in steel was on the way. He went to Jarrow in October 1934. His experienced eye at once saw the possibilities of Palmer's site for a vast new integrated steel-plant, of which he well knew the need in Britain. There was the harbour on the Tyne at which the largest ore-carrying ships could dock, the network of rails and sidings which had been built to meet the needs of the Shipyard. Salt could see the value of the Jarrow site for steel-making. What he could not see were the hidden politics of steel in Britain.

As a practical business man, Salt took the necessary preliminary steps to carry out his idea. He secured an option on the site, asked Henry Brassert and Co., the world's leading consultants on steel plant construction, to prepare plans, and proceeded provisionally to form a syndicate and to raise the money. The preliminary report from Brassert and Co., which was in his hands by January 1935, was so favourable to Jarrow as a site for a steelworks that Salt knew that on that report he would have no difficulty in getting the necessary finance. Brassert, however, added a warning, that Salt must first consult the British Iron and Steel Federation. This advice was immediately followed.

Thus began a struggle which was to shake the Government, to shock the

Conservative Prime Minister into public protest, and to expose the steel magnates of Britain as a group of men to whom national needs, even under the shadow of approaching war, meant nothing more than the opportunity for wringing profits out of obsolete plant. Looking back from 1939, one can see that the weakness of the country in armaments, which is now put forward as an excuse for Munich, was partly due to the obstruction of the steel magnates over the preceding years. They were determined to keep the vast new rearmament profits within the existing ring. To this end they refused to allow the radical re-organization of the steel industry necessary to meet national needs, lest it interfere with their private profitmaking. They maintained as long as they could their right to have their obsolete plant protected against competition, not only from the up-to-date works abroad, but equally from new works on modern lines at home. This country was put into a dangerous situation from which, even today, it has not been extricated because the steel magnates have been allowed to put their private interests first. The Government has protected them against all competition and built for them a monopoly, and better still a market which most, though not all, the steel-makers would not have been able to keep to themselves, even with a 33.3 per cent tariff and a 40 per cent currency depreciation.

France had had the good luck to have had a large part of her old steel industry destroyed during the war. British subsidies and German reparations re-built and re-equipped the French and Belgian industries. Germany, having lost 42 per cent of her pig-iron and 37 per cent of her steel ingot capacity, and 34 per cent of her rolling mills, had managed to rebuild a steel industry of the latest type within her restricted frontiers. No money could be raised on the London Stock Exchange for the badly needed re-organization of the British steel industry.

In Britain the banks found themselves with the heavy steel producing industries on their hands. They could not get even part of the money they had advanced. If they forced liquidation there was no one in the market for out-of-date steel plants. Even had the banks been prepared to accept a fantastically low price ... they would have got nothing from such sales, because they came after the debenture holders, except where, as in some cases, they were actually the biggest creditors, and also trustees at the same time for the debenture-holders! They were therefore in the awkward position of having to provide further money to keep steel plants going for which they saw no likelihood of profits ahead. All the steel-making countries after the war had to face similar difficulties during the period when men's minds were turned to disarmament. It would be interesting to work out to what extent Hitler was backed in Germany by international interests who saw in the rise of his movement a lever by which the steel trade, through armament demand, could be made once again a good profit-making proposition. If this be the case, his backers have not been disappointed in their expectations.

In England the bankers saw a tariff on steel as the most immediate means of getting something back. But they were bitterly opposed by the steel-using industries, who said that the reason why British steel-makers could not compete with continental prices was entirely due to their bad organization and largely inefficient and obsolete plant.

The imposition of the 33.33 per cent tariff and the creation of the British Iron and Steel Federation strengthened the British group in their struggle against their Continental competitors. Ever since the creation of the International Steel Cartel in September 1926 the British steel firms had remained outside because they were unable to reach any agreement on the share of the British market to be allocated to the Continental companies. With the imposition of the tariff the price advantage was lost to the Continental producers and they were more disposed to negotiate. They wished to have a quota of 1,000,000 tons of steel for the British market. On the other hand the British firms were anxious to limit the import quota of Continental steel to 500,000 tons only. No agreement was possible on this basis, and in spite of the tariff the Continental firms preferred competition to agreement.

Before any big reorganization scheme could be contemplated the Iron and Steel Federation wished to defeat foreign competition. The only effective way appeared to be by rigorously limiting their imports into Britain. To force the Cartel to accept the British terms, the Steel Federation obtained from Mr. Runciman a 50 per cent. tariff on semi-finished steel in March 1935. This imposition was too high for the Continental steel-makers. Even their more efficient plants were unable to compete successfully when their prices on the English market were increased by 50 per cent. Consequently they were forced to accept the terms offered by British interests. On May 1st, a temporary agreement was reached which led to a permanent agreement by the end of July. For the first year, imports of steel into England from the Cartel countries were limited to 670,000 tons, but for each succeeding year the quota was to be reduced to 550,000 tons. Having achieved their object the British steel-makers acquiesced in the reduction of the "penal" tariff. By it they had obtained a fixed share of the world's export trade and had strictly limited the market in Britain for the Cartel countries. With Britain a member of the Steel Cartel, the steel consumer and the taxpayer – paying for the armaments in all the countries concerned – were handed over to the greatest and tightest steel ring of all time. With this enormous power placed in their hands ... and without conditions ... the British steel masters were in a position where they could free themselves from the banks who were so inconvenient in their insistence on modernization. There was no danger of competition from abroad, and they could use their power to ensure freedom from fresh competition at home. They were ready to exploit the market.

It is important to realize just what were the conditions in the industry about which all these complaints were being made ... an industry thus heavily protected by Mr. Runciman and the National Government.

The position in the British iron and steel industry when Vosper Salt went to Jarrow to look at Palmer's site was that out of 308 blast furnaces in Great Britain, over 100 had been out of blast for over five years. There were less than 100 in active operation, and it was not expected that 150 of the more out-of-date ones would ever produce pig iron economically again.

Owing to the modernization of certain plants the output had doubled since the war, and the output per worker had increased by two-thirds. But the expert view, as expressed in the reports of the time, was that many of the blast furnaces, because of their inadequate size and out-of-date planning, were unable to compete unaided in modern world steel production. Only behind a prohibitive tariff, or in an emergency when anything would have to be used, could pig iron be again produced in these plants. Both tariff and emergency have been provided in 1939.

There were, of course, exceptions ... modern steel plants equal to any others in the world. But such firms as Lysaght's at Scunthorpe, and Stewart and Lloyd's at Corby were hampered by the existence of the old inefficient plants, absorbing orders, often actually making profit in bad times, because the big plant must work to capacity for its full economy to be effective.

There are four basic necessities for the efficient operation of a modern steel plant ... a minimum of inter-process transport, economy in the treatment of ore and coke, economy in fuel and, fourthly, a sufficiently large plant. Judged by these standards a good part of the British plant was out of date. The National Federation of Iron and Steel Manufacturers, in figures published in 1932, gave the transport costs for three blast-furnace firms in Cleveland, using local coal, iron ore and limestone, as 18s. 2d. per ton, actually 28 per cent of the cost of the pig. But this pig itself had to be sent elsewhere to be made into plates. From the Tees to its sister river the Wear, a distance of a few miles, added 6s. per ton for railway transport. A firm not having the advantage of local supplies, and using bought pig iron and scrap, paid a total of £1 per ton of steel produced, in transport charges alone. These facts prove to the hilt the case for geographical planning and for the integrated steel plant.

The Jarrow site had advantages which meant great economy in railway costs. The harbour had been deepened by Palmer's to launch large battleships. The *Olympic* and the *Berengaria* have been docked there comfortably for breaking up in recent years. This is an important consideration when the local ore deposits at Cleveland are largely worked out, and when more and more of the high-grade ores have to be brought in by sea. Ore used to come in large quantities from Northern Spain. Political questions have rendered this source of supply uncertain, so ore is now being sought for in West Africa and other hitherto untapped areas of the Empire.

The bigger the vessel the cheaper the cost of transport per ton of ore. The Bethlehem Steelworks in U.S.A. brings ore in from Chile in 21,000-ton boats to Baltimore. Germany brings ore in big ships to Rotterdam, and transfers them to 4000-ton lighters for the rest of the journey down the Rhine. At Jarrow there is direct access to the site of the steelworks itself for the largest boats, while the Tees can only take vessels of 7000 tons.

From every technical point of view the Jarrow site was ideal for a really up-to-date steel plant. As was indicated by Sir John Jarvis in his letter to *The Times,* the City was interested and finance was available. Everything in fact was ready for a great new project which would be today a great national asset. The one objection was on the score of productive economy. The new works would produce steel too cheaply. In a personal letter to me, one of the promoters, Mr. R. C. Whitfield, said: "One British iron and steel company produces steel ingots for about 83s. per ton. Another company using similar raw materials but possessing a more modern plant produces steel ingots for about 78s. a ton. A modern works at Jarrow taking advantage of the unrivalled facilities of that site and possessing the modern plants proposed is estimated to produce the steel ingots for about 65s. per ton."

This estimate was evidently accepted by the existing steel firms, for, as Sir John Jarvis revealed in the House of Commons, one of the terms that was proposed by the steel masters as a condition if Jarrow Steelworks were allowed to be constructed was that a fine of 15s. per ton should be paid into a pool, as being the margin between the Jarrow cost of production and that of the existing works. The Federation, of course, denied that this was ever suggested. In fact, issuing denials about their obstruction of the Jarrow scheme became a prominent activity of the Federation at this period. But it was clear from the way steel men in the House received this statement by Sir John Jarvis that they regarded such a demand as being in no way out of the ordinary.

Salt planned to produce at Jarrow high-grade Bessemer steel using English iron ore as well as imported ore. Until recent technical improvements had been devised the production of suitable pig iron for basic Bessemer steel from the English carbonate ores had been regarded as impossible, owing to the percentage of sulphur in the ore. As the ore yielded iron too high in phosphorus for the open-hearth system it was thought that the ore would be useless for steel production.

Discussing the significance of the technical changes an expert has written ... "Mr. H. A. Brassert in his studies and reports made in recent years on the rehabilitation of the British iron and steel industry, realized the enormous importance of this vast body of iron ore as a basis of low cost production in close proximity to the greatest markets of Britain. At the time of his investigation, Britain was importing between two and three million tons of steel, mostly of basic Bessemer quality, while at the same time her own industry was suffering from depressed conditions and serious unemployment. The replacement of this imported tonnage by steel of British production was therefore of great national importance in order to give employment to British labour instead of abroad."

In experiments in U.S.A., Brassert had shown that it was possible, by treating the molten pig iron with soda ash, to get rid of the sulphur content of the low-grade ore. It was possible by this means to produce good quality steel with a low fuel consumption. As a result of these technical developments Stewart and Lloyd's have established a new modern plant at Corby in Northamptonshire. The importance of utilizing local ore for the manufacture of high-grade steel in times of national emergency is immense, because our dependence on oversea supplies is reduced.

It is significant that the German authorities have been quick to appreciate the possibilities of this new method of dealing with low-grade ore. Hitherto Germany had depended too much on the iron resources of Sweden and Lorraine – both supplies being liable to interruption in wartime. The Nazi campaign for self-sufficiency to minimize the danger of a successful blockade encouraged schemes for the development of Germany's low-grade ore resources in the Swabian and Franconian Jura and in the Harz region. The Brassert process was the means by which these could be used. Hermann Goering has hurried on the construction of steelworks to use these ores.

The drama begins in November 1934, when the news about the option of Palmer's site by a new steel syndicate got around. The production of steel in 1933 had been 7,024,000 tons. Brassert had predicted that by 1940 British steel production would be up to 10,500,000 tons. This was laughed at by the steel producers, who declared that there was and could be no market for the steel of the projected works at Jarrow. When Salt had Brassert's favourable report, the finance houses became interested. In March 1935,

Salt submitted the Brassert Report to Sir Andrew Duncan, as chairman of the Iron and Steel Federation. Duncan was interested. The North-east coast members of the Federation were alarmed, and asked that Brassert should prepare a report on steel production in the Northeast, and a comparison of the Jarrow site as compared with the Tees, where Dorman Long and Co. had been trying to get a merger with South Durham Steel. This report was completed and sent to Sir Andrew Duncan in June 1935, though later the Federation claimed that it was only received in August. In either case, it was known that every obstruction had been put in the way of information being given to the framers of the report.

In its defence in *The Times* (July 1936) the Federation stated that during the autumn of 1935 the report was being "discussed". Since March pressure had been brought to bear on the City to prevent the syndicate raising capital, and the time was used to quicken up a stop-gap policy at the works on the Tees. By this time, public opinion on Tyneside, infuriated by the activities of National Shipping Security, had become thoroughly interested in the projected Jarrow Works. The opposition of the North-east firms was known, and Government spokesmen were being asked whether this new hope for the terribly hard-hit town of Jarrow was to be snuffed out to suit the steel combine.

So great was the feeling that Mr. Baldwin, in his eve-of-poll speech at Newcastle, found it necessary to be reassuring. There was, he said, the project of further steelworks for the North-east coast. There had been considerable discussion ... a desire on the part of all concerned to be helpful! "I want to say," he continued, "with regard to many statements that have been made, that there is no truth in any of the reports that either the banks or any other authorities interested in these matters are making a dead set to prevent anything of the kind being done in the area. It is not true."

In view of the real situation behind the scenes, and the amount of "desire to be helpful" really displayed, this speech deserves a place as Exhibit A in any museum of political orations.

Sir Andrew Duncan, however, really was doing his best to get the Federation to agree. He must have been in the confidence of Mr. Baldwin, who, as he was to tell the House of Commons later with "appalling frankness", as he said, that though he had fought the election, ostensibly on peace and the League of Nations, he had really made up his mind to a vast rearmament programme. The demand for steel was rising rapidly with the general upswing in the trade cycle. Sir Andrew Duncan must have known that shortly the demand would be higher than at any point since the last war.

Whether he took the steel men into his confidence is not known, certainly he did his best to get them to agree to the new works at Jarrow. Privately, he told Mr. Arnold Forster, who was now concerned with the project of raising the money in the City, that general co-operation in the new steelworks was impossible, owing to the attitude of the big Tees-side North-east firms, but that the Consett Iron Co., one of the big three of the North-east steel companies, was willing to help the Jarrow scheme "with cash and counsel" … and that in any case "the obstruction to the wider co-operation was no bar to progress." Consett had a lot to gain by this, as their present works are a long way from the river, and heavy transport charges have to be paid on their sea-borne ore. On this assurance the syndicate renewed their option on the Jarrow site.

Soon after the new Parliament met, there was in December a debate on the Jarrow scheme in the House of Commons. In view of what we now know was in his mind regarding rearmament, the speech of Mr. Baldwin on this occasion is interesting.

> "Perhaps some hon. Members did not read what I said in the country and I repeat it: A great many people and a great many industries have benefited by the protection given to them by this Government, and there are many industries to-day – I instanced the iron and steel industry particularly – which, had the condition of 1931 been allowed to go on, would have been bankrupt at this moment, and they are now enjoying great prosperity. No one grudges them that prosperity. There are many more. But I do say that where men for years could not have expected to have enjoyed the prosperity that they have enjoyed – largely, I admit, by their own efforts, but their own efforts would have been futile without the help of the Government – it is their duty to see what they can give the country in return for what they have had."

The strong "hear, hears" from the "non-steel" M.P.s in the House encouraged the Premier to continue:

> "There can be no better work for the men who have received so well at the hands of the State to pay back their debt to the State, to those who are most in need. There are many cases in which this can be done. The difficulties of doing it compulsorily are almost insuperable, as hon. Gentlemen opposite, if they were to try it, would find, but I believe that help in that way and help that can be given would do more than anything else to make a change, not only a material change but a veritable spiritual

change, in those neighbourhoods, and such work would be a blessing to the country."

By the next month, January 1936, the demand for steel had reached and passed the production which Brassert had been sneered at for prophesying might be obtained in 1940. There was a conference between representatives of the syndicate and of the Steel Federation. "Jarrow has got to go forward", said Sir Andrew Duncan. The steel masters had other ideas. They put forward the argument that a serious shortage of steel faced the Federation ... the shortage that the experts of the Jarrow scheme had been prophesying since November 1934. But, argued the Northeast coast firms, this means an immediate extension of the capacity of the existing works, and the Jarrow proposals must take cognizance of this fact. In other words, the situation that made the Jarrow Works more urgently needed than ever, that justified to the hilt the contention that a new integrated plant was needed, was used as an argument by the steel masters to prove that the Jarrow Works were not needed at all. They would hastily hatch up and extend their own works to meet the need.

In March of the previous year, Brassert had been asked by Sir Andrew Duncan and the Federation to report on this very point – a comparison between a new integrated plant at Jarrow, and the extending of existing plants on the Tees. Brassert had reported that the cost would be much lower at Jarrow. "From a national standpoint", he had added, "a modern steel plant situated on one of the world's best coking deposits and on one of the country's finest industrial harbours would be a distinct asset, especially in the export trade." That asset, with its much lower costs, the Steel Federation was determined the nation should not have.

It was this national need, not the rival claims of two sets of capitalists to a share of the steel market, that was rousing the country's interest, and which prompted the Commissioner for the Special Areas (Sir Malcolm Stewart) to write in his Report, published in February 1936:

"I have not been directly concerned in these negotiations which have experienced many setbacks, but representations were early made by me in appropriate quarters as to the desirability of carrying out this scheme which, apart from any claims for consideration based on need of relief of distress, had the advantage of expert opinion as to the good economic position of Jarrow for the establishment of a steelworks there."

In March, one year after having received the original report asked for, Sir Andrew Duncan got from Brassert detailed proposals regarding the new plant. When this was put to the Federation, the North-east firms replied by demanding such eliminations and reductions in the scheme as would have reduced the Jarrow plant to a completely uneconomic figure of production. Brassert had put the necessary minimum at 350,000 steel ingot tons annually. This demand for reduction was made at a time when, with the 50 per cent tariff in operation, the demand for home steel was rising far more quickly than the Federation firms could meet it.

By this time (April 1936) the costs of construction which had been at their lowest when Brassert made his original plans in 1934, were now rising rapidly. More capital would be needed for the Jarrow Works than if construction could have started early in 1935. In addition the syndicate had had to find large sums merely to keep their option. At this period, Consett, which had promised "cash and counsel" and agreement "in principle" withdrew their offers of co-operation "in view of the expansion initiated since January by other members of the Federation".

Under advice from several importance people who had been influenced by the favourable attitude of Sir Andrew Duncan, the syndicate made one last effort to secure consideration for such parts of the original scheme as would at least provide an economic basis on which it was possible to operate. They received the reply that "the Federation is not concerned to investigate or to secure the commercial soundness of a new venture". At the same time, owing to letters in *The Times* and the general indignation of people whose views count in such matters, the Federation issued a denial that they were preventing the Jarrow promoters from proceeding with an independent scheme at Jarrow "if they saw fit to use the site for which they held the option". In other words, they did not keep the man out of the wood, they only told him that if he came in they would shoot him. The Federation could now distribute both orders and raw material. By the new arrangement with the Cartel, the control of the industry was completely in their hands. As Mr. Brassert himself said, under these conditions it was impossible for any expert to advise anyone to go on with the scheme. Nevertheless, there was, of course, nothing to prevent anyone decorating the Jarrow site with a steelworks purely for his own amusement if he wanted to do so. As *The Times* remarked in a leading article: "The Federation has no power to prevent the construction of new works, but there are other ways of killing a project than those expressly forbidden." Yet Mr. Runciman, throughout the debates at this period, maintained the fiction that really no one had stopped the Jarrow Steelworks ... the Federation had only felt that they could not co-operate.

There was just one snag left in the summer of 1936, before the Federation and Mr. Runciman between them had nicely finished off this dreaded new steelworks which would have upset the projects for patching up the old works on which profits might now be earned. The arrangements with the International Steel Cartel had in fact been working for some little time, but it was necessary to get formal sanction in the Finance Bill of 1936. These were included in the famous Clause 6, which would have slipped through the House easily enough except for the bitter row about Jarrow. The Jarrow Town Council had circularized all the Local Authorities and M.P.s asking for help. There was a good deal of misgiving among Government supporters, especially as Lord Nuffield was angrily threatening to start a steelworks himself, so great were his difficulties in getting the steel he wanted from the Federation firms. Mr. Runciman, however, could be trusted to deal with any situation where postponement of the trouble might get round the difficulty. In the thick of the angry debate, he rose and while assuring the House that everyone in the steel industry had the best possible intentions to everyone else, and the kindliest feelings to all newcomers, announced that as President of the Board of Trade he had asked the "Import Duties Advisory Committee to examine all the data available, and to report on the present position of the iron and steel industry and in so far as practicable the general lines for its future development". This, of course, as it was meant to do, quietened the Opposition among most of the Government supporters.

Not all, however. Major Hill, the late Conservative M.P. for Ripon, wrote to *The Times*:

> "The best brains, and unlimited money have been directed to starting industries in the special areas. When it is proposed to build a modern works, to produce a needed article in right quantity in the right place without costing the taxpayer a penny, it is allowed to be torpedoed."

Major Hills might really have added that far from costing the taxpayer a penny, the cost of armaments with steel at so reduced a price would have saved him a considerable bill, to say nothing of the vast saving in the cost of keeping men in idleness.

Commenting on the appointment of the Inquiry, the Commissioner for the Special Areas wrote:

> "It is difficult to see how this belated action can bring any hope to Jarrow. What appears to have happened is that, owing to much delay in settling

the policy to be pursued, and to lack of co-operation, opportunity has been lost to improve the future position of the industry by the erection of steelworks offering the advantages of reduced manufacturing costs and favourable facilities for distribution – conditions which are essential to the improvement of the country's capacity for meeting foreign competition and reducing the price to the consumer at home."

One further quotation from *The Times,* from Mr. H. Arnold Forster, a pillar of orthodoxy and supporter of the Government who had been in the negotiations from their early stages, though never himself financially interested in them. He wrote (July 6, 1936):

"A system which permits the adjudication as a proposal of admittedly national importance being delayed for more than a year, and permits such adjudication to be left in the hands of parties whose financial interests may run counter to that project, is not conducive to the enterprising development of the steel industry."

The Jarrow Steelworks was dead ... strangled at birth. Attempts have been made to minimize this as an isolated incident ... worked up to far beyond its real significance by sentimentalists about the Distressed Areas and interested politicians. "You can't run a steelworks as a charitable concern to relieve distress" is the kind of sneer that has been frequently used in arguments about Jarrow. Malcolm Stewart is neither a propagandist nor a sentimentalist. He has expressed his opinion – the opinion of a business man – very clearly and very decisively.

"The establishment of more economic manufacturing conditions in the future", he wrote, "has been sacrificed to procure profits made available by the present good demand influenced by the granting of a materially increased tariff in imported steel and by the defence programme. ... The advantages accruing from tariffs should be utilized to promote efficiency and ability to meet foreign competition and not merely as a temporary shelter for making increased profits."

But the killing of this new steel plant was not an isolated incident. It is part of the deliberate policy of the Federation to prevent these new integrated plants, with the latest technical devices for reducing costs of production, being set up to compete with the old plants. Not only when the projects are put forward by newcomers to the British steel industry like Vosper Salt and Lord Aberdare, but even when they are promoted by such well-known and experienced members of the Federation itself, as Sir William Firth of Richard Thomas and Co., the restrictions are applied.

The story of the Ebbw Vale Works bears an instructive resemblance to Jarrow's. Firth conceived the idea of a new fully-integrated plant which he proposed to erect in Lincolnshire to be near the beds of cheap ore from which the basic bessemer process makes steel at a lower cost than the open-hearth, which needs the better-quality ore. Every kind of obstacle was placed in his way ... to be just, not only by the Federation. There was considerable pressure brought to bear on him to use the Ebbw Vale site to keep the works in a distressed area ... a point worth noting in view of the sneers against the Jarrow Works as being "a charitable steelworks" made by the same Cabinet Ministers who urged Firth to remain in South Wales. The delay brought the construction of Ebbw Vale also into the period of rising construction prices. This and the difficulties of the new site made it necessary to raise more capital than the original project needed.

When Firth went to the market for additional capital he found that, wherever he turned, the sources were blocked. Opposition from established firms was sufficient to stop financial houses supporting him. Capital was available, on terms, and eventually these terms had to be accepted. The Bank of England undertook to see that the money was raised, but the directors of Richard Thomas, Ltd., had to accept a controlling committee, the chairman of which was Mr. Montagu Norman. It included a representative of established firms. By such a committee control is maintained over the production and prices of goods from Ebbw Vale. Established interests, by imposing price limits on the new firm, and by restricting its production, can safeguard their own position.

Capitalists protect themselves when an industry is modernized by ensuring such control of it as will prevent their particular product being undersold. They safeguard their own profits, and in so doing prevent the full advantages being derived from improved techniques. It is of little advantage to be able to produce steel 15s. a ton cheaper than existing plants if that 15s. has to be paid over to one's competitors. Capitalism saves its own profits at the expense of industrial progress. But while it seeks compensation for itself no concern is expressed for the workers who are displaced when the new rationalized plant goes into operation. In South Wales some 8000 workers will be displaced when the new Ebbw Vale plant is working to the full. There is no compensation for them. Similarly in North Wales there is anxiety that the modernization of the steel plant of John Summers, Ltd. – another scheme backed by Montagu Norman – will throw 1500 men idle. Capitalists arrange compensation to their own kind, but the workers are left to idleness and the allowances of the U.A.B.

It may thus be argued, as Dorman Long's did in fact argue, that it would do no good to employment in Tees-side to have the new works at Jarrow. The comment on that is supplied by the facts. At the time when the Jarrow Works, had it been started when first projected, would have been coming into production, the demand for steel was such that the Federation was forced to increase the quota of imports from abroad to about the same amount as what Jarrow could have produced. Yet at that time, the Jarrow men were still idle or tramping round the countryside desperately looking for work. We had to pay higher to the foreign firms to increase their quota and £386,000 a year was being paid into Jarrow as unemployment and public assistance doles to keep the men and their families alive. In addition to the skilled workers, there would have been all this time the vast amount of unskilled labour needed for the clearing of the site and the construction of the works, which in itself would have paid wages that would have gone to increase demand in the consumption industries.

It is urged that the improved technical processes, while undoubtedly cheapening steel production, needed less men than the processes they would displace. But here was a new market. While the rearmament orders were available there was a new demand. In addition, the cheaper process would in itself have improved our industrial position. Every steel-consuming industry is today complaining bitterly of the handicap caused in its export trade by the high price of British steel, which is all it is allowed to buy under the Cartel arrangements. The high cost of steel for shipping has helped to drive British orders for ships abroad, as has been noted in the shipping chapter. The worst of the position has been covered by the rearmament orders and the fact that so many firms are working to capacity on Government orders that they have no time or desire to look for orders abroad. But when the rearmament orders are over, what then? True, strides have been made in bringing up-to-date existing plants, but the armament boom only covers for the time being the fact that they are in uneconomical sites and cannot be properly planned as a new works would be. It is when these old plants, albeit reconstructed, have to compete with the new integrated plants in Europe that the draught will be felt to the full. The Steel Cartel may be some protection ... at the expense of the British steel consumer ... but it is not likely to be the main purpose of an international Cartel to keep the worst of the world's winds from British steel concerns.

The story of Jarrow, and the attitude of the Iron and Steel Federation, is a vivid illustration of the obstacles put in the way of technical progress by modern monopoly capitalism when it can secure a complacent government to provide the necessary legislative conditions for a closed market at the expense of the taxpayer. The money which has been wasted because of the steel monopoly could have given this country a highly integrated, new steel industry, able to produce at far lower than present costs. Money thus saved could have provided for the displaced workers ... not the semistarvation standard of the "dole", but at proper maintenance rates. It could have met the demand for highly skilled workers by giving the younger men the best technical training at special schools, and provided the older men with pensions on which they could live decently. But to the banks the all-important consideration has been to ensure that the existing firms be given a monopoly, at the taxpayers' and steel-users' expense, and thus be able to pay back moneys advanced on plants that have become obsolete. It is one of the joys of our private banking system that modern progress should be starved to pay interest on old debts. One cannot blame capitalists for behaving like capitalists ... but such actions provide the overwhelming reasons for getting rid of the system which is strangling the older industrial countries. It is important to note just what is the effect of such actions in terms of human life and misery, for on that a policy to deal adequately with the situation must be based.

CHAPTER TWELVE
Jarrow Marches

JARROW HAS many visitors. Journalists from all over the world come there as to the classic town of unemployment in England. It has a way of impressing itself in odd dramatic flashes. My first visit remains a vivid memory. I went to help in the election of 1922, when my colleague in the National Union of Distributive and Allied Workers, Mr. R. J. Wilson, was the Labour candidate. There was a great meeting in the old theatre in the centre of Jarrow, now completely derelict and unused. Row after row of men, densely packed, mostly unemployed. Not all, for at that time Palmer's Yard, though doing as badly as all the other firms on the river, seemed an eternal part of the town. There was a feeling of "kick" in that audience. "There are possibilities of backfire here", I remarked to one of the Boiler Makers' Union officials on the platform with me. "Well, don't start one", he replied warningly. "There's always the possibility of trouble at Jarrow."

Immersed in the problems of my own constituency of Middlesbrough, I did not return to Jarrow, except for an occasional meeting, until 1932, when, after my defeat in 1931, I was selected as Labour candidate for Jarrow. Mr. Wilson, who had been defeated by a local conservative in the 1931 election, retired on account of age.

At Middlesbrough I had thought that I had known what poverty could mean. But in that town some industry was going on, some people had work. Compared to Jarrow, things on Tees-side were moving. Jarrow in that year, 1932-33, was utterly stagnant. There was no work. No one had a job, except a few railwaymen, officials, the workers in the co-operative stores, and the few clerks and craftsmen who went out of the town to their jobs each day. The unemployment rate was over 80 per cent. "Six thousand are on the dole, and 23,000 on relief out of a total population of 35,000, was the estimate given at the time by the Medical Officer of Health.

Yet even then, ten years after that meeting in the old theatre, I sensed again that atmosphere of "kick". When a whole town or a whole area is unemployed together, especially if it is dominated by one industry, the unemployed are not isolated, separated from their natural leaders. If only some industry is working, it is generally the most skilled, the most self-confident, the most ambitious who can get what is going. When all is closed down, the highly skilled man, the ambitious young foreman, the keenest trade-unionists provide the leadership for the unemployed. When industry revives, these leaders are taken first. It is then that the remaining unemployed have the most difficult time.

In 1932, here was a mass of over 6,000 unemployed men with their natural leaders in among them. Alfred Rennie, one of the finest types of Tyneside skilled men, now the Mayor of the town, young, strong, solid; George Rose a similar type, David Riley, J. R. Drummond, now a trade-union organizer, and a dozen other such men who since have run the town as leaders of the Labour majority were then in the unemployed queue ... and fine use they made of their enforced leisure. Rose ran a Labour College class which he tried to keep down to 100 members. But 300 men would jam themselves into the room to listen to the lectures. Drummond was running the unemployed organization, Rennie and Riley the Labour Party. The town was down and out. The shops were closing one by one. But the old Labour rooms, nearly falling round our heads, were the centre of a vivid, intense communal life, which no social service organization or welfare worker can ever arouse ... or for that matter understand its passionate independence.

When George Buchanan, fighting in the House of Commons against dividing the unemployed into two sections under different parts of new Insurance Act said, "Leave us at least the comradeship of the unemployed queue. Don't drive a division between us there", he was voicing a desperate need of the men.

The Trades Union Congress, when mass unemployment started in 1921, took the view that the best organization to look after an unemployed man was the Union to which he had belonged when in work. They urged the Unions to provide for this. Some Unions did so at once with a special 1*d*. per week contribution. But there is also a horizontal solidarity among the unemployed. A man may have been a carpenter or a bricklayer. But out of work the Ministry of Labour becomes his "boss", against whom a mass struggle of a political nature has to be waged to get justice. Because the T.U.C. preferred not to set up this mass organization catering for the mass needs of the unemployed, it was only natural that some such organization should grow. ... The National Unemployed Workers' Organization which developed soon came under the ban against the Communists, who only dominated the organization in those areas where no one else was doing the job. When the local Labour Party or Trades and Labour Council took on the work, as at Jarrow, an effective local organization was developed, effective because it had the power of the whole local movement behind it.

To any visiting Continental trade-unionist Jarrow in those days would have seemed classic ground for a big Communist Party. If not Jarrow, then where?

There was a spot of trouble, because the local Labour agent was so antagonistic to them. After he had left, things settled down comfortably. The Communist Party secretary once told me that he had seven members, five of whom also held cards in the Labour Party. No one bothered much about that. The Jarrow Labour Party has on occasion duly passed resolutions in favour of the United Front, but it has never been a burning issue locally, largely because the local Labour Party has always taken the lead in the streets, as well as in the day-to-day work of a political party. It welcomed anyone who came along, provided they would settle down to hard work with the rest of us. Quarrels, deep and bitter, there have been, but these have been the inevitable clash of strong personalities in a small town, rather than due to any serious differences of opinion.

A real figure in Jarrow politics, then as now, is a frail looking, sensitive man, a highly-skilled carpenter, J. W. Thompson, who became the first Labour Mayor of Jarrow in 1935. He had had to leave Palmer's after the great woodworkers' strike in 1921. He got work in Newcastle, but fortunately did not leave the town. Deeply religious, as fastidious in person as in life, his socialism mingled with his religion, and he has spent himself in the service of the workers of Jarrow.

We were walking back to the Labour Rooms in early January 1934, oppressed with this terrible problem of Jarrow's unemployment. Buying an evening paper, we read that Mr. Ramsay Macdonald, then Prime Minister of the National Government, who was about to visit his Seaham constituency, had refused to meet a deputation of Government M.P.s on Tyneside (there were no others then) who wished to put before him the plight of the area. "I wonder if we could persuade him to meet a deputation from Jarrow", Thompson said thoughtfully. "He *will* see us ... he must," I replied, for to me it seemed impossible that the man with whom I had worked since I first joined the socialist movement until that dreadful betrayal in 1931, could refuse to see me if I stood on his doorstep.

So, instead of asking first, we decided on a mass deputation. On a January Saturday, when it was blowing a gale, a crowd from the whole constituency, Hebburn and Felling as well as Jarrow, assembled. To walk all the way in face of that driving rain would have been impossible. We counted our resources and decided to take all those we could raise the money for, a few miles by train, and walk the rest. We managed to get the fares for 300 people, and the others accompanied us on foot for the first part of the Journey.

From the train, we had a walk of nine miles in face of the gale, mostly uphill. Some of the marchers were real "mothers in Israel", those indomitable middle-aged women who are the backbone of all the local Labour Parties. For me there was the anxiety ... would it be in vain? Would the door be kept shut in our faces? There were enough police and detectives to have kept us in check if we had been bandits ... but all was orderly and the police were helpful.

A mile down the road, William Barkley of the *Express* and Ernest Hunter of the *Herald* came to greet us. "We hear he is going to see you", they said. At the house of Dr. Grant, where the Premier was staying, eight of the leaders and myself were invited in. Tea was offered, but we felt that we could not accept that until the tired men and women outside could be fed.

Mr. Macdonald came into the room ... the first time we had met since the election. It was always difficult to resist Macdonald when he himself had determined to be charming. Our backbones were like ramrods when he entered, but soon he had us sitting in chairs round the fire, listening to us attentively as we told the pathetic tale of the woes of Jarrow. Two of the women in particular were most moving as they told him of the difficulties of trying to bring up a family on the dole.

I tried to be hard, unimpressed ... to remember what this man had done to the movement that alone could help these men and women. But the whole atmosphere under J. R. M.'s skilful handling became like one of those "socialist firesides" which had formed the perorations of his best speeches in times past. He asked us for a special written report, promised special consideration. Jarrow would be kept in his mind, he said, and the memory of this talk round the fireside on the hill.

We stood to take our leave. Mr. Macdonald put his hand on my shoulder. "Ellen, why don't you go out and preach socialism, which is the only remedy for all this?" Which priceless remark from the Premier of a predominantly Conservative Government jerked me back to reality ... the sham, by the soft firelight, of that warm but oh so easy sympathy.

When we got back to where the blessed women of Seaham Harbour Labour Party had provided hot tea and pies for the marchers, the pressmen came in for a story. Bill Barkley's roar of cynical laughter when I reported the Macdonald remark was a heartless but probably fitting comment. Yet I am sure that at that moment Macdonald was as sincere as he had ever been. The tragedy was that he knew the real cure for the evils of which we told him ... but had run away at the moment of the trial that he had himself forecast so accurately years before.

What good do such marches do? Are they just stunts for politicians exploiting, the miseries of the unemployed? The men and women who had been on that march realized its value. The Premier had met them when he had refused everyone else. It gave them some hope to carry on the struggle ... which is so difficult to do when there is never any success, when no one ever seems to take any notice. The great publicity given even in the national press to the event, brought the plight of Jarrow to public notice. Jarrow began to be "news". People who sneer at such things as trifles have no idea of the awful sense of helplessness that comes in the narrow streets when weeks and months of unemployment stretch into years. If only something is being *done* about it ... somehow it helps to keep the spirit of men alive.

English men and women differ from French and Germans, and for that matter from Scotch and Welsh, in that they hate going on to the streets. Marching to a demonstration in some square or park of their town is about as much as the most enthusiastic among them can be persuaded to do. Even for a May Day procession, or a strike, they prefer to watch the other fellows from the pavement, and then rather shamefacedly push along to the meeting with them. The English worker dreads even feeling that he may possibly be looking a fool in the eyes of his neighbour. Not that he has much fear of the boss, if he has one, seeing him. His real fear is the chaff of the man next door.

Refugees from socialist movements on the Continent have commented on the smallness of even our largest English demonstrations compared to those they used to have. But when the Englishman turns out in any sort of numbers for a march, it means that individually he is roused. Otherwise the most persuasive organizer agitates in vain.

In the months that followed the march to Easington, things in Jarrow got steadily blacker. The unemployment and relief figures were only altered by the numbers who left the town, and by a few of the most skilled workers who got work along the river. The final closing of Palmer's by National Shipbuilders' Security, Ltd., came as a terrible shock. Deputation after deputation from the town and from Tyneside went to see Mr. Walter Runciman, the President of the Board of Trade, himself a member of a great ship-owning family. The local Council sent several. The business men of Jarrow sent a very impressive and representative delegation, without even a shade of pink among them. Tyneside boroughs struggling with their own terrible problems lent a hand, for they too were menaced by N.S.S., Ltd.

These deputations met a figure of ice. Icily correct, icily polite, apparently completely indifferent to the woes of others, Runciman as a minister in each office he held was one of England's minor disasters. For him, nothing can ever be done about anything. Nothing but the worst can be expected to happen. As a personality he is sunk in the negative. After my experiences with him, I understood during the Sudeten negotiations just what the Czech ministers would be going through ... and how constitutionally susceptible Lord Runciman, as he had become, would be to his German hosts at the weekends, who would have the easiest possible task in persuading him that the only thing for Britain to do in any circumstances was just precisely nothing at all.

Then came the crash of the steelworks' scheme; the realization that the Government were backing the steel combine, and that Walter Runciman would "do nothing" to prevent the steel masters from strangling the Jarrow scheme at birth. To the Town Council deputation which met him at the moment when the Cartel proposals were being forced through the House of Commons by the Government, in the teeth of protest from some of their leading supporters, Mr. Runciman coldly told them that the Government could do nothing for Jarrow. "Jarrow," he said, "must work out its own salvation."

That phrase kindled the town. All the respectable deputations had got nowhere. At a great demonstration of the unemployed, Councillor David Riley, as chairman, suggested that the unemployed of Jarrow should march to London, and tell the people of England on their way down of the treatment they had received. That was in July 1936.

The unemployed were enthusiastic, but enough cold water was immediately thrown on the scheme to smother the flame if enthusiasm alone had kindled it. David Riley was determined the march should go through. A big man physically, Irish by descent, given to strong enthusiasms, he showed those unexpected gifts of political organization which the Irish have in a special degree for any cause they really care about. Riley talked the matter over with the Jarrow Labour Party Executive and myself. Labour had just won its majority on the Town Council. The Mayor decided that if there were to be a march it must be a town's march, with the backing of the whole of the citizens ... from Bishop to business man.

That was ambitious, for class distinctions are pretty tight in Jarrow. But it was this idea which more than anything gave the march its kudos. Hunger marches of desperate men from the distressed areas there had been in plenty. The comfortable had dismissed these efforts as "Communist demonstrations", as though that accounted for everything. But the fact that the Town Council sanctioned the march, practically unanimously, meant that appeals for support sent out over the signature of the Mayor. When the time table had been worked out, the letters asking for the use of halls and services were sent to the towns on the way, not by a March Committee but on official Borough notepaper over the signature of the Town Clerk.

The correctitude of municipal service stood the strain of the unusual. Those letters were duly placed before the proper committees, and the requisite arrangements were duly made. The organization of the march was done from the Jarrow Town Hall, supervised by the Town Clerk, and all in a manner to stand the scrutiny of any auditor.

It was decided that the marchers should arrive in London for the opening of the new session of Parliament; that a petition signed by as many citizens of Jarrow as possible should be prepared; and that it should be carried by the marchers on the way, being handed to the Chief Magistrate of each town in which the marchers halted for the night for his safe keeping. Not Parliament alone was the object of the march … but the rousing of public opinion in England to the plight of Jarrow, and the forgotten areas like it. To do this effectively, it was decided that a public meeting should be held each night … which added to the problems of the organizers and considerably to the strain on the leaders of the march. We did not realize as we enthusiastically planned all this, what it was going to mean to march all day, get the men fed and installed for the night, and then take a huge public meeting each evening.

Tyneside helped us magnificently. Newcastle had a Labour Mayor that year, the fine old veteran Alderman W. Locke. He presided over a conference of all the Tyneside local authorities, which agreed to launch a petition to support not the march, but the town's demand for work. "We intend to make the Government sit up and take notice," he said. "Jarrow's troubles are our troubles. The promises to set up a new steel industry in the town have come to nothing … not because the promoters were not prepared to carry out their promises but because they have been hindered."

A large number of men volunteered to go, but we could not take an army. Finally 200 men were selected, everyone of them vetted by the borough medical officer, Dr. Dormer. There was so much disappointment among the men not selected that it was agreed to have a list of "possibles" to take the place of any who might be unable to go at the last moment. A man of sixty pleaded with me to be put on the first list. He wrote:

"I have suffered hardships for years. Rain and cold and wind on the way will mean nothing to me after that. I have suffered all that a man may suffer. Nothing that can happen on the road between here and London can be worse."

His tall thin figure and fine eyes remained in my memory. Before we returned from the march he had died.

Funds did not allow us to buy any clothes for the men ... but they are all expert at mending their own boots, so the committee provided leather and nails. A waterproof groundsheet that would also serve as a cape was issued to each man. Field kitchen equipment was lent by the Boy Scouts, and the committee decided to buy a second-hand 'bus to carry the men's kit and blankets, and the cooking apparatus. On the day the march started, the funds which Councillor Riley and the Mayor had raised by their appeals amounted to about £4 per head, about £800 in all. One pound per head had to be saved for the return journey by train, another £1 represented the overheads, including the 'bus. More money came in as the march proceeded, but to set off for a month's march to London on a basis of £2 per head needed a lot of faith as well as organization. But it was a good deal more than the marchers from Scotland and the other areas ever had.

Prayers were said for the marchers that Sunday of October 4, 1936, in every church and chapel in Jarrow. On Monday morning the men lined up for a final review by the Mayor outside the Town Hall. The men had done their best to look smart on the little they had. Faces carefully shaved ... but so thin. Broken boots mended and polished. Shabby clothes brushed and mended by their wives. The waterproof cape rolled over the shoulder bandolier fashion. We marched to Christ Church for a short service, which the men's wives and the Mayor and Corporation attended. The words of that grave and saintly man, Bishop Gordon of Jarrow, as he pronounced the blessing and bade us Godspeed gave to the men and their wives a sense of high purpose in their Crusade.

I still find it hard to forgive the vindictive action of Hensley Henson, Bishop of Durham, who wrote a letter to *The Times* denouncing our quiet and constitutional march as "revolutionary mob pressure". Harder still to forgive him for the difficulties he must have made for Bishop Gordon. That kindly man who had spoken to us so movingly in church had to write to the papers saying that he had only blessed the marchers "because the Chief Magistrate had asked him to do so". I blamed Bishop Gordon for his recantation in an article I wrote at the time. But when the march was all over, I received from him a beautiful letter, from which I could guess the difficulties he had had to face.

Odd how tradition lingers on ... how social strata run true to type. There were the Jarrow men ... in the tradition of the strikers of the 1840s and the Nine-Hour-Day men of the 'seventies ... they stretched behind us in the long struggle of the workers of the North for tolerable conditions of life.

And there was the Bishop of Durham in 1936 acting in much the same spirit as his predecessor in 1810 who had lent his stables for a concentration camp for striking miners, where they were chained to the mangers. When the class struggle comes to the surface, "progress" is seen to be a very thin veneer.

Quite independently of our march, unemployed from Scotland, Wales, Cumberland, Durham and Yorkshire were marching to London to expose their grievances against the Means Test and the U.A.B. regulations. Our men had received so much press publicity that I thought they might go rather "prima donna" about these other marchers, and treat them as rivals. That thought never seemed to enter their heads. To them, these other marchers were a welcome sign that other men felt the same as they did, and were kicking, too.

The Jarrow march was kept irreproachably "nonpolitical" by David Riley, whose powerful frame marched at the head of our column. In a lounge suit and a bowler hat that became famous, Riley was the complete expression of the civilian ... the citizen who puts on his hat and goes determinedly to London to tell Government and Parliament what he thinks about them. Councillor Paddy Scullion, an unemployed bricklayer, young, good-looking, and with a great gift of emotional oratory, and Councillor Symonds, dark, thin, consumptive, were with Riley in charge of the administration of the march. The Mayor and other councillors representing all the parties joined us when they could. With a certain humour, the March Committee had sent ahead as our advance agents the two political agents for the division, Councillor Suddick, the Conservative, and Harry Stoddart, the Labour agent.

Definitely this was where the Jarrow march departed from all tradition. But the idea worked wonderfully. The two agents, presenting credentials from their respective parties, induced mildly mystified chairmen of Conservative associations to join with Labour Party chairmen, slightly worried about Transport House bans, to bring along their respective Mayors to welcome us as Crusaders ... a blessed word that got us out of the poor law whenever there was anything else available. When either political party took us in hand we got by far the best treatment. I found out what a difference a white table-cloth and a paper serviette can make to one's outlook on life.

Because I wrote it on the march, while the events were hot in my mind, I quote from *Time and Tide*:

> "Sometimes we came in from the dark road to beautifully set tables, napery and crockery and bright lights. Immediately the men smartened up. Where it was not possible for them to wash before tea, they

surreptitiously combed tousled hair and rubbed soiled fingers on their handkerchiefs. But in those towns ... mercifully few ... where the tables were bare boards, and tea was poured from buckets into our own mugs, the men who had appeared so smart and alert at the well-set tables, suddenly looked 'poor-law,' and just as grubby as their angry M.P. who still had to smile and return thanks for the bread and marge as politely as she had done for the hot pies."

The March Committee had realized from the first the possibilities of strain on men who had been underfed. The Inter-Hospital Socialist Society came to our rescue. At their own suggestion, they supplied relays of two students a week, with a car and medical equipment. Dr. David Cargill and his colleagues improvised a clinic in a corner of whatever chapel, or drill hall, or casual ward the men were to sleep in. Often they shared the hard boards with them. These medical students soon diagnosed the complaints that ill-fed and wrongly fed men had been suffering from for years. They begged free dentistry en route for men with neglected mouths. They persuaded specialists in towns through which we passed to give unusual help in urgent cases, such as the removal of infected tonsils. They got men into hospital, and all but one rejoined the march within a few days. The blisters from which we all suffered at the beginning received such care that after a week we were all marching with hardened healthy feet.

What a blessing this medical care was I only understood to the full when, the Jarrow men having returned home, I went to help the men who had marched from Durham without such skilled assistance. I had to cut socks that had become embedded in broken blisters, and bandage the feet of men who must have walked in agony. Yet these men too had kept the road, and were not far behind our time schedule.

The effect of a whole month of such regular and devoted attention from the St. Thomas' doctors, medical care of a kind they could never get normally, with three meals a day, and steady exercise in the open air, improved the men's physique noticeably. "The fine thing is knowing when we get up in the morning there's something worthwhile to do," was a frequent comment of the men when asked how they felt. When we had taken all this care, it was a little hard to be lectured by the Press for "exposing the miseries of the men on the road", especially as these comments were in newspapers that had never so much as mentioned the hunger and misery of these men when they stayed quietly at home. Hardest of all, to be denounced from the platform of the Labour Party Conference for "sending hungry and ill-clad men across the country on a march to London" when we knew with what high hopes and in what good spirits the men were marching. It was a queer experience, that Labour Party Conference in Edinburgh, 1936 ... the last conference, fortunately, under an Executive every member of which was chosen by the block vote. Having got the men well started on their road, I dashed to Edinburgh for a couple of days for the unemployment and distressed-areas debates. Not so much because of the Jarrow march ... I thought that we were so guaranteed 100 per cent respectable. With the blessing of bishop, priests and clergy, subscriptions from business men, the paternal interest of the Rotary Club and the unanimous vote of the Town Council, could anything have been more constitutional? But I wanted to put in a word for the other marchers as well as get the general backing of the movement for our protest. I went from the warm comradeship of the road to an atmosphere of official disapproval. The Trades Union Congress had frowned on the marches, and the Labour Party Executive followed the lead. No one could say that the Jarrow march was "Communist-inspired", but indubitably there were two Communists in our ranks as there were several firm Tories. I expressed to the conference the pious hope that when certain eminent Labour leaders arrived at the Pearly Gates, St. Peter would be able to give them a guarantee that there were no Communists inside. But whatever the official attitude, the warm sympathy and helpfulness of the delegates made up for it.

The Executive decided to have a commission of inquiry into the Special Areas ... though why the need for another commission when every pore of every unemployed man was indexed by this time, it is difficult to see. At that moment, in October 1936, the time was set for *action* regarding the distressed areas. Their neglect of this grim problem was the weak spot of the National Government. The Cabinet were pouring out gifts to their own class in the form of subsidies, tariffs and quotas, which were substantial presents to the big industrialists, as we have seen in the case of iron and steel. For the Special Areas just nothing had been done at all, except, of course, the inevitable commission. And the Special Areas were not isolated phenomena. At that time, 47 per cent of the industrial population of the country were living in the areas either scheduled as "distressed", or in places like Liverpool, South Lancashire and Tees-side, with such a high rate of unemployment, and therefore of municipal rates, that they were demanding to be so scheduled. In a fine speech to that conference, Barbara Gould, moving the official Executive resolution on malnutrition, said that "in the distressed areas, men and women are being destroyed body and soul. What experts would call malnutrition, you and I would call semi-starvation." And the Labour Executive proposed another commission!

It was in itself a very good commission. Dr. Hugh Dalton and Mrs. Gould did a fine piece of work, but it necessarily took a long time. By the time their complete report was ready, the opportunity for effective action had passed. Interest was being diverted to the temporary possibilities of employment contained in the rearmament programme. Had the Labour Party put its power behind the marchers, sent out the call for solidarity with them, then by the time these men had reached London ... not only from Jarrow but from all parts of the country, the support that would have been roused everywhere would have been enough to shake the complacency of the Baldwin Government. It might have shaken even more than complacency. The Labour Party, however, drew out, and the T.U.C. circularized the Trades Councils advising them against giving help. So in places like Chesterfield, where the Trades and Labour Council obeyed the circular, the Conservative Party weighed in with hot meals and a place to sleep. Mostly, of course, the comradeship of the trade unions and the Labour Movement was circular-proof on such an occasion ... and the warmth of their welcome remains as the finest memory of the march.

To be quite fair, there was a certain justification for the attitude of the General Council of the Trades Union Congress. If for every grievance, or because some set of people wanted to do a stunt, a march was started across England that could demand hospitality from the Labour movement in every town through which it passed, a situation might soon arise which would be intolerable. But as has been proved over and over again by events, English workers only go on to the roads at times of great misery and when intolerable conditions at home force them to do something drastic to call attention to their plight. Clearly every case should be judged on its merits. And that I was given to understand was what the T.U.C. circular really meant. But when Jarrow and South Wales ... fully guaranteed as official by their respective movements, claimed to be judged on their merits, the National Council of Labour took the view that if they gave countenance to one type of march they would have to do the same for all! It is rather trying to have two alternatives applied against one's efforts at the same time.

But it seems to me that from their own point of view the Labour leadership make a mistake in frowning on any unusual methods of stating the case of the victims of capitalism. Speeches are made so often that they make much less impression than some practical object lesson. A worker who has little to offer the movement except the skilled work of his hands delights to have the opportunity to lay that offering on the altar of the struggle. We marched into Leicester with the men's boots coming to pieces. There was no money for new ones. So, on their own initiative, the Co-operative

Society's boot repairers sat up all night, and worked without pay to repair the boots, the Society giving the necessary material. I was taken round at two o'clock in the morning to have a word with them and to thank them. The boot-repairing factory was eerie in the stormy October night. I only went in for a few moments, as we had to be away early on the march next morning, and after a day's marching and a big meeting, one wasn't feeling like making more speeches. But I came from that comradely atmosphere far less tired than I went in. There was such gay enthusiasm for this unusual bit of help, that it was great fun being among the men. One boot-repairer, pulling to pieces an appalling piece of footwear remarked, "It seems sort of queer doing your own job, just because you want to do it, and for something you want to help, instead of doing it because you'd starve if you didn't. I wonder if that's how the chaps in Russia feel about it, now they are running their own show."

This cannot be a day-to-day chronicle of the march. A few high spots stand out ... wealthy Harrogate where the Territorial officers looked after us ... Leeds where the chief newspaper proprietor gave us a meal the men still talk of ... and with free beer! Barnsley, where Joseph Jones the miner's leader and Mayor – how we blessed him! – had the municipal baths all heated ready for the men, and where I had the muscle-easing luxury of the women's municipal foam bath. Or the awful days like the twenty-mile stretch from Bedford to Luton when it rained solidly all day, and the wind drove the rain in our teeth. Except for the hospitality at the end of the day, one day's tramp was much like another. The one thing that mattered was the weather. The men were up at 6.30, the cooks having got up earlier to prepare breakfast. They had all slept together on the bare boards of a school or drill hall ... or if lucky on palliasses borrowed from somewhere. This was rare except in the casual wards. To keep spruce when men sleep in their clothes is difficult, but they managed it. Daily shaves were the order. Parade was at 8.45, with everything packed for the road. I joined them then, having taken whatever hospitality was offered the night before usually in the home of the secretary of the local Labour Party. The men had improvised a mouth-organ band. The journalists who accompanied us had subbed together and got a collection in their offices to buy some mouth organs, and we had expert players. We swung out of the town by 9, the 'bus having gone ahead. Most of the men had been in the army, so we marched by army rules, perfected as they have been through long years of experience ... fifty minutes to the hour and ten minutes rest. The field kitchen cooked us a midday meal when the weather let them. A fine day meant stew, tinned fruit, and hot tea ... and greatest of blessings a long stretch out for a sleep on the grass. On wet days, luck was out. We stood in the rain under mackintosh capes, eating sandwiches ... with always the blessing of hot strong sweet tea ... no room for individual fads about China tea and lemon! At night, there was always the big meeting. The men, of course, were excused attendance at this. The meetings, with very few exceptions, were always crowded. In one or two cases there hadn't been time for proper advertising, but the Press did their best for us ... and we learned to be very grateful for that steady support of union journalists everywhere. It makes such a difference if the ordinary decent reporter is with you, whatever his proprietor may think.

We had looked forward all the way to our march through London. In fancy, we had seen ourselves carrying our box with the petition inside it through sunlit streets and smiling citizens. Actually, rain soaked us through to the skin. The pressmen told us consolingly that we all looked so utterly shabby and weary in our wet clothes that we presented London with the picture of a walking distressed area. But their assurances of dramatic effectiveness were not as comforting as the hot meal provided by St. Peter's Kitchen, or the good supper which the co-operative workers of N.U.D.A.W. gave us, when we finally got to the L.C.C. Institution that night.

How to get Jarrow's case to London before Parliament opened? There seemed no time to organize a Hyde Park meeting. But we hastily got permission to hold one in the Park, and hoped for an audience from the crowds there. The Communist Party had gathered a big demonstration on a general unemployment protest. They generously gave way for an hour and asked their great audience to swell our Crusade meeting, which grew to enormous size when it was known that Jarrow Crusaders were there.

When Parliament re-assembled there were two petitions to be presented. The one, bound in the book we had carried across England, of nearly 12,000 signatures. The other, of 68,500 from the towns on Tyneside, presented by Sir Nicholas Grattan-Doyle, the senior member for Newcastle. The Jarrow petition stated that the town had been passing through a long period of industrial depression without parallel in its history ... its shipyards closed, its steelworks denied the right to re-open. Whereas formerly 8000 workers were employed, only 100 were now at work, and those on temporary schemes. "The town cannot be left derelict, and therefore your petitioners humbly pray that His Majesty's Government and this honourable House will realize the urgent need that work should be provided for the town without delay."

It was a tense moment. As many marchers as could be got in were packed in the galleries. The members, flooded with postcards and letters from their constituents, to whom we had appealed en route, were interested and sympathetic. But, of course, there could not be a debate. A few questions were asked by Mr. Lawson, Mr. Magnay and Mr. Chuter Ede, who had put them on the order paper previously ... and the House passed on to consideration of other things.

The men, who were entertained to tea in the House, were rather disappointed. They had imagined an imposing ceremony and a long discussion. But they were very sporting about it, as we explained that that was just how the most important petitions of the past had been presented to Parliament, and that the interest and value of the presentation was seen in the later debates on the subject, not at the actual moment.

The actual presentation at best could only be a gesture. What mattered more, in a practical sense, was the crowded meeting of members of all parties in the biggest committee room in the House of Commons to hear the Labour Mayor, Councillor Thompson, the Liberal ex-Mayor, Councillor Dodds, and the Town Clerk state the case about the shipyard and the steelworks. There was a dramatic moment when the Mayor held up his chain of office. "This chain," he said, "was given to the town by Sir Charles Mark Palmer. Its links form a cable, its badge is an anchor ... symbols in gold of the cables and anchors of the thousand ships we built at Jarrow. Now, owing to National Shipbuilders' Security, Ltd., the Jarrow shipyard is closed. Ships for Britain's food and her defence will be made in that famous yard no more. God grant the time may not come when you members of Parliament will have need to regret that you allowed the scrapping of this great national asset in the interest of the private profit of a bank's shareholders."

M.P.s were made distinctly uncomfortable. So much of a case is discounted when made in the House itself, because the speaker is Government or Opposition by definition. But when old and firm Government supporters like Sir Nicholas Grattan-Doyle and Councillor Dodds backed the case; when in coldly official terms the Town Clerk, in his wig and gown, gave figures and chapter and verse for everything that was said, even the oldest shell-backs began to feel that Jarrow had a case, and that some nasty work had been afoot.

The Press were able to dispel a little of this feeling of discomfort when at the marchers' meeting in the Memorial Hall, Sir John Jarvis announced further details of his scheme for a new tube works. The newspapers next morning gave the impression that a rich Santa Claus had suddenly appeared to solve all Jarrow's problems at one stroke. Sir John was rather hurt because neither the Labour Mayor nor the Jarrow members of his own party seemed very enthusiastic about such a speech made at such a moment, when we had got the attention of London, and when it really contained very little beyond what he had said already in the North. Some of the criticism of Sir John Jarvis has been perhaps unfair, but he has never understood the basis of the resentment he caused at such moments. He attributed to party feeling an irritation felt by members of all parties at the times he chose for the announcement of plans, which, when he announced them were not very near fulfilment, and which, in any case, were no substitute for what we were demanding from the Government.

These, shall we call them misunderstandings, are only of importance to a wider public than Jarrow, in so far as they form a continually recurring problem in all the distressed areas. Sir John Jarvis is the type of rich man who, with the very best of intentions, desires to be fairy-godfather to what he assumes to be a derelict town of down-and-outs.

In the case of Jarrow, he found a town of workmen accustomed to a high degree of trade-union organization, many of whom had been skilled craftsmen. They were used to organizing and managing their own affairs. Many of them were politically educated men, who through the long, bitter struggle knew who and what was their real enemy. They were not up against a Conservative Government just because it was not of their political colour. At least 30 per cent of the workers of Jarrow vote Conservative pretty steadily. But all of them had seen their industries closed down by one set of capitalists, a great new project blocked by another, with the open support of a Government that was subjecting them to all the barbarities of the Means Test.

They were determined to make the Government face up to its duty to Jarrow and to the distressed areas. The problem, as they saw it, was too big for private charity. Though any work that could be brought to the town by a private employer was welcome, and they were prepared to be grateful ... they were gravely concerned that such private activity should not be done in such a way as to give the Government the excuse they were looking for to get out of the awkward situation in which events like the Jarrow march and its nation-wide publicity had placed them.

The march had struck the imagination of the people of Jarrow. They gave the marchers a great welcome when we returned by train the day after the petition had been presented. Railwaymen had put fog signals on the rails. There were bonfires in the streets near the line. The whole town turned out for the greeting. There was great emotion in the town that night ... a feeling that at least some move had been made, that at least the marchers had told the world.

The struggle we had to capitalize that publicity into a steelworks at Jarrow is told in another chapter. The marchers had done their bit. After that, the fight had to be fought week in and week out in Parliament. Mr. Oliver Stanley became President of the Board of Trade. He, at least, was a human being instead of a block of ice. And after endless negotiations with Consett, we have got a new steelworks ... not the big, integrated plant of the Brassert scheme, but a steelworks with big possibilities of expansion is rising rapidly on the site of Palmer's Shipyard. Early this year I walked over the site, where gangs of men were busy on the concrete foundations of the new rolling mills. I stood by the big concrete mixer, which one of the men who had marched was looking after. A group nearby fixing wooden moulds looked up and greeted me with: "This is what we marched to London to get." They and the gangs of men digging near them felt a certain special satisfaction in digging those foundations, making the concrete and fixing it in place ... they had a sense of having a share in the new works.

And if I were "social service" instead of Socialist, it is on that note of triumph that I should close the chapter. But the grim thing is that the workers have no share in these mills. When the works are built they will still be subject to the toll of profit, the exigencies of a system where they can be closed at the will of people far away to suit a financial policy. People have said to me with a sneer ... "You can't have a steel mill for charity." That's true and we wouldn't want it. Plenty of charity has, in fact, been given to the steel industry, but it has not been the workers who have got the presents. Actually, the main hope of the new Jarrow steelworks is that not only have practical business men been concerned in it, though they have done their share, but that the men of Jarrow forced the Government to take some share in getting that steelworks going. They were rated by a bishop for their revolutionary intentions in just going to London to ask nicely for those works. The real revolution would be for the workers of Britain to insist on a properly planned steel industry for national needs, run in the interests of the community and not to suit the short-term interests of a set of finance-men.

CHAPTER THIRTEEN
The Town of Initials

IN JARROW most people live in a world of initials. Their lives are governed by symbols. They are expert in terms unintelligible to the outsider who has not known the "queue". A man who has been unemployed for years has to know the exact and subtle differences between U.I.B., U.A.B., P.A.C., G.T.C., L.T.C., I.C., J.I.C., and the rest. The Boards and the officials these letters represent govern every detail of his life. For the family on U.I.B. (Unemployment Insurance Benefit), life for the first twenty-six weeks is comparatively straightforward. Little as it is, at least the wife knows what is due each week and can make her arrangements accordingly. After these first six months, the difficulties of the Means Test begin.

Here is the case of F. C., a Jarrow shipyard riveter, a good worker and a real personality. He was in work down the Tyne last year. There are seven in the family, man, wife, boys aged nineteen, thirteen, eleven, and girls aged nine and five. Theirs is a good type of independent Tyneside household. The son of nineteen is working as a machinist at 50s. a week. The father gets 39s. unemployment benefit for himself and family. The U.I.B. is due to stop, and the family will come under the U.A.B. (Unemployment Assistance Board). The son is regarded as the breadwinner of the family. In future, therefore, his father will receive, not 39s. unemployment benefit but 8s. unemployment assistance.

This will mean that this family will automatically drop below the scale which, after paying for rent and for necessary household expenses, the British Medical Association considers is the barest minimum for physical health. Soon one or both of the growing lads, not getting enough to eat, will start feeling "poorly". The Government will have saved some shillings on that family for the time being, only to have to spend a good deal more later on to get the boys well again.

This family is one of the lucky ones. The father will be at work again, perhaps before the malnutrition of his family becomes serious. Jarrow is a town of big families ... though the birth rate is falling, it is still well above the national rate. Here is a Catholic family. The father, an intelligent man, takes a considerable interest in politics. There are eight children, the eldest a boy of fourteen, the youngest six months. The boy earns 9s. 8d. a week. The allowance under the Means Test is 45s. The only other help received is that the three children of school age get free meals and milk at the school canteen, having been certified as under-nourished. Owing to the large size of the family a rent of 16s. 6d. a week has to be paid. The "overcrowding officer" insisted on their removing from the old house, where they paid 8s. 10d., and of course they got some allowance for this. The man carefully made out his weekly budget for me.

	s.	d.
Rent	16	6
Coal	3	6
Light	2	0
Clubs (clothing) etc.	5	0
Insurance	2	0
Cheap rate dried milk for babies		6
£1	9	6

This leaves 25s. 3d. a week for food and such necessary expenses as cleaning materials, medicine, renewals, etc., for ten individuals. The school officer called attention to the state of the children's boots, so one week's rent had to be missed to pay for them. That was weeks ago, and the father is still trying to catch up on those arrears. Except for the free milk, the children get no fresh milk. Fruit or salad is never bought. The boy, Edward, working for too long hours in all sorts of weather, never has any of the protective foods. The staple diet is tea, bread, margarine, potatoes, cheap jam, with stew at weekends. The mother is always ailing, obviously taking less than her share, but is considered a "good manager who cooks when she can".

Another personal friend of mine in Jarrow gave me his story. (I quote such cases because they are far from being the worst … nor are they stories of the so-called "feckless", whom poverty and malnutrition, continued over a long period, has reduced to tired indifference.) A. K. was a hewer until Hebburn Colliery closed, when he got work at the Jarrow shipyard. He is forty-seven years old … which means sentence of economic death on Tyneside if you are once "out" at that age. He hates enforced idleness and is continually trying for work. He has three children, a boy aged sixteen getting 8s. a week "sick pay", a boy of fourteen, chronically rheumatic, and a child of eight. The wife is ailing and bloodless and gets 2s. 6d. a week extra sick allowance from the U.A.B. The eldest boy went to work as an errand lad at 6s. a week. He became ill simply because he was not getting enough food to stick the long hours and carry the weights required. The Unemployment Allowance of the family is 35s. 6d. Doctor's notes have to be sent in periodically for the mother and sick boys. What is really wrong with all of them is the effect of a long period of semi-starvation. The doctor says so. The 2s. 6d. extra allowance for the mother is conscientiously spent by the father in milk, eggs and two ounces of fresh butter for her each week. When it does what it is given for and improves the mother's health, then it will be stopped and cannot be given again until the doctor again has to say that the woman is suffering from malnutrition.

None of the "moral" reasons for poverty so complacently advanced by the comfortable as "causing poverty" apply in these cases. The men are intelligent citizens taking an interest in their town's affairs.

They add to the horrors of poverty the knowledge that if their children do not get protective foods and vitamins no amount of doctor's medicine will keep them well. As one of them remarked after we had discussed this aspect of his budget in detail: "If they are going to keep us poor, they ought to keep us ignorant. Perhaps it hurts less when you don't know."

The entire question of the Unemployment Assistance Board, and the administration of the Means Test in the distressed areas like Jarrow and South Wales, is one of the major social problems of our day. It needs much more thinking about, and less mere propaganda. As things are, we have the expansive Minister of Labour, Mr. Ernest Brown, in one of those goodwill speeches for which his pulpit training has so well fitted him, insisting that the basis of U.A.B. assessments is a "NEEDS test" not a MEANS test. After one of these perorations an audience who had no personal acquaintance with the system would think that the man on U.A.B. has only to go to his local office, point out that his family is in need of anything from a holiday to a garden roller, and, as from a beneficent Father Christmas, the need will be met.

To be fair, the U.A.B. is a considerable improvement on the old Poor Law. Its officers can take into account circumstances other than actual destitution. The family can be kept together and helped through a bad patch, instead of the old poor-law idea that the household must strip itself of everything before it can be considered sufficiently destitute to receive help. Apart from medical needs, which must be attended to by the Public Assistance Committee, there is almost nothing in reason, and in *theory*, which the U.A.B. officer cannot provide for a family or an individual on his books. To quote the Board's own report: "The basic principle of the Board's administration is to look at any household with which it is concerned as a group of persons with a history and a future and decide on exceptional needs accordingly."

This being the excellent principle, why then is the Means Test so bitterly resented, that in an area like Jarrow a local speaker has only to hiss out the words to rouse any working-class audience to the same fury which they would have shown at the mention of the Poor Law in pre-war days?

It is not the personnel that is resented ... at least not in Jarrow. Women have spoken to me with appreciation of the kindly understanding displayed by some of the Means Test officers. But in such a town, with its problems of longstanding unemployment, the Means Test and its horrible counterpart the "wages stop", work as a kind of double-acting hammer, by which if an unemployed family shows reason why it should not be driven down by one regulation, it is pushed back by another.

The original idea of the Household Means Test was to prevent the payment of benefit in those cases, greatly exaggerated in the House of Commons at the time, where the household income was so high that the family might reasonably be expected to look after an unemployed member. Immediately it led to far worse and more widespread abuse than its advocates had ever dared to suggest existed on the other side ... only, as these abuses were against the unemployed instead of against the fund, complaints went unheeded. A son saving to get married compelled to keep step-father and brothers; a sister, working as a skilled typist, made to keep a father and adult brothers, thus depriving her of the possibility of saving for old age, or getting the clothes and nourishment needed for her work. Families broken up through children leaving home either to qualify for benefit themselves or to make it possible for parents to receive assistance.

In a town like Jarrow, it has meant that the few who are working are compelled to bear a portion of the national burden of unemployment out of all proportion to their resources. The idea is that the son *ought* to bear such weight as his family duty. But this weight, as we have seen, is placed there to suit the convenience of the big business taxpayers, who thus thrust the consequences of their inefficiency not only on to communal shoulders, but vote to push it on to the frail resources of those still at work.

The excuse is usually made that the local officers of the Unemployment Assistance Board have "discretion" in such matters. This discretion is severely limited by the Board's own regulations. But in an area as wide as Jarrow and with so many unemployed the decision which involves the actual life and happiness of thousands of families should not be a matter of individual opinion. It is said that an official is not subject to local influences as would be a local committee. But an official has to live in the place ... the only difference is that the influences become hidden instead of public. And in practice, since staff is cut to the lowest in the interests of economy, the issue of health and life instead of dragging illness and malnutrition is more often settled according to the rough rules of arithmetic with an eye on the need for economy, than on that "basic principle" which sounds so well in the Board's own reports. It is true that every applicant has the right of appeal against the amount given him as an allowance, but very few know their rights unless they have someone to help them, and of course from the Board's point of view this immediately brings him under the local influences which are said to "poison the springs of good administration".

In the distressed areas particularly, the deterrent force of the regulations acts like a pall of crushing weight on all individual effort. Every penny that is earned, or that comes by any other means into a U.A.B. household, must be reported to the Means Test officer. The allowance is reduced in proportion. A portion of the earner's wage is allowed him in the Act itself. In some cases that I have had reported to me, where a son has got a rise in wages, an amount greater than the rise has actually been deducted. This leads to every kind of subterfuge. A daughter, already giving more of her wages to keep the unemployed members of her family than she thinks just, has an advance, say, of 2*s*. 6*d*. She says nothing about it at home, feeling that she is entitled to that much for herself. Her father does not know, but the employer is bound to report it to the U.A.B. office. The father is then put on the carpet, perhaps threatened with prosecution for not having told the officer. Already smarting with the indignity of being so largely dependent on his children when he is only too willing to work himself, the man goes home in anger ... a family row, and perhaps the girl leaves home.

If a worker loses all or most of anything extra he earns by such deductions, then all incentive to earn goes. We hear so much about the necessity of providing the capitalist with an "incentive" to go on making profit that it seems odd that the same order of society should be shocked because his "duty to his family" is insufficient incentive to a worker to put in extra effort in order to save a few shillings on the accounts of the Unemployment Assistance Board. A man whose duty it is to organize the sale of newspapers in Jarrow told me of the difficulty of getting lads whose families were on U.A.B. to go out in all weathers to sell the papers. "Why should they go out in the heavy rain to sell, they say to me, when the Means Test man takes practically all the difference?"

Now whatever may be said ... and I don't think there is much that can be ... for this procedure in areas where there is some work to be had, the effect in an area like Jarrow is psychological damnation. It reinforces all the tendencies there may be to sink down to whatever level of living is permitted by the officers of the various controls. Add this to the debilitating effects of malnutrition and the ennui of compulsory idleness ... and the result in individual lives can be devastating.

The wages stop is another device ... designed to save a shilling or two on a number of cases ... the effect of which is to crush all enterprise out of the men, apart from the serious results to the health of their families. The idea is that an unemployed man should not receive from the Board as much or more than he would receive at any employment he is likely to get. This cuts doubly hard in the distressed areas. In a place where work is fairly plentiful, trade-union wages are likely to be paid. In a badly distressed area, men have to take any job at practically any wages. If they don't they are cut off benefit. It is rather wonderful how the skilled and organized craft unions have managed to maintain their rates, but, generally speaking, a distressed area tends to be a low-wage area. Once a man, however skilled at his normal job, has accepted a wage lower than his former wage, then that becomes his "normal" rate, and when he is unemployed his allowance is reduced accordingly.

This produces curious results. People in Jarrow have complained to me that "with all the unemployed about you still can't get a man to do a few odd days' work". Let me give an actual case. W. E.'s wage when last in work was 52*s*. The U.A.B. assessment for himself and family was 45*s*. 6*d*. He was offered a temporary job as handyman by a local tradesman for £2 a week. The job lasted three weeks, which was, of course, not sufficient to bring him back to benefit. When he went back to claim U.A.B., he was assessed at *38s.*, because in the absence of "exceptional circumstances" his allowance must be less than his last wages ... and not only must actual earnings be considered, but the deductions for the insurance he would have paid had he been at work. The State gets the advantage of that ... which is as though the unemployed man was still paying health and unemployment insurance. But the man gets no corresponding advantage in benefit. So for three weeks work the man pays a permanent fine of 7*s*. 6*d*. a week, plus the loss of the 22*s*. 6*d*. for the three weeks actually worked. Then that Jarrow tradesman grumbled to me and said that men really don't want work when it is offered to them. What I find so odd is the moral indignation shown by the heads of the U.A.B. when employers put their side of the case. But in justice, I must say that I have never heard any local official defend this monstrous system.

The answer to "You can't pay a man more on relief than he could earn" surely is that no wages ought to be so scandalously low as the scales of relief which are calculated on the barest necessities of a life lived without strenuous work. It is urged that in exceptional circumstances, such as a large family, the Board allows its officers to waive the wages stop. But in practice this "stop" is pretty rigorously applied. Officers are directed "to look with special closeness at cases where allowances of 45s. or more would be payable". If the U.A.B. were considered as a social service rather than a means of screwing down allowances to save money by an elaborate espionage system on the individual worker, it would be possible to provide for the exceptionally large family, and have a statutory minimum wage enforced. But actually it is not only the large family which suffers from the wages stop. In the low-wage areas, like Jarrow, girls can be got to serve behind the counter for 6s. to 9s. a week. When they are unemployed they cannot then claim the 15s. which has been laid down as the U.A.B. rate for the single woman worker. By means of all these stops, and regulations and deductions, families and individuals are kept in that vicious circle of low-wage, lower allowances malnutrition, passing on to one or other of the deficiency diseases. There is no mystery about the high tuberculosis rate of Jarrow.

The special tragedy of Jarrow is that these men and their families are being punished for what everyone admits is not their own fault. The industry of the town was killed in the interests of one set of capitalists, its revival hindered to suit the pockets of another. Yet each man on U.A.B. or P.A.C. has to submit to the pressure of all the punitive clauses of the regulations as though it were in some way his fault that the works were closed down.

Much is said of what the State has done for the depressed areas. In detail these are all of them bribes to employers to start some work in a Special Area. For this the employer is offered land at very favourable terms. Factories are built for him, roads, power and other services provided. Assistance in raising capital is given, freedom from rates for a period, concessions on income tax. There is no Means Test for him, no inquiry as to whether the firm in question really needs this assistance from the public purse. When the employers were de-rated ... so that the flourishing industries of a town like Birmingham only pay altogether about a quarter of a million pounds in rates per year ... this was applied without any Means Test. Firms, like a flourishing gramophone company that was and is making fantastic profits, received the rates concession in exactly the same way as Palmer's Shipyard, then struggling to keep its head above water in a bad time. It is said that the cost of administration would be considerable ... but obviously it would be nothing like so great as the expensive apparatus of the U.A.B. which exists to save these few shillings per family which will have to be paid out over and over again in the attempt of the community to cure the ravages of disease and malnutrition which are the main results of this policy. For what this cheese-paring has meant in death and the manufacture of the unfit, the health statistics of towns like Jarrow show. It will be brought home to the nation more sharply now that compulsory military service is introduced. The rejections in the distressed areas will be an eye-opener. Already it is said that the medical standards for conscripts from the distressed areas have been lowered. The unemployment administration as a whole is beginning to take more interest in jobs likely to be available now that employers are complaining that they cannot get the type of men they want. During years while the young people ran wild, losing their normal period of apprenticeship and training, the Ministry's only remedy for Jarrow was to get as many of them as possible away from the town. Now there is a definite shortage of "improvers" and skilled workers on Tyneside, who might have been trained during these years of idleness ... a policy repeatedly urged upon the Government by those who knew the position in the area. Fantastic as it seems, firms have been bringing men up from the South, with all the difficulties that arise about accommodation and keeping two homes on one wage, while the Ministry has been paying considerable sums of money to pay fares and allowances to young men to go from Jarrow to the South to meet precisely the same difficulties there. The question of training has aroused a lot of prejudice among the unemployed because of the grudging way in which it has been done. The "dole school", as the Juvenile Instruction Centre is called, is disliked in Jarrow, not, as is often said, on " political" grounds, but because the boys feel that it is useless and that they are humiliated by going there. If they don't go they will get no unemployment benefit. Instead of this invaluable opportunity for a longer training and education being used to build up their morale and give them pride in themselves ... which a good type of higher elementary school like the Jarrow Central School does, the boys feel like "unwanted kids" ... as one of them described it to me. Periodic strikes, consequent punishment and a generally reduced morale is the result. No wonder there is a prejudice among Jarrow mothers against their boys going to the "dole school," in spite of the terribly hard work of an excellent "head", who himself once worked in Palmer's. Some of the boys take a pride in being "tough", pulling their caps down on one side in imitation of their favourite film gangster, and a cigarette-end picked up anywhere when they dare. That is a natural reaction ... just to show the kids going to the elementary school that they are men now. There is fine stuff among these adolescents. Once their interest is aroused they will work their heads off, as we find when we use them to deliver handbills for the

Labour Party, or similar jobs. But the school curriculum is designed to keep them under control with the least possible amount of expense ... and they react accordingly. The lot of the teachers is consequently a hard one, with unsuitable buildings, insufficient staff and very little equipment of any kind.

A number of young Jarrow men have gone to one or other of the centres set up by the Government. There has been a good deal of severe national criticism of these camps as "slave" camps, "concentration" camps and the like. I discussed their attitude in detail with some of the Jarrovians who had been there. Their case was a reasoned one ... certainly not wild and whirling propaganda.

They had few complaints about the food, which they dismissed non-committally as "better than we can get at home on the dole anyway". Nor did they allege any military discipline at Brandon, which was the camp to which they had been sent. But they said that they had not been taught anything. They were put on a different job each week, and as soon as they began to get interested in it were switched off to something else. The result, they said, was that it was no easier to get a job than it was before, and that on construction jobs and navvying there was a prejudice against them when it was known that they had been to a Government training camp.

The Local Training Centre at Low Fell and the Government Training Centre at Wallsend are more popular, because the men say "they teach you something". The difficulty about this kind of adult training is that it is of use only to unmarried men. After six months training, they cannot be considered "trained" as the unionized North understands it. All that can be hoped for, therefore, is a job as an improver in one of the Government-subsidized, largely unorganized factories of the South. This means leaving home, and it is not possible to keep a wife and children on an improver's wage. The trainees themselves have not complained to me about the union attitude. Those who come from trade-union homes understand fully that if the skilled and organized trades are swamped by semi-trained, or demi-semi-trained Government dilutees, all hope of preserving standard conditions built up after long years of trade-union effort would be at an end.

For a government that was serious about solving the varied problems of mass unemployment, Jarrow would have been a useful area to have tried out methods of dealing with some of these problems on intelligent lines. Instead, everything has been done on the most grudging and economical scale. The theory during the whole grim period has been that the cheapest (and therefore, of course, the best) method is to give the men just enough to exist themselves and keep their families alive, not even in good health, but just alive. The result is colossal waste ... waste of men, waste of intelligence, waste of physical strength, waste of invaluable national assets. ... England is beginning to discover her shortage now that she wants skilled men at her armament trades and strong men for her defence.

CHAPTER FOURTEEN

How Charity Helps

JARROW HAS had such nation-wide publicity as a distressed town that it has naturally attracted the attention of the charitable. Other needy areas have looked upon Jarrow with a feeling that its "publicity value" was attracting a disproportionate amount of assistance. There are towns and villages which have suffered as much as Jarrow and have had little publicity and scant assistance from outside sources. Because of this publicity it has often been assumed that Jarrow has received a much larger degree of assistance than most of the other distressed towns. That may be so. Here are the facts of the assistance which comes to Jarrow. I must say quite frankly that for much of this material I have had to rely on the facts as supplied to me by others. For it has been difficult for me, as a Labour M.P., to make the necessary contacts amongst the social-service workers ... and that, I think, is symptomatic of the attitude of the well-intentioned people who administer and run these charities locally, for the benefit of, but seldom by means of, the unemployed.

The present social-service movement is the outcome of an attack of conscience, or apprehension, among the more socially-minded of the well-to-do as the worst period of the last slump was ending. Before 1933 there was no club organization for the unemployed men except the one in the Labour Party rooms and one or two rooms in empty shops which the Town Council allowed for their use as rest rooms, and for playing indoor games. In that year Dr. Mess, then director of the Tyneside Council of Social Service, addressed the Westminster Ruri-Decanal Conference, as a result of which the meeting decided to provide £300 a year for three years (later extended to four) to found and maintain a club for the unemployed of Jarrow. The club was not put under the direction of the Tyneside Council of Social Service, but was "a gift from the Churches in Westminster to the Churches in Jarrow". An organizer, Mr. Lloyd Greening, was sent down by the Industrial Christian Fellowship to run the scheme. He took over a disused mill in Jarrow and within a few months he had the scheme running well. There were many difficulties, but he solved the greatest problem by his readiness to allow a committee of members to have a considerable say in the affairs of the club. The men felt comfortably at home there. There was none of the segregation between employed and unemployed which has been so bitterly commented on to me by the unemployed men in connection with the much-publicized Power House scheme at Hebburn. The membership has seldom fallen below 200 at a subscription of one penny per week. Over one thousand articles of furniture have been made by the members. On my visits there I have admired the elaborate wardrobes and sideboards and other pieces of furniture which they have made. For the twelve hundredth anniversary of the death of Bede the club members made a very fine altar-piece for the Old Church.

In 1937 the Westminster grant came to an end. Sir John Jarvis was approached in the hope that a grant for the club could be made from the Surrey Fund. But he replied that he saw no useful purpose in continuing the club. However, another patron has been found. Many of the Government Ministries have developed associations amongst their staff with the idea of helping the distressed areas. In Jarrow's case the staff of the Board of Admiralty have agreed to provide the Jarrow Club with £300 a year for an indefinite period. Under Mr. Greening's successor the club has now been affiliated to the Tyneside Council of Social Service. The principle of running the club by a committee of the men has been continued. Though the rooms are draughty and sketchily heated, the general view is that it is certainly one of the most vigorous unemployed centres of its kind on Tyneside.

Apart from this club there are other social-service movements in the town. During the worst of the depression there seems to have been little help from outside coming into Jarrow. There was a long time before the conscience of the comfortable middle class was sufficiently moved to do anything. The publication of the startling figures of the Bradbury tuberculosis report in the national Press, and the publicity resulting from such events as the march to Easington, drew public attention to the terrible rate of unemployment in Jarrow. In 1934 the staff of Carreras, the London tobacco firm, began to subscribe about £5 per week which was sent to the Mayor, Mr. R. J. Dodds, for the assistance of needy cases. Until his death Mr. Dodds administered this little fund at his own discretion, without any elaborate organization for the investigation of the circumstances of each applicant. After a lifetime among them he knew his Jarrow folk better than any investigator. This fund has naturally diminished with the passage of time and now Mr. Hervie Clerk, the well-loved young Rector of Jarrow, is chairman of the small responsible committee. All the various churches have their own charities, of course. There is a branch of the Personal Service League which distributes the supplies of second-hand clothing, mainly sent from the South. Now that the worst days of unemployment have passed there has been a sharp decline in the quantity of clothing sent up to Jarrow. Less than one-third the amount is sent up now.

Another social-service organization in Jarrow is a Welfare Committee. Actually this committee controls no funds. It has a group of investigators who consider any application which might be made for assistance, and after investigating the applicant's circumstances, refer him to the appropriate organization. A private organization, it offers advice only after an inquisition which the independent Northerners dislike.

In a different category to these small committees, and with far bigger resources, is the Surrey Scheme, started by Sir John Jarvis when he was High Sheriff of Surrey. Ably assisted by Mr. Chuter Ede, now Labour M.P. for South Shields, Sir John appealed for funds from the more prosperous county of Surrey to give assistance to Jarrow. As chairman of the Surrey Education Committee Mr. Chuter Ede was able to interest the schools, with the result that the children made contributions to the fund which finally amounted to about £40,000. The administration of this fund has been completely in the hands of Sir John Jarvis, whose leading idea was the excellent one of using the money to provide work of benefit to the town rather than individual charity. But the whole history of the fund in Jarrow illustrates the difficulties of private benevolence in dealing with so vast a problem. One purpose for which some of the money was used was to provide free material to enable the unemployed to redecorate their own houses. An approximate allowance of about 30s. per house was made for the cost of paper and paint. The unemployed men did the work themselves. But new paper and paint did not minimize the results of overcrowding in Jarrow, nor did redecoration do much to improve the health of those who lived in the defective houses which were so strongly criticized in the Bradbury Report. There was no doubt that the houses needed decorating. And the housewives were glad of the opportunity of having their houses cleaned. But money collected in Surrey for the benefit of the unemployed was thus actually used to subsidize the landlords. For it was their duty to keep their houses papered and painted.

Of more permanent value is the laying out of the Jarvis Park and sports stadium. Unemployed men were given work on the laying-out and making of this park. The Town Council purchased the ground and raised a loan of £3000 to provide the materials needed. From the Surrey Fund came the money to pay the wages for the men. Men were engaged for monthly spells, with the idea of spreading the four weeks work to as many men as possible. Relays of eighty men worked at one time. There was very little additional financial benefit for the men in the work. The difference between the allowance they got when unemployed and the wage they received for a week's work was less than 10*s.* per week, and in some cases was not 2*s.* 6*d.* per week. Even so, there was no hesitation on the part of the men in trying to get a month's work. It did give them a short spell away from the idleness of the dole.

Out of this earlier experiment of Sir John Jarvis with the money of the Surrey Fund came the realization that something more than charity was required. His subsequent efforts have been directed towards bringing commercial employment into Jarrow. The bringing of the *Olympic* and the *Berengaria* for shipbreaking, and to provide the steel for the tube works and the metal works do not in any way come under the heading of "social work". The advantage of Sir John Jarvis's work for Jarrow has been the sense of drive which he has given in his own strong personality and his emphasis on the need for new industries, rather than on the difficult and anomalous position in which he is frequently placed as the dispenser of large charitable funds in the town.

Many of the unemployed take advantage of the allotments which are made available to them by the local authority. The Council has endeavoured to see that allotments are available for all those who desire them. From an allotment a man can gain a useful supply of fresh vegetables and its cultivation helps to give an unemployed man a feeling of purpose which might otherwise be absent. The Commissioner for Special Areas has provided the money to equip one group of allotments with small greenhouses, to enable the men to cultivate a greater variety of produce. It is a wonder what the men have been able to do with their slender resources and the poor land, which, in some cases, is little better than a coal tip. Good use is being made of the scheme organized by the Society of Friends, which enables unemployed men to buy their seeds, tools, fertilizers, and other requisites at cheap prices.

It is regrettable that the young people in Jarrow are especially handicapped by the absence of suitable facilities for recreation. Early in 1937 a Juvenile Organization Committee was formed to deal with this problem and to co-ordinate the work of various youth organizations. By arrangement with the Town Council certain parts of the parks are available for football and cricket. A football league has been organized among the various youth associations, and attempts have been made to get a netball league for the girls. It is generally admitted that the girls have far less chance of healthy exercise than the boys. Most of them work in offices and shops. Many have to travel out of Jarrow to their jobs. As a result it is often quite late in the evening when they are free. To increase the facilities some sort of community centre is needed for the new housing estates. In view of the campaign for physical fitness this is the sort of facility which might well be encouraged by a grant from the National Fitness Council.

What is the reaction of the men of Jarrow to these various social services? Sometimes the impression has been given that the Jarrovian workers are an ungrateful set of people because they have not been more appreciative of what has been done for them. Such a misconception arises from a difference in viewpoint. The Jarrow men do not want charity. Those middle-aged and elderly men who can be seen walking the streets of Jarrow during the hours when their more fortunate fellows are at work, were, until Palmer's collapsed, efficient workmen, some of them highly skilled. The ships they built were amongst the best that sailed the seas. And, like all workmen, they are deeply conscious of the high tradition of good workmanship which they had established. Men with that record, and that ability, do not take easily to charity. They do not wish to answer a barrage of questions in order to obtain a new pair of blankets. They wish to live their own lives as independent units. All they want is the chance to work. As one of them said to me: "And as for being grateful for what is done for us – why should we be? We are willing to work for what we get." Personally, I think that such an attitude is healthy, and it is one which has my whole-hearted sympathy. These men have done nothing that they should go cap in hand to seek assistance. Their jobs have been taken from them as part of the price we pay for our outworn economic society. It is not for those who are comfortably well-to-do to expect obsequious gratitude from those who are paying the price of rationalization.

A number of the problems of social service arise from this feeling that the "unemployed" are a class apart to be assisted and provided for by various well-meaning people. When the widespread and severe effects of unemployment were eventually realized in the early years of the present decade the conscience of the country was affected. It became fashionable to "do something for the unemployed". Out of this feeling came the social-service movement as we now know it, with its clubs for the unemployed. The movement has been based on the idea of teaching the unemployed how to spend their leisure usefully. It has not been concerned with a frontal attack on the problem. By attempting to get the men interested in carpentry, in amateur dramatics, or in lecture courses little work of real value is achieved. For the social-service worker, in these circumstances, is working in very artificial conditions. Above all else the unemployed man wants a job. He wants his independence – he wants the right to earn his own living. And until he has the right it is impossible for him to join fully in the work of the community centres. Almost all of the problems which our social-service movement thinks that it is trying to deal with would disappear if an adequate wage level was substituted for the present unemployment allowance. A man without a job is no subject for experiments in social organization. It is this fact which has caused such a bitter reaction from some of the middle-class social-service workers. They approach the unemployed as benefactors and expect – sometimes not consciously – to be greeted as social saviours. The men do not want charity. They want jobs.

This position is made more difficult by the way in which some social-service centres have been set up. Insufficient attention has been paid to local connections. An organizer, to justify his job, decides that certain towns must have centres. Perhaps a few sympathizers are collected, premises are taken, and then the unemployed are invited to become members. Often a young University graduate arrives and commences to "organize" men old enough to be his father. These men have a hatred of being organized in that way whether for education or for recreation. Men who have been independent and efficient workmen – and often taking a responsible part in the activities of their union – cannot be regarded as social casualties in need of guidance. Many of them have the ability to organize their own activities. And in the best social-service centres the members have a great deal of the responsibility in their own hands. If social-service clubs are to be a success their system of self-government and self-control should be encouraged and extended. The movement should be organized on a democratic basis and administered by the men. The staff should not appear as organizers but rather as "advisers" and "tutors". If a group of men desire carpentry lessons arrangements should be made for an expert to teach them, or to assist them. By giving the men a greater degree of responsibility, and by recognizing the fact that they are men of experience, a much better spirit could be produced.

Already, as a result of the way in which the social-service movement has been organized, a kind of stigma is being attached to social-service activities. I discussed the problem with a few of the leading men in the unemployed club at the Labour Rooms. They hated everything connected with "social service". Their attitude was that they wanted to organize themselves in their own way. The very word "recreation", they said, had a sort of stigma in Jarrow. As the industries on Tyneside are nearly all heavy trades the men have had all the exercise they want by the time they return from work. Many of them are too tired for organized recreation. So "recreation" comes to have attached to it the idea that it is the sort of thing provided for the unemployed ... for the failures. This feeling has deepened as more and more men have got work in the recent armament boom. "Other men have got work. Why not you?" The unemployed man hears that daily ... from his wife, from his children, or if they are too kind, then from the U.A.B. or the P.A.C. officer. As many of the men who were once members of an unemployed club find jobs there is a tendency for those who remain to feel that their continued association with the centre is a mark of inferiority. Because of this some are leaving the clubs. They are trying to provide their own recreations without any forced organization.

Social-service clubs ought not to exist in isolation. If their membership is limited – either actually or in effect – to unemployed the result is that the sense of isolation which the unemployed man feels is only heightened. Successful social-service clubs are those which are working as community centres. And, if social service has any future it lies along those lines. There is little room in English life for a charitable organization trying to "organize the unemployed" as a class apart. A community centre, the organization of which is based on local groups and controlled by the local people themselves, particularly if premises are provided by the local authority instead of being planted on the town by an outside body, can serve a useful purpose by providing facilities of various sorts for the public it serves. There is room in most places for an organization providing lectures and various informal classes. By bringing together employed and unemployed, and people of different wage groups and interests, in some forms of activity the community centres could serve a constructive purpose.

These Jarrow men and women are not ungrateful people, unappreciative of what has been done for them. They want just what everyone else wants – that feeling of security, independence and fulfilment which comes from having a job to do. In the seven years in which I have been intimately connected with Jarrow, first as candidate, then as Member of Parliament, and have been going in and about the streets, and into many of the poorest homes, I have never once been asked for money. That I think is a pretty good indication of independence. I have been asked, of course, for subscriptions to clubs and charities, to help in the provision of a dart board, and the other various appeals which reach an M.P. Often I am asked for books. The women ask me for clothes for their "jumble" sales. But never, in all my connection with Jarrow, has any individual asked me for money.

This, I think, is the traditional attitude of Tyneside, for it is not confined to Jarrow alone. It is the same in each part of my constituency, some parts of which, such as Bill Quay, suffer poverty as bad as anything which Jarrow can show. If Britain leaves these old areas to rot, with the convenient feeling that they are derelict anyway, a fine tradition will have been lost from our national life.

CHAPTER FIFTEEN
Housing and Health

BAD HOUSING, overcrowding, underfeeding, low wages for any work that is going, household incomes cut to the limit by public assistance, or Means Test or whatever is the cutting machine of the time ... these mean disease and premature death. No goodwill speeches, no glowing perorations about "the patience of our people under misfortune" alter the plain fact that if people have to live and bear and bring up children in bad houses on too little food, their resistance to disease is lowered and they die before they should. Their babies die, too, at an unnecessary and an easily-preventable high rate.

This is the basic fact of our whole social problem. Yet the conscience of the better off, and the doctors who know this but find it inconvenient to admit, jib at the conclusions of which towns like Jarrow supply the living proofs. It is more comforting to say: "The women do not know how to cook" ... "The Irish have a racial susceptibility to tuberculosis" ... "The families are too large" ... "The geological formations are unfavourable" ... all of which reasons have been put forward by various medical authorities and seized on to prove that "the trouble after all is not poverty". Any excuse will do to veil the awkward facts that a system which allows houses to be run up overnight like mushrooms to serve an industrial magnate ... and then scraps the industry while leaving the houses and their inmates derelict, to suit another set of financial interests condemns to premature death and preventable disease an excessive number of Jarrow citizens every year.

From 1871, when the rapid industrialization of Jarrow was intensified, the death rates and birth rates of Jarrow have been consistently and considerably higher than the general rates for England and Wales and for the grouped average of towns of comparable size. The war conditions increased but did not cause the overcrowding. Bad housing has always been the most acute of the difficulties that the Jarrow health authorities have had to face. A census taken by the Borough Engineer in 1919 showed that, taking the low standard of more than two persons per occupied room, 13,450 persons or

35 per cent of the population were living in overcrowded conditions. Over 5000 persons were living more than three persons to a room. Over 70 per cent of the population was living in conditions of more than one person per occupied room. In the three areas declared to be "insanitary" over 50 per cent were found to be overcrowded ... many grossly so. The Medical Officer of Health at the time, anxious to be duly moderate, remarked that while the housing outlook was "gloomy", it must be remembered that "the careless tenant of the slum house may be as large a factor in causing its bad conditions as the careless owner" ... a curious comment seeing that he had himself listed as the chief housing defects of the borough, defective roofing, want of damp-proof courses, ash-pit closets and bad construction. It is a little difficult to see how the worst tenant could have been responsible for such basic faults.

The census of 1921 gave a much higher rate of overcrowding, 42.32 per cent on a slightly lower population figure, which probably means only that the census figures were more exact than the survey of the local borough engineer could possibly be. What this appallingly high figure meant in human lives is shown by the vital statistics. The general death rate in Jarrow in 1921 was 17.29 per thousand as compared with the average for England and Wales of 12.1. The rate for grouped towns the same size as Jarrow was 11.7. The infantile death rate was 116 per thousand as compared with the general rate for the country of 83. The deaths from tuberculosis and respiratory diseases was 39 per cent of the total, an extraordinarily high figure. 1921 was not a "bad" year like 1919, when the infantile mortality rate in Jarrow reached 153 per thousand. Yet as the medical officer of health points out: "Had the Jarrow death rate been on the same level as for England and Wales, there would have been only 438 deaths instead of 626. "Which is to say that in the condition of 1921, 188 people died for the reason that they lived in Jarrow.

Faced with this high density of 46.2 persons to the acre the corporation tried to seek relief by extending the boundaries. The bill was thrown out on Second Reading by that House of Commons whose members, according to J. M. Keynes, looked like "hard-faced men who had done very well out of the war". They had no time in their anxiety to get rid of all the war controls on private enterprise to concern themselves with such problems as overcrowded Jarrow. The result of this rejection meant that Jarrow could not find land on which to build houses within its own rating authority ... a serious matter to a town with so low a rateable value. It was not until 1936 that this difficulty was met by securing parliamentary sanction to the inclusion of the new housing estates within the borough boundaries.

But years of overcrowding and preventable deaths and suffering were the result of the earlier decision of the House of Commons. Fifty houses were built in 1921 on a new housing estate, but as the Medical Officer regretfully remarked, the rents of these were too high for the incomes of the poorer workers in the town. A few more houses were built the following year ... at rents of 9s. plus rates, "more than the labouring classes could afford to pay". The subsidies under the Addison Act were cut too soon for the Act to make any difference to Jarrow.

In 1923 the Medical Officer reports that the conditions of overcrowding remain unaltered. "Of the total population of 36,000," he adds, "6000 are drawing the dole, and another 23,000 are receiving poor law relief." Under such conditions the Conservative Housing Act of 1923, which aimed at "stimulating building by private enterprise", was of no value in meeting the problem. More advantage might have been taken of the Wheatley Act with its £9 per house for forty years, had the Town Council of the period with its moderate majority really taken energetic action.

Seven years after the war the evil remained as bad as ever. A comparison of the different wards showed as usual the enormous discrepancy between the Grange Ward, where are situated most of the good houses that Jarrow had then, and the crowded East, Central and North Wards.

Ward	Death rate per 1000
East	20.57
Central	19.38
North	19.27
West	14.66
South	12.44
Grange	9.12
Borough Average	15.5

The tuberculosis rate in the Central Ward was 3.46, its respiratory disease death rate 4.84; in the North Ward 2.03 and 5.07 respectively. For the Grange Ward, in the same town, with the same "geological formation and rainbearing winds", a 0.96 tuberculosis and 1.78 respiratory death rate.

The Medical Officer says grimly: "Under the present conditions of overcrowding in which many of the people are living the chances of anyone having a reasonable prospect of recovering from pulmonary tuberculosis are poor, and in addition the patient may be a source of considerable danger to the other inmates of the house. To provide adequate treatment in an overcrowded house for a case of pneumonia is practically an impossibility."

In 1929, though 628 houses were reported as not reasonably fit for human habitation, only 52 new houses were built ... and not of course for the people who needed them most. The following year the Medical Officer of Health deplored the fact that the overcrowding figures were practically the same as those given by the borough engineer in 1919. The 1931 census revealed that there had been a net loss of population of 20 per cent since the 1921 census, and the birth rate had fallen to the lowest recorded in Jarrow. There was therefore some decrease in the overcrowding. The percentage had dropped from 42 to 33, but a third of the people were still living at a density of more than two persons per room. Thirty-five per cent of the families still occupied dwellings of not more than two rooms, practically the same figure as the 1921 census. The density per acre in the Central Ward, with its sensationally high death rate from respiratory disease, was 139.2 per acre as compared with the 41.6 per acre in the Grange Ward.

Following a conference in Newcastle of the National Association for Combating Tuberculosis, an expert, F. C. S. Bradbury, M.D., D.P.H., was asked to make a report, which was published early in 1933. An intensive survey was undertaken of Jarrow, using the neighbouring district of Blaydon, where the population was roughly the same as Jarrow, as a control for comparison.

The facts produced startled the country, though they were only too familiar to those who worked among the people of Jarrow. The general death rate in Jarrow for the period 1929-30 was 14.9 per thousand, for Blaydon 9.5, the average for England and Wales. being 12.4. The percentage of deaths due to tuberculosis was 13.2 in Jarrow compared with 9.3 in Blaydon and 7.5 for England and Wales. Combining the deaths from respiratory diseases but excluding tuberculosis, the rate for Jarrow was 3.1, 1.5 for Blaydon, 2.1 for England and Wales. The tuberculosis death rate in Jarrow over five years, 1926-30, was *greater* than in the five years 1896-1900, although in this period the tuberculosis death rate for the whole country had fallen by 50 per cent. In the later period the death rate from (sputum positive) tuberculosis in Jarrow was greater than the total pulmonary death rate for all urban districts of England and Wales for the same period. The death rate from non-pulmonary tuberculosis in Jarrow exceeded that for England and Wales in all the age and sex groups dealt with, especially in children, among whom the Jarrow rate was more than three times the rate of England and Wales. The death rate among Jarrow children from one cause alone ... abdominal tuberculosis, exceeds the total death rate from *all* forms of non-pulmonary tuberculosis in the children of England and Wales. That there was less spinal and bone and joint tuberculosis was attributed to the fact that so little fresh milk was drunk in Jarrow. This saved the children from one form of tuberculosis, only that the consequent under-nourishment should make them more susceptible to another form of the disease.

The average proportion of deaths of children in Jarrow from all forms of tuberculosis was found to be 24.4, the corresponding figure for all children in urban districts of England and Wales being 10.5 per cent. A particularly significant fact is that children under fifteen formed 37 per cent of the population of Jarrow, but 44.8 per cent. of the patients at the tuberculosis dispensary. For England and Wales as a whole the highest mortality from tuberculosis is in the older age group, 45-65, but excessive mortality from tuberculosis in Jarrow is specially marked in the two youngest age groups, 0-15 and 15-25. The deaths of children from tuberculosis on a statistical rating per million gave a figure for Jarrow of 113.5, compared with 16'5 for Lancashire, usually regarded as a high tuberculosis-rate county.

Having ascertained these statistics, Dr. Bradbury went on to examine the causes which made Jarrow the worst place in England for tuberculosis. He found, for example, that among families examined who lived in one or two rooms paying less than 3s. per week per room in rent the incidence of tuberculosis was 63.7 per cent, but among those living in three or more rooms paying 3s. per week or more per room in rent, the tuberculosis percentage was 38, even though the families paying the higher rent were within the overcrowded category.

Dr. Bradbury stated in his report that "no attempt will be made to establish the thesis that undernourishment is in any sense a factor which leads specifically to tuberculosis". But he found that "there is greater undernourishment among tuberculous families than among families with other sickness, so that there is a progressive increase, from families with no sickness, to those with sickness other than tuberculosis, than to tuberculous families". Of the families with no sickness examined, 31.1 in Jarrow, 6.8 in Blaydon were undernourished. Of the families with sickness other than tuberculosis 38 per cent were undernourished in Jarrow, 10.6 per cent in Blaydon. But of families with tuberculosis, 48.9 per cent in Jarrow were undernourished, 18.9 in Blaydon, giving a joint figure for the two areas of 43.7 undernourished in tuberculous families, as compared with 21.1 undernourished in families with no sickness.

An interesting section of the Bradbury report deals with the relation of individual foodstuffs to the incidence of tuberculosis among the Jarrow families studied. Meat, butter, bread and milk were the foods chosen. There is in each tuberculosis case an excess of bread ... being the cheapest of the staple foods. But meat, though the dearest, was not the food most lacking among tuberculous Jarrow families. Milk showed the greatest deficiency. In Jarrow at this time, an average for all families of only two-thirds of a pint per head per week was being consumed. The amount of milk consumed was found to vary in accordance with the tuberculosis rate. To quote the report: "The tuberculosis rate of Jarrow is approximately twice the proportion found in Blaydon. The proportion of non-tuberculous families who consume less than the standard amount of milk is approximately twice the proportion found in Blaydon. The amount of milk consumed per head in nontuberculous families in Blaydon is almost exactly twice the corresponding amount in Jarrow. These proportions do not hold good for any of the other foodstuffs studied." Dr. Bradbury adds the significant comment: "Ordinary cow's milk appears to differ from most other foodstuffs in being *par excellence* the food which must be consumed fresh. This fact suggests that shortage of milk has possibly more important aspects than mere undernourishment and that perhaps vitamins, enzymes, or unknown serological constituents of fresh milk have an important bearing on the body's defences against tuberculosis." Then one thinks of the lack of opportunity for keeping milk fresh even for a few hours in the overcrowded conditions in parts of Jarrow today.

The high proportion of tenements in Jarrow is one of its features. Blocks of tenements, common even later than 1933, have four or eight families in what is virtually one house divided into several apartments. There are blocks of eight dwellings, each block having a common yard. Twelve to forty inhabitants used the same yard, common water tap and two or four common sanitary conveniences.

Dr. Bradbury took as his standard of "poverty" anything below an income of 10s. per head in the family. Using figures from groups in which variations of poverty had been eliminated, it was still found that families living in these tenements showed more tuberculosis than those with the same incomes living in separate dwellings. Of the total families examined it was found that 55 per cent of those classified as "poor" had one or more tuberculous members. In Blaydon it was noticed that tuberculosis was less common among miners' families than others. It was also shown that unemployment in this area was less common among miners. Incidentally, tuberculosis was then and is now more rapidly fatal in Jarrow than elsewhere. The average duration of the disease before death is 2.5 years in Jarrow as compared with 3.3 years in crowded Lancashire. Actually it takes, in one-third of the cases, less than one year to reach the end.

The case which Dr. Bradbury allows the figures of his survey to build up ...

that overcrowding, undernourishment, insanitary conditions are the main causal factors of the high tuberculosis rate in Jarrow, seems unanswerable. "These findings," writes Dr. Bradbury, "lead to the considered opinion that poverty is to be regarded as a factor of prime importance in the causation of a high incidence of tuberculosis in Jarrow." But when he comes to his practical suggestions for reducing the horrible disease, his proposal regarding the food problem on which his report laid such stress was:

"In view of the apparent importance of undernourishment as a predisposing cause of tuberculosis, it appears desirable that *something should be done* to improve the defences of poor families against tuberculosis *by the issuing of information* by local authorities on the subject of better housekeeping – particularly in the matter of providing adequate and balanced diets at the cheapest possible rates. "

The italics are mine, and comment seems unnecessary. In fairness to Dr. Bradbury it must be added that he was emphatic as to the necessity of reducing overcrowding.

One feature of the Bradbury Report which received very wide notice in the Press at the time, and to which attention was specially directed in the Committee's own preface to the Report, was the theory that the racial factor helped to account for the disproportionately high rate of tuberculosis in Jarrow. "Dr. Bradbury's figures appear to show that the high proportion in Jarrow of persons of Irish race is directly concerned with the high incidence of tuberculosis." The local Press leapt joyously at this useful excuse. It is therefore of particular interest that the recent inquiry into tuberculosis in Wales and Monmouthshire, published by the Ministry of Health (1939), devotes some space to the consideration of the racial factor in a high tuberculosis rate. This latest report comes to the conclusion that "for practical purposes we may safely assume that racial susceptibility *per se* is only a comparatively minor factor in causing high mortality from tuberculosis in this country".

The Bradbury Report gives an unforgettable picture of the Jarrow up to 1932. What is the position now? From 1932 to 1936 were years of the blackest slump. There was no work in the town. Unemployment stayed at well over 6000. The product of a penny rate fell steadily to its lowest point of £365 in 1935. Under such conditions and with such slender resources what could even the best intentioned local authority do? Jarrow death rate, both the general and the tuberculosis rates, remained steadily higher than the average for the country. In 1934 the percentage of deaths from tuberculosis in Jarrow was 11.84, as compared to the average for the country of 6.4. In

1935 infantile mortality was 112 per thousand as against a rate of 57 for England and Wales and 55 for smaller towns like Jarrow. In the East Ward the rate was 200 per thousand, as against the average for the Grange Ward of 53 ... and in that year the live births in East and Grange Wards were equal. It was still four times as dangerous to be born into the East Ward as into the slightly better-off Grange Ward in the same town. I say slightly, for the middle class of Jarrow consists of a few officials and professional men and their families. The greater part of the Grange Ward is inhabited by working-class families, some a little better off ... but the overcrowding is nothing like so bad as in the East or Central Wards.

The Council had started tentatively on a policy of slum clearance under the Greenwood Act, with a first order for the North Ward in 1931. Progress would in any case have been slow because of the financial conditions that prevailed then. But in addition, although we have seen what effect the overcrowded housing conditions were having on the health of the town, the Town Council had to meet with the resistance from the owners of those hovels of death and disease. The North Ward No. 1 clearance area included part of a district poetically known as Poets' Corner, from the names given to the streets. Milton, Spenser and Shakespeare would lift an eyebrow if they could see the property to which their names were given. But as always happens when a place gets a nickname, Poets' Corner bred a local patriotism, and there were some good Labour fighters who lived in the bad conditions of this area and fought desperately for a closing order, who would claim a sort of pride in living in Poets' Corner. Their source of satisfaction was its 100 per cent Labour solidarity. Its tuberculosis rate was exceptionally high, even for Jarrow. Four hundred people lived in ninety-six dwellings, with a total of 184 rooms.

The Ministry of Health confirmed the Clearing Order after an inquiry, but the owners fought it bitterly. It was taken to the High Court, where the owners' appeal was dismissed, and they then went to the Court of Appeal. They won their case, and in October 1934 the order was quashed ... three years after the original order had been made. Proceedings to clear No. 1 area had to be begun all over again.

My political work takes me a good deal among these clearance areas, visiting the houses, talking to the women. Property-owners should have been liable to prosecution for even allowing people to live under such conditions, much less be allowed to receive rent for them. The floors were rotten. A mother showed me a scar on her baby's face which had recently been bitten by a rat as it lay in its cradle. No money spent by tenants or Council on insecticides seemed able to keep down the swarming beetles in the rotting woodwork. The roofs leaked, the walls were damp. Paper hung away in long strips. In some houses the fire grate was loose in the wall and looked liable to fall away at any moment ... perhaps when full of live coals, and with a pan of boiling water. To keep food or milk fresh was impossible. Every drop of water had to be carried up a rickety flight of wooden stairs from the tap in the yard by the upstairs housewife. In the midst of all this, the women were trying to bear and rear babies well, to wash, clean, make meals, keep up a home on the pittance of P.A.C. And the grave gentlemen who make official surveys of such areas gravely suggest as a remedy that the wife should be given information on how to cook and where to buy the cheapest supplies available!

Houses were built to rehouse the tenants of one such area under the Slum Clearance Act, but the owners were able to prevent the Council allowing them to be occupied. For months the houses stood empty while the tenants struggled on in the old bad conditions. Every time a councillor appeared in the street he was besieged by women asking why they could not go into the new houses now that they were all built and ready. One woman told me how she and some friends used to push their prams up the long road to the new houses on fine afternoons, to peer through the windows and imagine what it would be like to live in a house that had a tight roof and dry walls, and actually water laid on over the kitchen sink. "It was awful to go back to our old house," she said. Yet a property owner chuckled to me of the cute way in which the lawyers had been able to keep those nice new houses empty "until they had got satisfaction". Satisfaction takes curious forms.

Labour won its first majority and its first Labour Mayor, Alderman J. W. Thompson, in 1935 ... after all those years of struggle. The new chairman of the Housing Committee was Alderman Symonds, an unemployed man who had himself lived, until very recently, in overcrowded conditions. The Council started on an energetic slum-clearance policy. The new houses had to be built outside the borough boundaries, but their rateable value came to the town when the boundaries were extended in 1936. Under Part II of the Housing Act, 1936, a determined effort was made to reduce the number of tenements. The 1st July, 1937, was the date "appointed" by the Minister of Health, after which overcrowding would be a punishable offence if the occupier refused suitable alternative accommodation or if a house were let after that date under conditions which cause overcrowding. The overcrowding survey of Jarrow in 1936-37 revealed that of 7724 dwelling-houses inspected, 1350 were found to be overcrowded ... which means that 17.4 per cent of the families were living in overcrowded conditions, the number of persons involved being 6664. An alarming enough figure for a small town, but not nearly the whole truth, for in determining the number of persons under this Act a child under one year is not counted, and a child one to ten years old is only counted as half an adult. As these families are those with the largest number of children, the number of people, men, women and children, in Jarrow still living under overcrowded conditions must be well over 7000.

The Council's proposals to remedy overcrowding, which were submitted to the Ministry of Health, included the erection of 337 additional houses specifically to rehouse the worst cases of overcrowding. But as the Council's heavy slum-clearance programme is far from being complete, despite all the Council can do with its limited resources, none of these houses have as yet been begun. The Medical Officer has to take what comfort he can from pointing out that from all sources during 1937, the number of overcrowded families was reduced by 50, from 1350 to 1300. Under the Slum Clearance Orders the number of persons displaced was 2218 persons, mostly from the bad tenement houses. The majority of these have been re-housed by the Corporation.

There is air and light on the new housing estate of the Council. The wind sweeps freshly from the sea some eight miles away along the river. There are green fields nearby. The very worst of the Jarrow slums have been cleared ... but it is too early as yet to say what effect the new houses will have on Jarrow's tuberculosis scourge. It has improved appetites. An unemployed father complained to me that since going into the new estate "the children could eat a horse between two mattresses". The latest figures available at the time of writing are the Medical Officer of Health's report for 1937, at the top of the trade boom for the country as a whole. In Jarrow the crude death rate was practically unchanged since 1930. The pulmonary tuberculosis rate had fallen only by 0.06 per thousand in seven years, though the non-pulmonary rate has been halved. The cheap milk scheme under the Milk Marketing Board, which has been in operation since 1937, has allowed families to obtain fresh milk at 2d. per pint.

The infantile death rate in 1937 has been much reduced ... it was 73.3, though high as compared with the average for towns of similar size, whose rate was 60. It was, however, also the year with the lowest birth rate ever recorded in the borough. Dr. Dormer, the medical officer, adds: "Of the infant deaths more than half are due to three causes, gastro-enteritis, premature birth and pneumonia. Overcrowding and poor housing conditions contribute largely to the deaths under all three headings, while malnutrition and ill-health are contributory causes in those classified as being due to premature birth." This was Dr. Dormer's last report as medical officer. He used practically the same words in 1937 as in his first report for 1924. A grim commentary on fourteen years of the life of a distressed area, while elsewhere fortunes were mounting and the wealth of the country was unparalleled.

CHAPTER SIXTEEN
The Rates and the Child

WHILE WRITING this book I asked Mr. Herbert Morrison, the leader of the L.C.C., how much a penny rate brought in for his Council. "Oh, just over a quarter of a million," he replied casually. Sir Sidney Herbert added that Westminster's penny rate produced £42,000. These are figures with which something can be done. Holborn, with a population about the same as Jarrow, collects £6800 and Bedford about £1500. But for the last ten years each penny on the rates in Jarrow has produced round about £400 – sometimes as low as £350, never higher than £450.

Work in Jarrow, and in all the distressed areas, is conditioned by that ever-tightening bond, the product of a penny rate. It becomes the nightmare of every progressive mind in the place – the despair of councillors and officials. Every attempt to improve the condition of the people, all that valuable local desire to organize things better communally, which is the most hopeful thing in Britain's local life, is damped and crushed by this terrible problem of the rates.

When the industrialists complained of the cost of the rates, Mr. Neville Chamberlain, then Minister of Health in the 1924-29 Government, relieved them of three-quarters of the burden. That relief continues even to firms making the fantastic profits of the arms boom – and the relief now is mainly at the expense of the cottager and the small shopkeeper. For them no hope is held out. Mr. Chamberlain refuses to reopen the question, and the distressed areas have to struggle on under the ever-increasing load.

This book could be filled with nothing else but the effect of this low product of the penny rate on Jarrow. Here is a "slanting shot" on one aspect of the problem.

In 1938 the Board of Education wrote to the Jarrow Town Council pointing out the existence of serious malnutrition among the school children and requesting that something be done to increase the number of free meals. The Labour chairman of the local P.A.C. replied hotly that if they had to deduct the cost of the meals from the P.A.C. allowance, then the mothers could not afford to let the children have "free" meals, especially when several children were attending school. Permission was given to readjust this. The estimate of £2400 for this service was increased. £3900 was actually spent in the year 1938-39. The cost for 1939-40 was estimated to be £7300, subject to the 50 per cent special services grant from the Board of Education.

But the total for the year 1939-40 was growing alarmingly, not because of any extravagant schemes but just to meet the expenses necessitated by Jarrow's terrible burden of poverty even in the "boom" years of 1938-39. Very reluctantly, and despite the figures for malnutrition in the town, the Council has had, despite its Labour majority, to make every conceivable economy, and as everything has had to be cut, so has the amount to be spent on such items as cheap dried milk for nursing mothers, and the cost of the school meals. The estimate for this latter item has been cut from £7300 to £4500 for the year 1939-40.

To ensure that all classes bore some share of the burden, the Council cut the compounding allowances, which are paid to landlords who collect rates with rent and transmit them in a lump sum. This allowance was reduced from 15 per cent to 10 per cent. Because of this cut, the produce of a penny rate was proportionately increased. But the distressed areas grant is based on a complicated formula – an old-fashioned set of rules on to which new sets have been grafted by regulation. The result is now the kind of historic monument of a muddle in which a certain type of subtle official mind delights to wallow. To the basic sums are made an addition and deductions, and these deductions are based on the product of a penny rate.

Now because the Council raided one of its remaining few nest-eggs the product of a penny rate seemed to be increased, though there was no actual improvement in rateable value. So the Board of Education rate dropped proportionately. The result is just silly. The Jarrow houseowners – some of them are very small people, very little better off than their tenants – might have consoled themselves with the loss of 5 per cent by thinking it would help their town. But what consolation is it to anyone that this sum, insignificant in the Board of Education's accounts but very important to Jarrow, is taken from a town which has just had to cut down the grants for its school children's meals and for the food of its pregnant mothers?

In a fury of indignation I met the Accountant-General of the Board of Education, and all the appropriate officials at the Ministry of Health. Sympathetic men – but the rules of the Board of Education Grant Regulations No. I are sacred.

Are these meals needed? The present Medical Officer of Health, Dr.

Good, who is also the health officer for the schools, is just undertaking a nutritional survey of the school children. The total number of inspections to the end of 1938 were 3092. The children fell into four classes.

		%
A (excellent)	596	19.27
B (normal)	1543	49.9
C (Slightly sub-normal)	828	26.78
D (bad)	125	4.04

A special survey was made of the East Jarrow primary school. Here the total inspections were 103, divided according to categories as above.

		%
A	19	18.5
B	53	51.4
C	29	28.0
D	2	1.94

These figures are too small in number to make a proper comparison with the wider survey, but the following additional facts are interesting. Of the thirty-one children in the C-D categories, twelve get milk free and nineteen buy it. Only five in the whole school get the free dinners. Twelve of the thirty-one C-D classes get no milk at home, the other nineteen get an average of five pints per week at home. The average home consumption of milk for the children in the A and B categories is only three pints.

East Jarrow is a poor district, but the worst off is Dunn Street. There the D class (seriously undernourished) reaches the high figure of 5.9 per cent. In London anything over 2 per cent is considered very serious indeed.

It is usually objected to such figures that they are too "subjective" – that everything depends on the standard of the individual doctor or medical officer. In the absence of any universally accepted clinical standard of malnutrition that must to a certain extent be true. But in so far as it is true, it works against the Special Areas and prevents their state being seen in its really comparable grimness. For a medical man, working all the time in distressed-area conditions, inevitably takes a lower standard for his norm than one who works in the South or prosperous Midlands. A medical officer from a neighbouring town to Jarrow had a doctor from a Midland town staying with him at the time he was doing a nutritional survey of his worst schools. Because of his interest, and to help an overworked host to get away on a holiday, the guest helped in the work, using his own usual clinical standards. The result horrified the Medical Officer of Health, his guest's figures for cases of malnutrition being about four times those of the local officer. Dr. J. L. Burn, Medical Officer for Hebburn in 1935, who discussed this difficulty of an objective clinical standard with me, wrote in his report:

"It is curious to notice, in this area which has suffered severely from poverty, that not one of the returns of the death certificates indicate that malnutrition has played any part as a primary or contributory cause of death. Yet I calculate that only one-quarter of our population has been able to afford over a period of years the dietary which is regarded as a minimum by the British Medical Association or by the Ministry of Health Advisory Committee on Nutrition. I consider that death return statistics either cannot or do not throw any light as to whether a community is suffering severely from nutritional defects. It is surprising that no reference to nutrition has been made on any death certificate of Hebburn children or adults over a period of years. Yet personal contact with mothers and children at Clinics, and when on Housing duties in their homes, convinces me that serious undernourishment does exist, whether we get to know of it or not by statistical methods."

Perhaps because the tradition of the learned Bede is still alive in the town, less romantically but more likely, because of the interest in education always shown by the skilled worker, Jarrow has maintained a good educational tradition through the years. We have seen in an earlier chapter that there were schools in Jarrow long before elementary education was made compulsory. The old School Board formed in 1871 was put under the chairmanship of a man whose views on education would be considered advanced even in some quarters today. Temporary schools were quickly opened, and the first permanent Board School in the County of Durham was at Jarrow.

As long ago as 1880 there was a demand for higher education for the older boys. The upper standards were then put in one school, so as to give them better teaching, instead of leaving them as errand boys for the teachers in a number of schools. Three years later a specially designed school for this purpose was started with an organized science school at the top. Immediately after the war, this school became a Selective Central School. The Roman Catholic managers, who have done pioneer work for education in Jarrow, were the first to open a Selective School for Girls. A report in 1929 states that the R.C. schools were already organized on the principles of the Hadow Report, some time before that report was produced.

The scheme of Re-organization and Development of Education in Jarrow, submitted by the Education committee in 1929, was described by the Board of Education as a "well-conceived scheme based on sound principles". In a letter written in 1934, the secretary of the Education Committee writes: "Had the managers of the two Church Schools fallen into line on March 1930 the work would have gone ahead. Instead they both stood out, and the committee kept postponing the question hoping for a settlement, until the economy stunt came along and swamped everything."

Since the war that handicap of the low yield of the penny rate has prevented badly needed work being done. Yet even when poverty has been at its worst the policy of the Town Council has been to put education first, whatever other services have had to be curtailed. The 1938 figures show that the amount spent on financing education (exclusive of the cost of free meals, milk, and medical inspection) was £74,566. Including these services, education was given a 4s. 5d. rate. In the worst year of all, the rate was 3s. 6d. Significantly, the next highest item in the Borough accounts was £14,000 for the main medical services.

There are things which cannot be done even with a 4s. 5d. education rate when that only produces £22,000, and when, even with the Government grant, there is only £75,000 to spend. The elementary school buildings are out of date and some are insanitary. They were all built in the years of Jarrow's prosperity at the end of last century. Several of them have not yet got electric light, which makes modern developments, like school films, impossible. In many the class-rooms are simply partitioned cubicles in what used to be a large hall. The mercy is that they are partitioned at all. The sanitary and washing arrangements are primitive, the playgrounds hemmed in by other buildings, for most of the schools are in the most crowded part of the town. Only one school has a playing field of its own. There are proposals for erecting new schools on the new estates, and a fine new secondary school has been built. But most of the children of today, and, for that matter, their children, will still be in these unsatisfactory conditions unless help is quickly given. The Board of Education will not pay more than 20 per cent towards the cost of renovating old schools. It is impossible for Jarrow to raise the 80 per cent or the amount needed for new schools; so the children will continue to suffer.

The total net expenditure per schoolchild in Jarrow, £12 18s. is well below the average of £15 4s. 5d. for England and Wales, though, be it noted, it is 34s. above that of a prosperous borough in the South like Lewes. Jarrow, unable to do much about buildings, has concentrated on the efficiency of its teachers. Only fourteen out of 196 are uncertificated, a fact of which the Education Committee have a right to be proud. Their expenditure on teachers' salaries is £9 13s., 2s. 1d. per child above the country's average, and above that of wealthy Harrogate.

The high quality of the teaching is reflected in the good standard of intelligence of the children. In 1936 a survey of Jarrow elementary-school children was undertaken by an educational psychologist, Miss Grace Hawkins. Her conclusion was that 20.6 of the children were of high intelligence for whom special provision should be made in central or secondary schools. No average for the country is available for comparison, but compared with other areas where similar surveys have been made this figure is regarded as a high one. Unfortunately only 8 per cent of the children can go on to higher education.

The Jarrow Central School with just under 400 children has all the difficulties of old and not very suitable buildings. This is made up for, to what extent that can be, by really superb devotion on the part of the staff.

There is no difficulty about persuading the parents to let the children go on to the secondary school. The Headmaster reports that the competition to get in is as great among the parents as the boys themselves. But over-crowded though the school is ... 400 pupils are crammed into a school built for a considerably smaller number, there are always many of proved intelligence who could benefit from higher education but for whom no room is available. The scholarship record is high, eight out of the forty County scholarships in a recent year. This is a marvellous record when the conditions under which the children work are considered. To do home lessons on the edge of the table in an overcrowded kitchen is not helpful to concentration on a mathematical problem. The Headmaster in an interview said rather surprisingly that he considered this a greater handicap than any actual malnutrition among secondary pupils.

That children of this poor area ... an area wider than the town of Jarrow itself, do so well under the difficulties prevailing is some indication of the wealth of brains, intelligence and toughness there is in the working classes of Durham and Tyneside. ... The national waste of such assets, merely in order to keep low the rates which the rich might have to pay if the burdens of these areas were more equally shared, is criminal folly. It is argued by the all-is-for-the-best-school that such conditions engender a higher resistance, and tougher calibre than the indulged sons of Eton and Harrow. But there is the damage rate to be considered ... the grimmer side of the picture. The corollary to the 20.6 of superior or high intelligence is the 16.4 of Jarrow children whom the psychological survey reported as "dull or backward to such an extent that they require special educational provision". And that figure is as relatively high in its way as the superior intelligence rate.

A small handful of Jarrow secondary pupils can get to the university. But if an earning job is offered, then parents on the Means Test or those at work with small wages cannot afford to let the child stay on at school. With the armaments boom there are now jobs of some kind waiting for the secondary-school boys when they leave, so that the pressure is not to let the children stay there longer than can be helped. The Headmaster says: "the lack of industries in Jarrow make the number of black-coated jobs very limited so that the most intelligent boys go away." Often the parents follow the boy. The Headmaster said that in one year as many as a hundred parents had left Jarrow to follow their sons to the place of the new job.

Facilities for other than black-coated jobs, mainly for apprentices at the two great firms in Hebburn, are provided in the "technical shop", where the boys come for two hours each evening. It is a five-year course, and only about a quarter of the boys can stay the course. After a full, long day in the works it is gruelling to give up every night for the five years of dawning manhood. Some physically cannot stand the double strain. The shop stands empty all day. It seems a pity that these boys could not be given the opportunity by their employers to put in a couple of hours during working time. If that is thought impossible then with the shortage of skilled labour, could not the machinery of the technical shop be used to train as apprentices some of the lads who are eating out their hearts at the dole school, or drifting rapidly into unskilled unemployability?

CHAPTER SEVENTEEN

Unemployment in Jarrow Now

THE LAST recorded percentage of unemployment in Jarrow was in September 1935 ... 72.9 per cent. As from June 1936, the Ministry of Labour decided to amalgamate the Jarrow and Hebburn Labour Exchanges. Hebburn is the neighbouring town to Jarrow, with a busy factory making electrical equipment, and the one part of the old Palmer firm that was saved from the wreck ... Palmer's Ship Repairing Yard, Hebburn, which has been working well under a particularly able and energetic manager from the Palmer staff. Nine months later, when the first figure of the joint register was published; the percentage for the two towns is given as 39.6 per cent. Amalgamating misery with relative prosperity improved the Ministry's figures, and enabled the Minister of Labour to talk of "great improvement", while it was still a fact that not a hundred men and boys had found work in Jarrow. Now it is only possible to arrive at an approximate percentage of the total number of insured workers in the town.

In 1932, the worst year of the national crisis, the number of insured workers unemployed was 7500 or over 80 per cent of the total registered for work. In January 1939, the number of adult males between eighteen and sixty-four who were out of work was 2152. Before assuming that a figure of just over 2000 means that Jarrow's problem is nearly solved it is worthwhile to examine this number in detail.

Unemployment only becomes dramatic to this country when it can be expressed in millions. In January 1939 the unemployment problem leaped into the headlines because the two-million level had again been passed, for the first time since February 1936. But it is unrealistic to think of two millions of unemployed as one mass. The problem has to be analysed in terms of units, of towns and the groups and industries in the different areas.

When the national figures of two millions was reached Jarrow was and is officially in a "condition of recovery". Of the 2152 adult males without jobs in January 1939, 510 were dependent on unemployment insurance payment for their income. Three times as many have been unemployed for such long spells in recent years as to have lost their claim to insurance benefit. They are the 1572 men who draw each week Unemployment Assistance allowances. Unemployment benefit, wrongly called the "dole", is a repayment by the Government of insurance claims to men who have contributed each week from their wages part of an insurance premium to entitle them to a weekly income in case of unemployment. But the severity of unemployment in England shattered the actuarial basis of unemployment insurance. In an effort to restore it the Unemployment Assistance Board was set up to pay allowances, subject to a "Means Test" to those who were unable to find work for a sufficient number of weeks in a fixed period to become an insurable risk. Of the total unemployed in Jarrow 73 per cent have been out of work for such long periods as not to be able to qualify for Unemployment Insurance benefit. Of the total number of unemployed there are 4 per cent who are unable to claim any allowance. These are mainly men who have followed an occupation which is not "insurable".

43.3 per cent of the men have been continuously without work for over a year. Ministry of Labour statistics record the number of weeks since a man last worked. Thus it may be that a man has been out of work for two years, but worked for three weeks two months ago. In that case he would be regarded as belonging to the group who have been unemployed for "less than three months". The man described as unemployed for over one year has never had a week's work in that period. Indeed, in Jarrow there are 251 who have never had a week's work in five years. Perhaps, when coldly read in print, that does not seem a significant figure. Translated into terms of individual lives – five years, 260 weeks, without work, without purpose, without an adequate income – and then regarded as one tiny fraction of the long-term unemployment problem in England, it becomes a bitter comment on our social system. To leave men without jobs and without wages for more than a year is to destroy lives.

Nearly two-thirds of the men – 63 per cent – are married and the effects of unemployment on their wives and families have therefore to be considered. More important still are their ages. One of the bitterest results of the twentieth century development is the rise of the "too old at forty-five legend". It is a myth which has gained ground and is now a serious social problem. Capable men are disqualified from jobs because of a manager's belief that ageing men are not worth a job. They say it is difficult for "old" men to keep pace with the machines, or that it is difficult for "old" men to adapt themselves to new processes. Once out, these men are unable to find work very easily. Often they have to rely on a succession of casual jobs. With the increasing mechanization of industry this process is likely to continue. Heads of families, after thirty or more years at work, ought not to be deprived of the economic security on which their happiness – and so often – their health depends, often for mere prejudice, or at the whim of a manager.

Jarrow's problem is not confined to the older men, however, for one quarter of the unemployed men are between twenty-five and thirty-four. They cannot be classed as too old or unadaptable. Nor can the 350 young men between eighteen and twenty-four. They are fit for, and ready for, any kind of a job. Yet only in the emergency of imminent war can work or a place be found for them. As recruits for the army, the percentage of rejects is high, for conscripts still higher. Arrangement will presumably now have to be made to feed conscripts into fitness.

625 of the unemployed men are classified as shipyard workers, 570 as general labourers, and 230 as workers in the building trades. Those three industrial groups account for two-thirds of Jarrow's unemployment problem. There are no other industrial groups with more than 100 unemployed. The remaining 700 men are from various groups – eighty--nine river workers, twenty-nine crane-drivers, sixty-three motor-drivers and horsemen, thirty-three shop assistants, and other occupations of that kind. Thus the industrial solution to unemployment in Jarrow is to find some outlet for shipyard workers, general labourers, or building workers. The majority are unskilled.

Of the shipyard workers unemployed, 226 are classed as skilled. It may be thought queer that they should be out of work while shipyard employers are bewailing the shortage of skilled men. Unfortunately, theirs is the tragedy of out-of-date skill. Among them are clever hand riveters, unwanted now in the days of acetylene welding. Some are too old to learn new high-speed techniques, but the manager of the Labour Exchange is taking advantage of the shortage wherever possible to persuade the yards to take men who are, after all, well used to the routine of shipyard work, even though they are unfamiliar with new processes. The reluctance to take men over forty-five, even in times of shortage, is hard to overcome. In desperation, skilled men will take any labouring job ... even though that means that they will be re-classified as unskilled at the Labour Exchange ... which, in turn, may later affect their U.A.B. allowance under the wages stop. Life becomes very complicated and the issues very involved for the long-term unemployed man. Which makes it difficult to bear with patience the type of advice which begins: "Why don't the unemployed do so-and-so" ... without any understanding of the problems involved.

There are so many well-intentioned people who can produce solutions for unemployment who will not take the trouble to analyse even the immediate difficulties. The lighter industries on the much publicized trading estates offer jobs suitable mainly for young girls and youths, when the real difficulty caused by the collapse of the heavier export industries is that of the adult man.

When the industry of a town has been killed, it seems as difficult to apply artificial respiration as on a human corpse. This is particularly true when the town or district has been a one-industry one like Jarrow or Southwest Durham or the cotton towns of Lancashire. All the traditions of the area, all the specialized skill, seem to cling to the dead industry. Though human beings prove themselves very educable and adaptable when they go elsewhere, the assumption is made that in their own town they can only do what they have always done.

In Jarrow, as subsidiary industries had not been developed in the recent past, the town is singularly short of sites for other industries. It suffers the special handicap of the overbuilt one-industry town. There are no vacant factories which can be immediately offered for adaptation to an industrialist. Several other Tyneside towns have benefited by the arrival of refugees from the Continent. Often they have been able to set up in England with their international trade connections, and introduce into this country some industry which has never been carried on here. The increasing difficulties of carrying on commercial life in countries under the shadow of Hitler is encouraging the transference of those industries here, despite the shortsighted opposition to giving them facilities. This is why the Town Council of Jarrow in 1939 promoted a parliamentary bill to enable it to acquire land for industrial purposes ... a useful measure at first vigorously opposed as "socialistic". It had to be modified considerably to conciliate the strong "capitalist" lobby in the House of Commons, but even in its present form it gives to Jarrow powers that few other municipalities have. The great area of Palmer's is such a magnificent industrial site that there was, not unwisely, considerable reluctance on the part of the Commissioner for the Special Areas, who acquired the site in 1938 to break it up for small industries, especially as there is hope that the new steelworks now being erected by the Jarrow Steel Company in connection with the Consett Iron and Steel Company may need the larger part of the land.

Sir John Jarvis, a London financier who was then High Sheriff of Surrey, started his work of bringing smaller industries to Jarrow in 1935. ... He began with a small furniture factory, which now employs about a hundred, mostly youths. His next venture was the Jarrow Tube Works, to meet the demand for small tubes mainly for cartridge and shell cases. In association with this, Sir John started Jarrow Metal Industries for light castings, which is now chiefly employed on aerial bombs and other munition orders. These two industries provide a welcome addition to the employment in the town. The Labour Exchange gives the figure at 200 men and boys at the tube works, and 300 employed at the metal industries. To provide scrap for these industries and to start a ship-breaking industry Sir John brought first the *Olympic* and, at the time of writing, the *Berengaria,* to be broken up at Palmer's old quays. The Jarrow Steel Company, which has been stimulated by the Government as a consolation for the sabotage of the great integrated works, and which was promised in June 1937, is now in course of construction, after long delay, despite the national emergency.

So that, as a result of all the hard work put in by Sir John Jarvis, the great agitation for the steelworks, the publicity given to the town by the march ... in fact after about five years' intensive effort, with the addition of generous terms of assistance given by the Commissioner for the Special Areas, the result is that about 800 men and boys have been provided with work. What then has happened to the other 4500 or so not included in the present number of unemployed, who were part of the 7500 out of work in Jarrow in 1932? Despite the expensive apparatus of government assistance, and the efforts of private benevolence, the vast mass have still had to solve the problem for themselves.

By 1939, seven years after the worst period of the slump, a considerable number, 600 men, are at work at the Mercantile Dock in Jarrow. By far the largest group have found work in the Tyneside shipyards. All the available "royals", as the specially selected skilled men in the shipyard were called, got work as soon as the new naval orders were given. Other shipyard workers have been absorbed by Armstrong Whitworths, Swan Hunter's, and Hawthorn Leslie's. In fact there have been complaints that owing to the publicity that Jarrow has enjoyed, the men from Jarrow have been given preference on Tyneside.

But before this movement consequent on the rearmament programme started, there had been a big loss in population at Jarrow. As soon as general conditions begin to improve there is a tendency to move out of the distressed areas. Schemes for arranged transference are valueless as palliatives on any considerable scale in a general depression, because there are no genuine vacancies to go to. But, naturally, as the rate of unemployed in the distressed area is always greater than in the country generally, there is a certain seepage of population out of specially distressed parts. In good times, when industries outside the derelict towns are prospering, there is a marked exodus, which slackens with the decline in industrial activity.

In Jarrow, abnormal unemployment started as early as 1921, before the rest of the country was badly hit. Between the censuses of 1921 and 1931, there was a net decrease of population of 3558 persons. The natural increase by excess of births over deaths was 10.3 per cent during that period. The total loss by migration, therefore, amounted to 20.3 per cent in ten years. Jarrow had thus lost about one-fifth of its 1921 population before the worst of the slump started. This loss in Jarrow is only equalled by the worst-hit area in Durham. The county lost 10 per cent of its population in these ten years. Only Bishop Auckland area comes higher than Jarrow, with a loss of 22.7 of its population in these years. As compared with this figure of voluntary migration in the bad period, the assisted Government transference schemes between November 1935 and December 1938 ... the better period of the present trade cycle only accounted for 345 transfers, which were transfers in some cases of families and in others of individuals.

The greater number of those who left Jarrow between 1921 and 1931 were those who had come in to work at the Shipyard during the war ... mainly from the South and Midlands, and who went back when it was clear that the best days of Palmer's were over. The slow rate of removals under the Government scheme illustrate the difficulties of transferring really settled population.

Taking single workers, or even families, from areas where trade is bad and likely to remain so, to the areas which need labour, seems so easy and obvious a solution of the problem when viewed with detachment from Whitehall. But as seen by the family to be moved ... it means a tearing up of roots, at best a gamble with the whole life of the household. Those easiest to move, the single young man or woman, tend to transfer themselves if really suitable jobs are going elsewhere ... but to the family the background of a lifetime is an asset not lightly to be sacrificed. In a town where you have always lived, and your father or mother before you, there are always relatives and friends who will give a hand in an emergency. Neighbours will help during sickness. Credit can be got at the local shops to tide over some unexpected bad patch. In a new town, one is a stranger with no one to turn to at a moment of crisis.

To move a long distance, after a prolonged period of unemployment, without a few pounds behind one for the absolutely necessary expenses, even when the Ministry pays for the actual removal of the furniture and the fares, is a worry. Its difficulties cannot be understood by those who talk glibly about transference, but who have never known what it is not to have any change at all in the pocket. There are the difficulties of the unknown, too ... the high rents, for example, for the newcomer on a commencing wage. To a Jarrovian the rents asked in London for the cheapest rooms seem simply fantastic. In areas of booming trade, prices tend to be higher than in towns where no one has any margin to spend.

Any enthusiasm for transfer that may be worked up by Ministry of Labour officials dies down as soon as there is a flicker of hope that industry may somehow revive in the town. Men prefer to hang on, in hope. Others even come back who have got jobs elsewhere. It is not a strange affection for Jarrow or Bishop Auckland or Dowlais as such ... it is the desperate need to get back to the economic and personal background of the days when one was fitted in firmly to a social group. In the early days, when Sir John Jarvis was optimistically promising to employ thousands soon in Jarrow, it was difficult for the Ministry to get families to move out of the town. In a lesser degree, these factors explain the reluctance of the poorest families to go to the new housing areas even in the same town.

It is urged that such considerations do not apply to young people who, it is said, ought to be got out of areas like Jarrow, early enough to start life elsewhere. But the transference even of young people seems to bring as many problems as it solves. The Minister of Labour, with full-throated emotion, can win approving "hear, hears" from the more comfortable sections of the House of Commons by describing the fresh hope of the young worker in his new home, as compared with the hopeless background he has left ... which, of course, ignores conveniently the most difficult problems that youngster has to face.

Juvenile and adolescent wages are based on the assumption that the young worker lives as part of his own family. In a way he is subsidized out of the family income, yet his small money wages, quite insufficient to pay board-and-lodging with profit to a landlady, mean real help in the home where the same rent has to be paid whether the youngster is there or not. The mother and father feel that it is unfair that they should have fed and clothed the child for fourteen years "in order that some other woman may get the benefit of their wages", as many mothers in Jarrow have bitterly complained to me. These mothers are not callous ... and they are right. Working adolescents are a real asset to the working-class family whose economic arrangements are based on the assumption of their help in later years. It is a serious matter when these props are not only removed, but sent so far away that all the ties are broken too. This is one of the most important arguments for planned movement of industry to the distressed areas, rather than moving the workers and their families to wherever the whim or interest of the employer may choose to put the factory.

In the new area, the wage of the adolescent is not sufficient to pay for his needs. When the grant from the Ministry ceases, or when the youngster moves to another job and goes outside whatever supervision is exercised by the Ministry, the hardship is both real and dangerous. There are more cases than the Ministry or the police will admit of lads and girls from thoroughly respectable working-class homes who get into trouble with the authorities because their wages provide no tolerable standard of living away from their homes. I came across a case where boys were brought down from the North, half-starved on their wages, and rotted with dermatitis through working in acid in a new factory in Aylesbury – a country area where the factory supervision, until we stirred up the Home Office and the Ministry of Labour, was as unsatisfactory as could well be.

The sense of distance from home causes often a homesickness that becomes hysteria. Many are the complaints of the housewives who insist on getting maids of really tender years from these areas, and are then surprised because the girls simply cannot stand the separation from their families and friends. It is difficult for an official, or a Member of Parliament who can get into a morning train at King's Cross, transact business in Newcastle and be back in town late the same night, to appreciate how final the separation of that six-hour rail journey seems to those who may never be able to afford to take it again for the rest of their lives. I have found that this sense of being cut off from home amounts to an obsession among the children of my constituents who have come to the House of Commons to tell me their troubles.

Transference therefore offers only a very limited solution to the problems of Jarrow, or any of the larger distressed areas. Nor should it be regarded as anything more. What Lord Runciman, who is not given to flights of rhetoric, described in the House of Commons as "one of the finest industrial sites in the world" ought not to be considered a derelict transfer area like Tow Law or Bryn Mawr.

In view of all the speeches made by Cabinet Ministers and others as to what the Government and private helpers are doing for the unemployed, this is what they all amount to in one of the most notorious cases. Jarrow has become the classic example of a stricken town. The swift murder, rather than the slow death, of its hopes have made it a dramatic rallying centre for much goodwill. In addition, the present President of the Board of Trade has a feeling of bad conscience ... though he, Mr. Oliver Stanley, has no direct blame for the actions of his predecessor, Lord Runciman. Yet all these efforts together, which only started when trade itself was beginning to revive, had helped barely one-eighth of the total unemployed, even up to the middle of a great arms boom. That is not an eighth of the highest figure, but calculated after 20 per cent of the population had already left the town after the closing of Palmer's Works. This 12½ per cent result, it must be admitted, is higher than the help given to any other English or Welsh town. I have no figures for Scotland, but there seems to be less done there than in England and Wales. I do not wish to decry the efforts, official and unofficial, that have been made to help the people in Jarrow. But it is worth noting that in the classic case, the best example with all sorts of favourable factors, and beginning when the trade cycle was already on the upswing, that 12½ per cent result is the best that can be done. And practically the whole even of this employment depends on armament orders.

Taking the two towns of Hebburn and Jarrow together there are now 19,000 employed workers, of which 10,000 are dependent on two industries-shipbuilding and electrical engineering. At the present time the prosperity of both is based on the Government rearmament programme. Of the other 9000 men a goodly proportion have found work in one of the industries whose prosperity has been based on rearmament. Such work is valuable for the improvement in morale which getting a job means to a man. But it does not touch the central problem of unemployment. What is going to happen when the rearmament programme ends? Gradually during the last few years the industry of the country has been organized for war. Whether war comes or not, there must come a day when the armament orders will slacken and, for most such factories, cease. Our capacity to bear the present heavy burden is limited. The Economic Advisory Council have reported to the Unemployment Statutory Committee that the rates of employment to be expected when the rearmament orders end will be increased above the normal cyclical unemployment by the specialized character of the falling off in the demand for labour. The slump at the end of the last war is only a taste of what lies ahead. Works have been wholly absorbed or have been newly erected for Government orders. In many cases normal business has had to be let go, to give priority to Government arms contracts. Our overseas markets have been neglected. When the armament orders come to an end where are the next orders to come from? Overseas buyers will have established their contacts elsewhere. The capitalists have looked after their interest by enjoying the phenomenal profits. The very justification the rich make for high interest rates is that "they won't last forever." Owners of aircraft shares can reap their fortune now. Workers in these industries have had to fight for their wages, and when the orders cease they have no reserves to fall back on. They will have to turn towards the Labour Exchange.

The moral of the analysis of these figures of Jarrow's unemployment is clearer than official sources care to admit. The distressed areas are the former exporting areas for our staple heavy industries. The slump in these industries has kept the "hard core" of unemployment steadily high. To say that Britain was once the workshop of the world, and that now other countries are catching up and making the things they once bought from us is a statement of fact ... but a milestone, not a signpost. Where do we go from here? The situation being thus; how can it be dealt with?

The chapters on shipping and steel in this book have described how the situation has been met by the private capitalists and bankers of Britain. In shipping savage rationalization has been forced through. The high cost of the dreadful social consequences has been thrown on the community, the heaviest rate burdens falling on the suffering areas. Yet the net result of that much-boasted piece of internal capitalist reconstruction has been that the shipping industry is on its back. The rationalizers have secured public subsidies ... not to build the needed ships but so to guarantee low prices and high operating profits to shipowners that they can be bribed to order ships from their own country rather than from a Germany which may be submarining before long the ships built at Hamburg for patriotic British owners.

In iron and steel, under the stimulus of an unprecedented armament programme, the problem was not one of rationalization but of expansion. The opportunity of this vast new market, controlled by the Government, paid for by the community, could have been so used that at the end of the rearmament period a completely re-organized and up-to-date steel industry would have been a great national asset to the country, able to take its full share in the world's trade. Instead, the leading idea of the Government has been to protect the existing old and inefficient plants and to guarantee their costly profits until they could patch them up and extend them ... not in the most suitable and economical sites but where old tradition had left them. In the doing of this behind a ferocious tariff the cost of steel has been forced so high that our steel-using industries, especially shipping, have been practically forced out of the world's competitive market and are existing on Government orders.

A neat way has been devised to keep the profits on the old steelworks. Where new and up-to-date plants have been erected they have been deliberately loaded with conditions such as those which the Steel Federation and the Bank of England have been able to force on Ebbw Vale. The limitations against their working to capacity have actually been designed to make them less efficient. It is an example of capitalism in decline, desperately fighting against that technical efficiency which, we are still assured, is the reason for the existence of capitalism as a system of industrial production. The high profits in aircraft manufacture show that vast fortunes can be made by the favoured under any conditions ... provided that a paternal government goes on giving orders and a docile taxpayer is prepared to go on paying. But there is a limit to this happy state.

The vast scale of our rearmament disposes of the plea that neither the country nor the industry could afford to re-organize and re-equip its old industrial plant from base to top. Today, according to Sir Kingsley Wood, the Minister for Air, we are spending on aircraft alone four millions a week. That sum will increase as the re-armament programme progresses through 1939. The capital cost of the new steelworks at Jarrow was estimated to be £4,000,000 when first proposed. Taking into consideration rising costs, say £6,000,000. Less than two weeks' cost of present aircraft production would have provided a great new steelworks producing the steel at so much less a cost than the old plants that the new works could have been depreciated to nil in the national balance sheet by now. Actually the new steelworks could have been built by the amount of good capital subscribed by the public for aeroplane and similar shares which has not gone into production but into the pockets of the professional share operators. This is to leave out of account the amount saved by having wages instead of unemployment pay. Obviously efficient plant would mean some displacement of labour ... but the pensioning of ageing and really redundant workers on honourable terms would be a far less serious social problem than the social cost of the idleness of men in their best working period.

CHAPTER EIGHTEEN

Conclusions

THIS IS the story of Jarrow. But not of Jarrow only. A similar story could be told of many other towns in Lancashire, in West Cumberland, in Scotland and South Wales. The outline would be the same. The human tragedy very similar. Only the details of the background would differ with the differences in the industry, cotton instead of shipbuilding, hematite instead of coal.

On the heavy industry towns like Jarrow, the industrial prosperity of Britain has been based. Out of the wealth produced in our Jarrows, our Oldhams and our Rhonddas British capitalists have financed industrial developments overseas and created the Empire of Tribute. Out of these capital investments has come the yearly payments of interest which in the past has kept the standard of living in Britain comparatively higher than in the Continental countries of the Old World. In that "tributary standard" the workers of Britain have shared, though they have had to fight for every bit of improvement.

It has been a hard fight, every step of which has been and is bitterly contested. But as we have seen in this story of Jarrow step by step with the growth of industry there has been some rise in the workers' standards and status. Gradually they won political rights-and in that the middle classes, with their own fight to wage, helped. Now the workers are fighting the key battle, the central issue in the class war, the struggle for economic control.

The story of Jarrow's industries, the fight in shipping and steel, reveal the weakness of British capitalism in its old unchallenged strongholds. The way is no longer easy and open. Other countries have developed to share the markets. But that is not the chief or the most anxious problem for the British manufacturer. The Anglo-Saxon technique in finance is old-established and clever in its developed ways. Britain still has advantages in material and in personnel, in her stable forms of government and the sense of security that until very recently has been a characteristic of these islands. Chairmen of directors are continually reported as saying in their shareholders' meetings that "given equal conditions British industry has nothing to fear from its competitors". But the central fact is just that conditions are no longer "equal". For that matter they never were, but while Britain had the advantage that fact was not stressed. British capitalists with their individualistic traditions and their gospel of *laisser-faire* are now facing competitors highly organized into national units. Russia with her socialist economy is, by that fact, almost entirely concerned with reequipping her own vast country and raising the standard of life of her own people. To the great competition for international markets the Soviet economy is, on the whole, indifferent.

Germany and Britain thus face each other in 1939, as they did in 1914, for a struggle for the economic mastery of the world, and each of the protagonists has taken measures in its own way to prepare for the day. Germany has put her industry on a war footing. Her whole equipment has been modernized, the trade unions and democratic movements smashed, and her whole economy placed under the control of the armaments ring and the army high command. There are no able-bodied unemployed. Nor are private interests allowed to interfere with the dominant interest of war preparation. This highly centralized economy, of course, is not intended only for war purposes. The idea is to win for Germany that economic self-sufficiency in raw materials which Britain enjoys because of her Empire. If this can be achieved without actual physical warfare as the munitions and highly organized industries of Czechoslovakia, the oil and wheat of Rumania, the metals, vegetables and meat of Yugoslavia and the ores of Spain have been taken without war – then Germany proceeds to an economic dominance of Europe and displaces Britain.

British capitalism has felt the effects of this direct challenge and has reacted in its own way. In place of the violent methods of the German high command in war and trade, the British have tried to make the transition slowly. With much the same end as the German Nazis they have been more concerned with preserving the position and increasing the share of the private capitalist. For instance, it is quite inconceivable that had they had a country so vulnerable as Britain, so dependent on sea-borne food, the Germans would have allowed a private company to rationalize the shipping industry to danger point. That one-third of the shipbuilding berths should be sterilized for forty years – some of them, like Jarrow, the finest sites in the world for the work, by the very year that war seemed most likely, is fantastic enough. But that when subsidies have to be hastily arranged to bring up the shipping strength, that the Board of Trade should confess itself helpless to prevent ships being sold to the ostensible enemy until fresh legislation had been passed, and then allow so long a time to elapse before obtaining the necessary powers can only be explained by this Government's intense reluctance to interfere with private profitmaking.

Consider the different ways in which the Brassert process for using low-grade ores to make steel was treated in Germany and Britain. The established steel-makers in both countries looked at it askance. Both wanted to make profit out of their existing plant. Neither German nor British iron masters wanted a competitive process which would make possible steel shillings per ton cheaper, but which would render existing plant obsolete. The difference therefore was not in the steel capitalists but in the attitude of the Governments. Goering saw in the Brassert process a contribution towards Germany's industrial self-sufficiency. There are low-grade ore mines in Germany, but to work them cost more than to import higher grade ores. Goering therefore formed the Herman Goering Stahlwerke to exploit the low-grade ores and use the Brassert process to make them into steel to supply the armament makers.

The English Government had had an object lesson in how much more cheaply with the new process steel could be made at Corby in Northants. The Government knew that many of Britain's steelworks, especially in the Northeast, were out of date, that an integrated plant was badly needed. By 1934 it must have known that the country was about to re-arm. Mr. Baldwin fought an election on peace in 1935 to rearm for war. Yet with all this evidence in its possession, Mr. Runciman allowed the Iron and Steel Federation to stifle the new invention, to strangle the projected steelworks at Jarrow, leaving 6000 workers on the dole, and in addition gave the Iron and Steel Combine the terrific, if temporary, tariff of 50 per cent to help the steel masters in their negotiations with the International Steel Cartel. Result – that Jarrow has consumed in unemployment pay far more than would have built the steelworks, that the country is in a war situation without a planned steel industry, that it has been dependent in moments of extreme pressures on its potential enemies of the Steel Cartel, while the Herman Goering Stahlwerke are just coming into production, a valuable addition to Germany's war potential.

In both Germany and England the real wages of the workers have had to be reduced, their standard of life lowered in order to pay for the readjustments that capitalism has had to make in order to make the price-profit system (built on scarcity) keep going in a period which scientific advance can make an age of plenty. Nazi Germany wants to use the surplus thus accrued for war preparation. Nazi leaders therefore want as many workers as possible producing as much on as little as possible. The English capitalists, relying on the resources of their Empire, want the profit surplus to be as big as possible. Hence they consider it better to strangle a Jarrow, to force an Ebbw Vale to work below capacity in order to keep the profits of the existing ring high. For the same reason they scrap Jarrow's shipyard and one third of the shipping berths of the country to retain the profit-making capacity of the remainder.

The cost of this British rationalization is very high – to the towns thus rendered derelict, to the workers whose livelihood is destroyed, and to the taxpayer who has to meet the bill for unemployment. Industrial lives in England have been as ruthlessly sacrificed to rationalization as in Germany they have been sacrificed to the Nazi war machine. Of that towns like Jarrow are the living proof. For the men who remain in the rationalized industries the future is also dark. Instead of sharing in what benefits are secured by rationalization, they are met with demands for further sacrifices. The Lithgow campaign for the grading out of the skilled men in the shipyards which we have noted in the text in Chapter Ten is the next stage. These skilled men have outgrown "their international value". In other words Nazi war-lord and British capitalist set the workers facing each other in an international wage-cutting competition with plenty of mutual hate propaganda thrown in – workers are set to hate workers while the Federation of British Industries signs the Dusseldorf Agreement with the Reichs Industrie Gruppe during the height of the war scare.

Only a planned socialist economy, producing goods for use and not for profit, can solve the basic problem of today. The capitalists are not solving it ... though they are planning on a wider scale than ever before. By their restriction policies they are only making the situation worse. The steel firms to save themselves get a tariff. The result is higher prices for shipbuilders. That leads to a demand for a shipping subsidy ... where is the process to end? With Colvilles supplying steel to the shipping firms of Harland and Wolff, and Lithgows, with which they are inter-connected, the various steel and shipbuilding firms in the Vickers ring supplying each other, the connections are sufficiently strong to keep the shipowners reasonably quiet about the effects of the steel tariff on prices, in return for which the steel firms support the subsidy demand. A nice big racket at the expense of the taxpayer.

A subsidy for a major industry like shipbuilding is, in itself, an admission of a defeat for capitalism as an industrial system, even though it wins this as a political victory. Now menaced by a war situation, the great decline in British tonnage becomes a national problem. The ships have not been built, the very places in which they were made, destroyed because individual firms did not see the prospect of sufficient profit in building ships. "Price economics" not only lead to sudden rushes of orders, alternating with periods of complete idleness with wastage of capital assets and bitter social consequences: we have now seen that it threatens the very life-lines of the State in time of danger.

Instead of panic subsidies now, we ought to have nationalized shipping and shipbuilding when the slump set in, and the yards could have been secured for the nation at bargain prices. It is not too late to do that now. Shipping is essentially a national industry. Our security depends on it. It is ideally suited for planned organization, as other states have proved. By placing the state organization and influence behind yards that they could call their own, their shipping has boomed, while the British yards have been idle. If a war is coming, we dare not leave the industry in private hands ... as we proved in our desperation in the last war. Their driving power. is the profit motive ... driving the companies to profiteer even out of the nation's needs. It is happening already. The cases of ships being moved from the national register during the war to get higher prices is paralleled this year by the ships sold at the moment of greatest danger to our potential enemies. From every point of view ... of efficiency and of national safety, this industry should be nationalized, not subsidized.

In the meantime, there remains the problem of Jarrow and the distressed areas ... still "distressed" despite the armaments boom. Can any immediate palliatives be suggested to a Government which has done and is doing so much for its own class, and so little for others?

The most obvious palliative is all that is implied in the shorthand phrase "planned location of industry". The more enlightened among the Government supporters have been pressing for some time that the Ministers of Labour and of Trade should take powers to prevent the cutting up of agricultural land for industrial purposes – the planting of big new works in rural areas quite unprepared to receive them. Social services have then to be hastily improvised of course at the expense of the rate- and tax-payer ... the industry itself being practically de-rated by the 1929 Act. The industrial areas which have all these services in being are left derelict. Often the main motive for planting the works so unsuitably is to get as far away as possible from the centres of trade-union tradition, in the hope of getting cheap and unorganized labour.

In May of this year, the President of the Board of Trade had to face a storm of protest because he said he could not prevent a company building a new steelworks in Edale, a famous Derbyshire beauty spot. There are no workmen's houses near. Roads, sewers, water supply, schools will have to be provided by the county, while there are excellent sites available in the industrial areas of the next county – Yorkshire.

The various war ministries are among the worst sinners. I have had correspondence with the justifiably angry Mayor of Bath, because a great munition works has been put down at Corsham, without the slightest attention being paid to the social needs of the hundreds of workers hastily dumped down there. In these days of 250-mile an hour bombers, to say nothing of the German and Italian aerodromes established on the North coast of Spain, it is absurd to talk of the vulnerability of the North-east coast as against the West country.

The excellent Report on the Location of Industry produced by "Political and Economic Planning" says:

> "The question of a policy for the location of industry did not arise when populations were tied to the soil nor to any serious extent so long as industrial civilization depended largely upon power from coal and on transport by rail and water. It has only been made acute by the development of electric power, road transport and mass consumption demands, which have conferred great mobility upon industry at a time when increasing costs of public administration and services have made it far more important for the State to anticipate and perhaps guide where industry and therefore population are going to grow. ... At the same time as the State has had to take on much of the burden of unemployment and depression resulting from industrial failure, public opinion is becoming increasingly aware that the forces which create such social liabilities are still operating unchecked."

The Government, which has so far refused to influence, or even to admit the possibility of a planned location of industry, necessarily exerts a very strong indirect influence through a variety of national policies ... tariffs, grants, governmental decisions regarding transport or subsidies, all have a "pull" on where this or that industry should go. The Government, thus, plans as it were by accident. It only refuses to plan by conscious design, and after proper investigation of the facts, less certain interests may be inconvenienced.

Some people of influence squeal every time a green field is taken for any housing scheme, however necessary to relieve congestion. That is absurd and selfish. But it is equally absurd to allow the creation of industrial slums all over this small island, peppering the countryside with what are potential Jarrows as soon as the arms orders stop, without any regard to the needs of the working population. If that argument does not appeal to the "right" people, the only powerful plea likely to affect them is that "it looks so untidy from the windows of the car ".

The argument of vulnerability, which has led to much munition work and aeroplane work being diverted from the distressed areas of the North-east, never seems valid to the Government as regards London. The South-eastern area, obviously the most vulnerable geographically and desirable to the enemy strategically because it includes the capital and the great ring of works in Greater London, now contains 54 per cent of the employed workers in the United Kingdom ... and is growing rapidly both in population and industries.

A planning commission for industry, which is the chief recommendation of the P.E.P. Report on Location of Industry, is attractive, except that it has the fatal defect of all such commissions ... that lack of personal drive and responsibility which acts like a creeping paralysis on all bodies whose duty it is to "influence, co-ordinate, advise". The President of the Board of Trade is crushed now under too great a variety of duties. A Minister for Industrial Planning, with the resources and authority of a state department behind him, responsible to Parliament would be the most effective way of getting the job done ... and very important, keeping it done ... that is provided, of course, that the Government wanted it to be done.

The problem of local rates has to be tackled from a very different viewpoint than that of the De-Rating Act, 1929. That act aimed only at relieving the burden of the industrialist. It reduced a cost on production, which in most cases was on shoulders well enough able to bear it. Actually it has had a deadening effect on the small consumer market. Rents which include rates, and therefore rise with the rates, the rate demand notes on owner-occupiers struggling to buy small houses in the highly rated areas, absorb an increasing proportion of the spending power. In such districts like Jarrow and Merthyr, where the rates are 22s. and 28s. in the pound, or even in the many districts where without being so spectacular the rates are 15s. and more, it is not unusual to find rents and rates taking more than one-third of the total of small incomes.

The State claims credit for assuming the burden of the able-bodied unemployed, but, as Durham County Council has pointed out in many memoranda, an enormous burden of poor relief is still left on the rates of distressed areas. The Old Age Pensioners' pittances have to be supplemented. Long-term unemployed come on to public assistance, as do the extra allowances which have to be paid to the sick and disabled. In addition local authorities have still to carry the burden of interest on funds which they were compelled to borrow at high rates of interest. In Jarrow, on one item alone, the ferry, this meant a 10*d.* rate for years, until extra grants were given last year. Some authorities were still burdened with interest on loans contracted to give assistance to the unemployed which the Government now admit must be a national charge. Yet the Government neither takes over such loan interest, nor in most cases has it allowed the local authority the power to pay off the principal of the high interest loans by borrowing elsewhere when money was at its cheapest.

Some form of rate equalization is obviously long overdue. It is clearly absurd that wealthy boroughs with no unemployed should be paying rates like 5*s.* 7*d.* while Jarrow has to carry the weight of 22*s.* in the pound. Patches on the evil, like variations in block grants, have been tried, but do not get to the real difficulty. A radical reform, a thorough overhaul of our antiquated and over-elaborate system of both local and national taxation, is badly needed. It is absurd for Ministers in answer to questions in the Commons to assume that "prosperity" ... a return to "normal conditions of trade" (whatever that can mean these days) will solve the problem. The country is considered to be in a state of hectic boom unknown since the days of high inflation at the end of the war. Yet Jarrow has just had to impose the highest rate in its history ... and most of the other Special Areas are in the same state or worse.

High rates mean the starvation of all the amenities that make life in industrial communities tolerable. This in itself has a deadening effect on the hope of getting private industry to these areas. Finding myself sitting near a high official of the Morris Cowley Works at a public function. I criticized Lord Nuffield for having spoiled Oxford instead of bringing much-needed work to Jarrow or South Wales. "Oh, I don't suppose Nuffield would have minded", was the reply. "He can live where he likes. But it would have been hell for us. He couldn't have got a first-class manager or technician to spend his life in Merthyr Tydfil."

"You might improve these places if you had to live there yourself. "

He laughed. "When I've finished work, I want some life ... not to run a Mutual Improvement Society at Jarrow or Blaina."

I know that I shall be blamed on Tyneside, particularly by the "Pro Bono Publicos", and the "Ancient Jarrovians" who send letters to the local Press, for writing this book about Jarrow. They will say: "Up here, we know how bad things are, even yet. But why tell the world? Let's pretend that things aren't too bad. Then maybe, they'll get better." If the problems of such areas as Jarrow, and Bishop Auckland, and Merthyr were purely a local matter, there might be something to that argument ... though I can't see what. But Jarrow's plight is not a local problem. It is the symptom of a national evil.

Anyone who takes the trouble to study the new forces at work in our urban civilization cannot deny the dangerous trend towards over-centralization that cheap power and quick transport have brought into this tiny country. London, already the biggest market, tends to draw wealth and initiative to the capital city, and thus become the prestige centre for commerce, for governmental activity, for art and literature, for political and social life. Newcastle was a capital city in the days when Charles Mark Palmer, the dashing, enterprising business man, thought he was in the van of progress when he got to London in a day's rail journey. His successor as member for the Jarrow Division does that journey in four and a half hours.

Every industry which comes to London creates new consuming power, a new market for other industries. Every cultural organization, every trade union which wants headquarters in London, every employers' federation which insists on being at the centre though its main industry is in the North all helps the pull. It is a problem which a Labour Government would have to face straightaway, for a lot of its strength would come from the older industrial areas. It would have to balance their demand to be allowed to live with the new interests of the vast and growing mass of London workers. This island is too small, its economic life too precariously balanced, its geographical situation too vulnerable, for its fate to be left to the casual workings of chance, or the insatiable unheeding drive of the profit-makers. Jarrow is an object lesson of what happens then. The profiteers, having ravaged a town or a country, can take themselves and their gains elsewhere. The workers have the main stake in their homeland, for in it they must remain. They have built it, and worked in it, fought for it. On their skill and their toil has been built England's industrial reputation. They were crowded into hovels, their children starved and died, and on their sacrifice great capital has been accumulated. It is time now that the workers took control of this country of ours. It is time that they planned it, organized it, and developed it so that all might enjoy the wealth which we can produce. In the interest of this land we love that is the next job which must be done.

Bibliography

Limitations of space exclude detailed references and a complete bibliography; but the following notes indicate some of the more important sources.

Files of various newspapers, including:

Newcastle Courant.
Jarrow Guardian.
Newcastle Chronicle.
Newcastle Journal.
Shields Gazette.
Press cutting collection of pre-war Jarrow lent by Mr. Peter Fanning.
The Times.

Annual Reports:

The Commissioner for the Special Areas.
Ministry of Labour.
Ministry of Health.
Unemployment Assistance Board.
The Health of the School Child.

Early Jarrow;

Victoria County History of Durham.
The Old Church. J. D. Rose.
Brief History of Jarrow. Johnstone.
The Bell Collection. Newcastle Public Library.
Jubilee History and Souvenir of Jarrow.
Centenary Souvenir of Primitive Methodist Church in Jarrow, 1822-1922.
Unpublished MSS.

Coal Mining:

History of the Durham Miners. Webb.
History of the Durham and Northumberland Miners. Fyne.
History of Coal. Fordyce.
A Voice from the Coal Mines. 1825.
Rules of the United Associations of Colliers on the Rivers Wear and Tyne.
The Pitman's Strike, 1844. A volume of original broadsheets in Wigan Public Library.
The Miners' Journal.

There are many valuable and interesting items in the various collections of local tracts and other material in Newcastle Public Library and in the offices of the Durham Miners' Association.

Rise of Jarrow:

The Palmer Record.
The Mid. Tyne Link.
The Making of the Tyne. Johnstone.
The Tyne and its Tributaries. R. W. Palmer.
Some Account of Palmer's. Malcolm Dillon.
Modern. Shipbuilding. (1894) Pollock.
Industrial Resources of the Tyne, Wear and Tees. 1863.
Proceedings of the British Association. 1861.
The Nine Hours' Movement. John Burnett.
A Shepherd of Sheep. Mrs. Liddell.
Records of Palmer's Shipbuilding and Iron Company, Ltd., at Somerset House.
Minute book and other records of Jarrow Town Council.
Jarrow Trades Council. Annual Reports.

Modern Shipbuilding and Shipping:

War Memoirs. David Lloyd George.
Some Economic Consequences of the Great War. A. L. Bowley.
Shipping. Labour Research Department.
Survey of Metal Industries. Committee on Industry and Trade.
Survey of the North-east Coast Area. Board of Trade.
Basic Industries of Great Britain. Lord Aberconway.
British Industries and their Organization. K C. Allen.
Britain in Recovery. Research Committee of the British Association.

British Maritime Policy. Sir Archibald Hurd.
Shipbuilding Rationalization. F. C. Pyman.
The Building of Ships – a British Survey. Sir James Lithgow.
Fact Finding Enquiries. Chamber of Shipping.
The Shipping World.
The Shipbuilder.
Fairplay.
Lloyd's List.
Journal of Commerce.

Iron and Steel:

Iron and Coal Trade Review.
The Economist.
The Socialization of the Iron and Steel Industry. By Ingot.
New Developments in Blast Furnace Technique. T. P. Colclough. M.Sc.
Report on the Iron and Steel Industry. Import Duties Advisory Committee.
Jarrow and its Plight, and other material prepared by Jarrow Town Council and Jarrow Industries Committee.
Correspondence columns of *The Times.*
Unpublished letters to the author relating to the negotiations for the steelworks at Jarrow.

Modern Jarrow:

Industrial Tyneside. H. A. Mess.
Various publications of the Tyneside Council of Social Service.
Causal Factors in Tuberculosis. Dr. Bradbury.
Reports of Medical Officer of Health, Jarrow 1875-1938
Durham and the North-east Coast. Report of the Labour Party to Distressed Areas.
Justice in a Distressed Area. Charles Muir.

General:

An Economic History of Modern Britain. J. H. Clapham.
A Short History of the British Working-class Movement. G. D. H. Cole
The Age of the Chartists. J. L. Hammond.
Capital. Chapters on the Working Day. Karl Marx.
Report of Conditions of Tuberculosis Service in South Wales and Monmouthshire. Ministry of Health.
Poverty and Public Health. G. C. M. M'Gonigle.

Problem of the Distressed Areas. W. Hannington.
Study in Location of Industry. P.E.P.
Minutes if Evidence before Royal Commission on the Geographical Distribution of the Industrial Population.
Public and Private Property. H. Campion.

Also from The Merlin Press

CLASH

Ellen Wilkinson

Clash is set against the backdrop of the 1926 general strike. It describes political and personal issues as Joan Craig, an activist in the trade union movement and Labour Party, lives through the excitement of mass protest and individual turmoil in her relations with two men friends. It draws on experience: the author toured the UK and spoke at a series of public meetings. *Clash* was first published in 1929.

"There are two distinct conflicts in this very clever and successful first novel. There is, to begin with, political warfare. Joan Craig, the attractive daughter of a Northern factory operative, becomes a Trade Union organizer, and Miss Wilkinson, in describing her heroine's experiences, takes us behind the scenes and shows us the General Strike of 1926 as she herself probably saw it. Then there is the rivalry between Joan's two suitors…"
The Spectator

About the author: Ellen Wilkinson (1891-1947) was a key figure in the socialist and feminist movement. She was born in Manchester and became the first woman on the city council. She supported women's suffrage, became Labour MP for Jarrow and helped lead the Jarrow Crusade. She was the first female Minister of Education, in the 1945 government.

ISBN 978-1-85425-119-0
198 x 129 mm. paperback

www.merlinpress.co.uk